VISUALIZING DATA
with MICROSOFT®
POWER VIEW

Brian Larson
Mark Davis
Dan English
Paul Purington

D1530533

New York Chicago San Francisco Lisbon
London Madrid Mexico City Milan
New Delhi San Juan Seoul Singapore
Sydney Toronto

The **McGraw·Hill** Companies

Library of Congress Cataloging-in-Publication Data

Larson, Brian, author.
  Visualizing data with Microsoft Power View / Brian Larson, Mark Davis,
Dan English, Paul Purington.
      pages   cm
    ISBN 978-0-07-178082-7 (alk. paper) — ISBN 978-0-07-178081-0 (CD-ROM)
  — ISBN 978-0-07-178082-7 (set)
  1. Business intelligence—Computer programs.   2. Microsoft Power View.   I. Title.
    HD38.7.L375   2012
    005.7'26—dc 23

                                                    2012025251

McGraw-Hill books are available at special quantity discounts to use as premiums and sales promotions, or for use in corporate training programs. To contact a representative, please e-mail us at bulksales@mcgraw-hill.com.

Visualizing Data with Microsoft® Power View

234567890   DOC DOC   109876543

ISBN: Book p/n 978-0-07-178080-3 and CD p/n 978-0-07-178081-0
of set 978-0-07-178082-7

MHID: Book p/n 0-07-178080-7 and CD p/n 0-07-178081-5
of set 0-07-178082-3

Sponsoring Editor	**Copy Editor**	**Illustration**
Wendy Rinaldi	Bill McManus	Cenveo Publisher Services
Editorial Supervisor	**Proofreader**	**Video Editor**
Janet Walden	Madhu Prasher	David Demyan
Project Manager	**Indexer**	**Art Director, Cover**
Sheena Uprety,	Karin Arrigoni	Jeff Weeks
Cenveo Publisher Services	**Production Supervisor**	**Cover Designer**
Technical Editor	Jean Bodeaux	Jeff Weeks
Carolyn Chau	**Composition**	
	Cenveo Publisher Services	

About the Authors

Brian Larson served as a member of the original Reporting Services development team as a consultant to Microsoft. In that role, he contributed to the original code base of Reporting Services. Brian is currently the Vice President of Technology for Superior Consulting Services, a Microsoft Managed Partner, in Minneapolis, Minnesota.

Brian has presented at national conferences and events, including the SQL Server Magazine Connections Conference, the PASS Community Summit, and the Microsoft Business Intelligence Conference, and has provided training and mentoring on business intelligence across the country. He has been a contributor and columnist for *SQL Server Magazine*. In addition to this book, Brian is the author of *Microsoft SQL Server 2012 Reporting Services, Fourth Edition*, and *Delivering Business Intelligence with Microsoft SQL Server 2012, Third Edition*, both from McGraw-Hill Professional.

Brian is a Phi Beta Kappa graduate of Luther College in Decorah, Iowa, with degrees in physics and computer science. He has 26 years of experience in the computer industry, and 22 years of experience as a consultant creating custom database applications. Brian is an MCITP: Business Intelligence Developer 2008 and a Microsoft Certified Database Administrator (MCDBA).

Brian and his wife, Pam, have been married for 26 years. Pam will tell you that their first date took place at the campus computer center. If that doesn't qualify someone to write a computer book, then it's hard to know what does. Brian and Pam have two children, Jessica and Corey.

Mark Davis is the Business Intelligence Practice Manager at Superior Consulting Services, in Minneapolis, as well as a consultant on all aspects of business intelligence implementations. Mark is an MCITP: Business Intelligence Developer 2008, and a Microsoft Certified Technology Specialist (MCTS) for Microsoft SQL Server Business Intelligence – Implementation and Maintenance.

An accomplished IT professional, after earning his Bachelor of Science in Business Education from the University of Wisconsin, Mark began his IT career as a contract programmer over 22 years ago, and within the first two years found his niche in business intelligence as a software developer, consultant, and trainer, providing consulting and training services throughout the United States and abroad. As an MCITP, Mark has tended to remain on the leading edge of business intelligence technology, creating solutions for clients across a wide spectrum of industries, including health care, finance, manufacturing, insurance, and numerous others. His talent and enthusiasm have helped establish him as a respected expert, with an extensive repertoire in the use of Microsoft and non-Microsoft report writing, database, and data analysis technologies. Mark is a member of the Professional Association for SQL Server.

In his spare time, Mark enjoys movies, filmmaking, theater, football, tennis, and reading a good book, as well as maximizing time with his wife, Pam, and their two children in the Minneapolis suburbs!

Dan English is a Microsoft SQL Server MVP and a Principal Business Intelligence Consultant at Superior Consulting Services in Minneapolis. He has been developing with Microsoft technologies since 1996 and has focused on data warehousing and business intelligence since 2004. Dan has presented for the Minnesota SQL Server user group, the Microsoft Minnesota BI user group, Minnesota TechFuse, along with SQL Server and SharePoint Saturday events. He is also an avid blogger and tweeter.

Dan holds a Bachelor of Science degree in Business Administration from Minnesota State University Mankato. He is an MCITP: Business Intelligence Developer 2005 and 2008, and a Microsoft Certified Technology Specialist (MCTS) for Microsoft SQL Server Business Intelligence – Implementation and Maintenance and also Microsoft Office SharePoint Server 2007 – Configuring.

Dan and his wife, Molly, live in Minnesota and have two children, Lily and Wyatt.

Paul Purington is the Vice President of Consulting for Superior Consulting Services in Minneapolis, Minnesota. He is also a partner in the company.

Paul grew up in Bloomington, Minnesota. He received his Bachelor of Science degree in Secondary Physical Science Education and went on to teach high school physics and computer science for several years. Paul's experience as an educator also includes being a computer software trainer.

Since 1995, Paul has been a software consultant. His first consulting gig required him to build some Microsoft Access 2.0 reports. He now designs and develops business intelligence solutions for clients that have databases containing many terabytes of data. Paul is an MCITP: Business Intelligence Developer 2008. (It's amazing how things have changed over the years!)

Paul and his family (wife Krissy, sons Jack and Ryan) live in the Minneapolis area. When he is not working or writing books, Paul enjoys playing softball in the summer and curling in the winter. His family also fosters rescue dogs.

About the Technical Editor

Carolyn Chau is a Principal Program Manager at Microsoft. Her focus is on leading teams to building rich and immersive experiences across Microsoft's Business Intelligence offerings. Her passion is around making data and insight discovery available to everyone. Most recently, she has led the product definition, design, and development of Power View as its product owner. With over 15 years of experience in project management, database design and implementation, and business intelligence application design, implementation, and training, Carolyn has lead the development of many business intelligence solutions, especially focusing on corporate performance management, Internet usage, and e-commerce behavior. Before joining Microsoft, Carolyn was Senior Consultant at InfoDynamics, LLC, a consulting firm specializing in data warehousing design, implementation, and education.

Contents

Part III   Appendixes

Quick Task Reference
(Learn By Doing Exercises)

Part III   Appendixes

Acknowledgments

This book is a team effort. That fact is obvious from the front cover, which lists our four names as co-authors. However, that team effort goes far beyond the four of us. We want to take this opportunity to thank all the members of the team.

First, a big thank you to Wendy Rinaldi for signing this team and for then having patience as we worked to figure out what it means to be involved in a multi-author project. Her guidance, understanding, and enthusiasm for the project are truly appreciated.

Another big thank you to Carolyn Chau, our technical editor. Her careful review of the content and her insight into the Reporting Services development team at Microsoft were important to the success of this project.

We also want to thank the entire team at McGraw-Hill Professional who shepherded this project through its twists and turns—correcting spelling and grammar, providing gentle reminders of deadlines, assembling videos, and generally ensuring a quality and timely result.

Our appreciation to John Miller for founding Superior Consulting Services (SCS), where the four of us are now employed. Without SCS, this team would not have come together.

We owe a huge debt of gratitude to our families for allowing us to take time away to complete this project. There is no doubt that this type of undertaking is not an individual commitment, but a family commitment. Also, a special thank you to Brian's wife, Pam, who served as an uncredited editor on this project, giving her own time to read every word and work through every Learn By Doing step in this book—not once, but twice!

Finally, we want to thank you for choosing this book to serve as your guide to Power View and the Tabular BI Semantic Model. We hope this book helps you to unlock the power of these truly exciting new products.

Best Regards,

Brian Larson
blarson@teamscs.com

Mark Davis
mdavis@teamscs.com

Dan English
denglish@teamscs.com

Paul Purington
ppurington@teamscs.com

Introduction

The world is filled with data. Today, electronic data is created and captured at an astonishing rate. This is probably just as true within your organization as it is elsewhere. In response, Microsoft has released a flotilla of data analysis, visualization, and reporting tools in the recent past to help organizations navigate the relentless waves of data. You may be familiar with some of these tools: the PivotTable Wizard and PowerPivot in Excel; PerformancePoint Services in SharePoint; and Reporting Services, with its Report Designer and Report Builder, in SQL Server. "Why then," you might be asking yourself, "with all these options already available, is Microsoft releasing another reporting tool?"

What Is Microsoft Power View?

Microsoft's brand-new report authoring product, Power View, is another step forward in the evolution of data analysis and reporting products. Microsoft's goal in introducing Power View is to make reporting not only simpler and more accessible, but also downright fun!

Video I-1   **Introduction**

Power View Makes Reporting More Accessible

Power View makes reporting more accessible in two ways. First, it moves the report authoring experience to the web browser. You can launch this brand-new reporting environment anywhere you have a compatible browser available. Second, Power View makes reporting more accessible by enabling anyone who has basic computer skills to easily access, explore, and visualize data in meaningful ways.

If you've had experience working with other reporting environments, you know that creating a report takes some effort and knowledge. During this process you have to access additional windows, properties, dialog boxes, and menu options, as shown in the Visual Studio example in Figure I-1. You have to learn how to use and interpret the reporting environment before you can learn anything from your data. Power View is

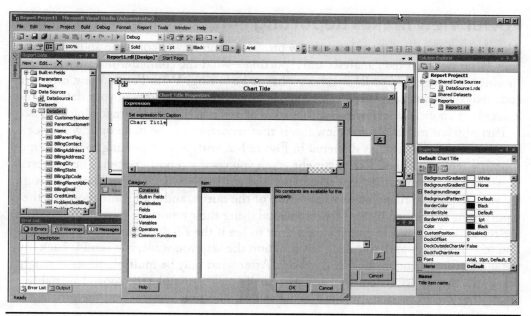

Figure I-1 *Example of current report development experience—not Power View*

designed to minimize the amount of time required to learn the tool so you are able to gain insights from your data as quickly as possible.

Power View is not meant to replace any of Microsoft's existing reporting tools. This new authoring tool is, instead, designed to provide a simplified and streamlined environment in which anyone can create reports. Imagine, if you will, the ability to create a table or chart from your data with just two clicks. Yes, just two clicks! With Power View, it is possible to do just that.

Power View is an offshoot of the reporting environment available with Microsoft SQL Server, called Reporting Services, and was developed by the SQL Server Reporting Services team. The team's vision for Power View is to provide an "interactive data exploration and visual presentation experience for ad hoc reporting." Their objectives for this tool are

▶ Be simple for end users

▶ Provide meaningful context immediately as data is added to the display and as the user interacts with that data

▶ Require no more than two clicks to visualize the data

We believe you'll agree as you explore Power View, the SQL Server Reporting Services development team realized its vision and met its objectives.

Power View Makes Reporting Fun

Along with its accessibility, Power View provides a fun way to consume and present data. Who says that data analysis and reporting—what the computer industry now calls "business intelligence," or BI for short—has to be boring? With Power View, exploring and analyzing your data is enjoyable and exciting. Finding insights in your data will no longer be a chore. You can see results as soon as you add data to the reporting canvas.

Part of what makes Power View fun is that reporting can be done by anyone, not just the IT department. As depicted in Figure I-2, with most reporting tools, you must submit a request to the IT department when you want a report created. The request is prioritized against other report requests and put into a work queue. Then, you wait for your request to make its way to the top of the queue, and wait some more for the report to be developed by an IT professional using their reporting tool of choice. After the report is delivered to you, it's then time to see if the IT department got it right. You test the report and, if it does not function the way you want, you send it back into the queue for reprioritization and rework. After what may be multiple times through this cycle, the report is deployed and you finally have a completed report. Invariably, after using the report for a while, a new business question surfaces and the process starts all over again.

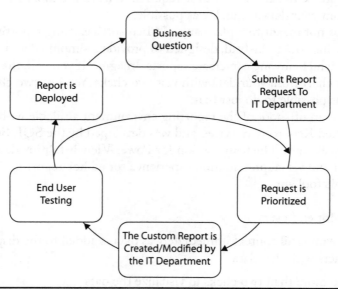

Figure I-2   *Typical report request process using the IT department*

With Power View, you no longer have to depend on the IT department to create reports. Instead, you, as a business user or subject matter expert, have the power to create your own powerful, dynamic, and fun reports. There is no waiting for your report to rise to the top of someone else's priority list. This expedited authoring process is shown in Figure I-3.

The fact that Power View makes report authoring highly interactive, easily accessible through a web browser, and enjoyable is amazing. The SQL Server Reporting Services team has taken the report creation process to the next level. They have provided us with a new and unique way to consume our data.

Power View Makes Reporting Simple

To make report authoring enjoyable, Power View keeps things simple. One of the ways Power View simplifies report authoring is to take the complex process of querying databases right out of the picture. Those of you who have created SELECT statements with JOINS and WHERE clauses know how difficult querying databases can be. Power View obviates this type of querying through its use of the BI Semantic Model.

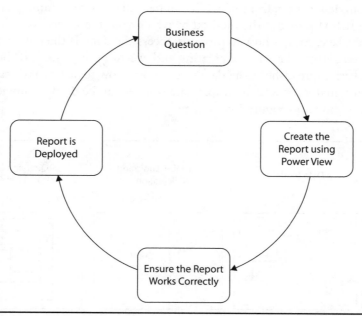

Figure I-3   *The Power View report authoring process*

The BI Semantic Model

Instead of having the report query the database directly, Power View uses a layer placed in between the report and the data. This layer is called the BI Semantic Model (BISM). The BISM contains three components that make it easy to access your business data, as shown in Figure I-4.

First, as the name implies, the BISM contains a model of your data. This model hides the complexity of the data as it is organized in the database. Instead, it presents the data in the way you think about it relative to your organization. Your organization deals with certain things every day. For example, it may work with customers, products, and purchases. In that case, the BISM would contain Customers, Products, and Purchases, along with all the information your organization collects about each of these items. The model also knows how these things relate to one another: Customers are related to Products by making Purchases.

Second, the BISM provides a place to store calculations that are used throughout your organization. A calculation might specify how to determine net profit, how to define the cost of goods sold, or any of a hundred other figures. These calculations capture the business logic specific to your organization right inside the model. Rather than duplicating these calculations over and over in multiple reports, your business logic is stored in a single location, from which it can be utilized across numerous reports.

Finally, the BISM provides the method by which your report accesses the data. This data access layer knows how to properly access the data. If the data is located in a database, the data layer takes care of creating and executing the query. If the data is in a text file or an Excel spreadsheet, the data layer knows how to access and read that file. You can mix and match, as well. Multiple data sources can be used to provide data to a single BISM, as shown in Figure I-5.

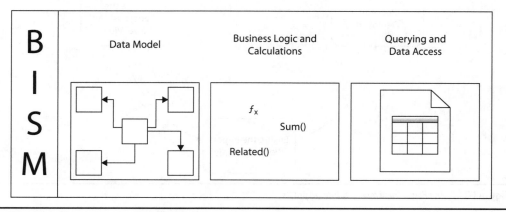

Figure I-4   *The components of the BI Semantic Model*

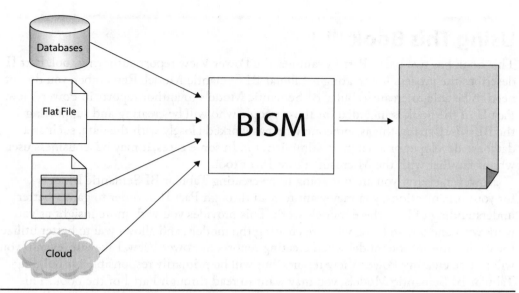

Figure I-5   *Using data from multiple sources to create a single BISM*

All of these BISM capabilities hide complexity from the report authors, making Power View one of the simplest reporting tools ever.

Power View Is Powerful

Power View's simplicity does not, however, make this report authoring tool simplistic. Power View enables you to create complex reports that allow for serious data interaction. Not only are you able to see the results instantly, but as you add items to the report, you will be able to interact with those items and they will interact with each other.

You can select one bar of a bar chart and that simple action will change which data is represented in a table on the same report. All of this can be accomplished with no programming required! How fantastic is that? This is a revolutionary step in the Microsoft report authoring roadmap, and it is very exciting when you see it in action for the very first time.

All of this functionality means you can ask questions on-the-fly and click on the report to see the answers. No programming is needed to provide this functionality. The reports actually tell you a story based on your data.

Using This Book

This book has two parts. Part I examines the Power View report authoring tool. Part II describes the process for creating a Tabular BI Semantic Model. Remember, you do not need to be able to create Tabular BI Semantic Models to author reports in Power View. Part II of the book is included for those people who will be creating and supporting the BISMs. Usually, this is someone who has worked closely with the data, such as a database developer or a database administrator. In some cases, it may be a business user who is familiar with the Microsoft PowerPivot tool.

However, even if you are not going to be creating Tabular BI Semantic Models for your organizations, you may want to read through Part II in order to gain a better understanding of how these models work. This provides you with more insight as you work with and advise those who are creating the models, and allows you to better utilize the capabilities of the model when creating reports in Power View. Likewise, even if you will not be creating Power View reports, but will be primarily responsible for building Tabular BI Semantic Models, you may want to read through Part I of the book. This will allow you to gain an understanding of the way the reports are created with Power View. This enables you to design and create models that work well in the Power View environment.

The Learning Environment

This book not only tells you about the features of Power View and the BISM. It also contains exercises that show you how to implement these features for yourself. These exercises use data for a fictitious company called Pan-Geo Hospitality and Travel (more about that in Chapter 1). The book includes video demonstrations that show how to complete each of these exercises. You can read through the chapters and supplement that reading with the video demonstrations.

If you would like to take your learning one step further, you can build your own learning environment and try these steps yourself. This will give you a more hands-on experience. If your organization has a development or testing environment that supports Tabular BI Semantic Models and Power View, you can use Appendix A and its accompanying video to install the sample data and sample model used for the Learn By Doing exercises in this book. (Appendix A lists the software required by such an environment.) If your organization does not have such an environment, you can create your own virtual learning environment using limited-time, evaluation versions of the necessary software from Microsoft. Appendix B and its accompanying videos will walk you through the steps necessary to create and configure this virtual learning environment.

About the Media Included with This Book

Visualizing Data with Microsoft Power View contains several dynamic learning tools that will aid you in your mastery of Power View, including

- ▶ More than four hours of video demonstrations

- ▶ A complete package of sample data: a Power View–optimized BI Semantic Model with source code, a SQL Server database, and additional underlying data sources

- ▶ Comprehensive instructions for creating a learning environment, including Windows Server, SharePoint Server 2010, and Microsoft SQL Server 2012 with PowerPivot and Reporting Services SharePoint integration

- ▶ Six completed Power View reports that include multiple views, visualizations, and performance dashboards

- ▶ A BI Semantic Model with advanced extensions using DAX functions, including date and time, mathematical, logical, informational, and statistical functions

All of these tools are available on the enclosed DVD (for purchasers of the print book) and via download from the McGraw-Hill Professional Media Center (for purchasers of the ebook).

Print Book Users: Running the DVD

If the disc enclosed with the print book does not auto-start in your CD/DVD drive, do the following to display the menu:

For Windows 2000, Vista, and XP:

1. Open Windows Explorer.
2. Navigate to the drive containing the CD/DVD labeled Visualizing-Data-with-Microsoft-Power-View.
3. Locate the file Visualizing-Data-with-Microsoft-Power-View.exe.

NOTE

The .exe filename extension may not be visible if your system is configured to "hide extensions for known file types."

4. Double-click the filename to open the menu or right-click and select Open.

For Windows 7:
AutoPlay: Select Run Visualizing-Data-with-Microsoft-Power-View.exe.

DVD Technical Support

For questions regarding the content of the DVD, please visit www.mhprofessional.com or e-mail customer.service@mcgraw-hill.com. For customers outside the United States, e-mail international_cs@mcgraw-hill.com.

Ebook Users: Downloading the Media from the McGraw-Hill Professional Media Center

If you purchased the ebook edition of *Visualizing Data with Microsoft Power View*, you can download all of the example material included on the print book DVD from the McGraw-Hill Professional Media Center. Instructions for downloading are included at the end of the eBook Table of Contents.

What's Next

Chapter 1 shows you how to get started with the Power View reporting tool. After you see how to launch the application, you'll take a tour of the product and learn some associated terminology. This will be followed by an introduction to the Pan-Geo sample data that is used throughout the rest of the book.

So, let's get out there and have some fun with data analysis and reporting!

Part I

Using Power View

Chapter 1

Getting Started

In This Chapter

- ▶ **The Evolution of Microsoft Business Intelligence**
- ▶ **Launching Power View**
- ▶ **Microsoft Power View User Interface**
- ▶ **Sample Data**
- ▶ **Wrap-Up**

I n the introduction to this book, we discussed the design goals for Microsoft Power View and explained how Power View allows users to design and build their own reports in real time, bypassing the lengthy process of designing reports and having the IT department build them. We also discussed the fact that Power View provides a simple interface for building reports so users can start building reports soon after starting up Power View.

In this chapter, you'll first learn how Microsoft business intelligence (BI) tools have evolved, culminating in the development and release of Microsoft Power View. Then, you'll launch Power View and get a tour of the Power View user interface. Finally, this chapter introduces you to the sample data that is used in the examples throughout the book.

The Evolution of Microsoft Business Intelligence

Before we get into the details of Microsoft Power View, let's take a look at how Microsoft business intelligence has evolved over the years. This background should give you a better understanding of how Power View works. It can also provide insight into how Power View is intended to be used.

In the "old days" of data warehousing and business intelligence, data marts and data warehouses were created using a top-down approach. Business users had to work through the IT department by following a traditional application design methodology. The process started with design meetings that took place over a period of weeks, months, or even years depending on the size of the project.

These design meetings would be attended by IT employees and business users in order to accomplish the following:

- ▶ Determine and document the reporting and analysis requirements of the users

- ▶ Identify the sources of data that would be used for making business decisions

- ▶ Design processes to import data from these data sources

- ▶ Plan out the database structure for the data warehouse

- ▶ Design the reports and/or applications that would be used to analyze the data

- ▶ Estimate the effort and cost to build the solution

Once the design was complete and management had approved the budget and timeline for the project, the IT department would build the data warehouse according to the design. Unfortunately, most data warehouse projects did not (and many still do not) complete within the budgeted time or cost. In addition, the users—for whom the project was originally started—did not have the ability to actually analyze any data until months, or oftentimes years, after the project was started.

There are several consequences to approaching BI projects in this manner. First, the information needs of the users are likely to have changed from the start of the project to the time the first analysis is delivered. The data warehouse is already obsolete by the time it becomes available for use! Second, users often find that the reports and applications do not provide all of the necessary information to make business decisions. Reports designed on paper look very different once they are loaded with actual data. Many times these reports lead to further business questions and users discover that the reports were not designed to answer these new questions. Imagine management's perspective, spending thousands or millions of dollars on a project only to find out that core business decisions cannot be made using the tools created! I wouldn't want to be the person delivering that news!

Microsoft's approach to the BI methodology has evolved to be more user-centric. The users are the ones who know their data the best and know what they want to learn from that data. Instead of having the users sit down with the IT department to build a solution on paper, why not give the users access to the data along with easy-to-use analysis tools? That is the approach Microsoft has chosen to pursue, as evidenced by Power View and the Tabular BI Semantic Model (BISM).

PowerPivot

Many business users are very comfortable working with data in Excel. The main problem users experience with Excel is the limited number of rows allowed in a workbook and the poor performance that results when working with large amounts of data. If users could effectively use the data analysis tools in Excel with a workbook containing millions of rows of data, they could fulfill many of their data analysis needs. This was the inspiration for PowerPivot.

PowerPivot is a data analysis add-on for Microsoft Excel 2010 that allows large amounts of data to be collected, aggregated, and analyzed in one workbook. PowerPivot workbooks use a powerful data engine to quickly query a large volume of data. Using PowerPivot, many business intelligence questions can be answered efficiently and responsively directly within Excel.

The data to be analyzed may come from a variety of sources. The user imports this data into the PowerPivot workbook. Once the data is loaded, the user can utilize tools such as PivotTables and PivotCharts to calculate totals and find trends in the data. Figure 1-1 shows a sample PowerPivot analysis. Very powerful!

PowerPivot allows business intelligence to be more of an evolutionary process than a discreet project—providing a return on investment (ROI) almost immediately. Users can make business decisions based on results in PowerPivot in very short order. The need for a huge business intelligence project that does not provide deliverables for months is gone!

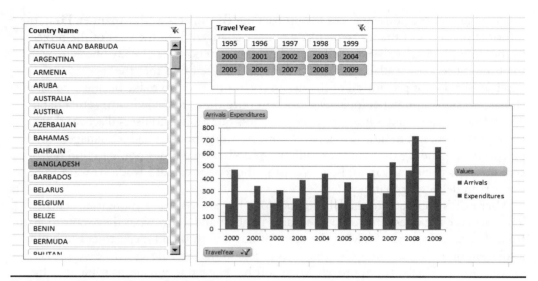

Figure 1-1   *The output of a PowerPivot workbook*

In addition, Microsoft provides a way for analysis work done by an individual user in PowerPivot to be shared at various levels throughout an enterprise. PowerPivot has two editions—PowerPivot for Excel, which works within Excel on a user's workstation, and PowerPivot for SharePoint. Using PowerPivot for SharePoint, analysis can be shared by a number of users in a work group or department.

For example, say Bill in accounting has analyzed the general ledger data and created some useful charts illustrating trends in gross profit. Others in his department have seen his PowerPivot workbook and would like to use those charts to create their own charts using the same data. To meet their needs, Bill publishes the PowerPivot workbook to a document library within the accounting department's Microsoft SharePoint site. The entire department can then use and enhance the workbook. The workbook has gone from being an individual tool to an important departmental resource. It has been escalated to the next level of use without the intervention of the IT department.

To make the leap from departmental resource to enterprise-wide tool, we leverage another Microsoft product, SQL Server Analysis Services.

Analysis Services and the BI Semantic Model

Microsoft SQL Server Analysis Services has provided the support and capabilities for corporate-level business intelligence for over ten years. Analysis Services efficiently delivers large amounts of aggregate data to many corporate users for use in reports and interactive tools. It accomplishes this feat by using objects called *cubes*.

Cubes are loaded with aggregates of numeric quantities such as sales figures or inventory amounts. These aggregations are calculated when the data is loaded into the cube. The aggregates don't need to be calculated when the user queries the data. As a result, totals can be retrieved from Analysis Services cubes very quickly.

For example, if Ashley needs a report listing the sales for the company, totaled by department and year, Analysis Services will have already calculated these values in the cube. Instead of having to sum up the thousands of individual sales and group the totals by department and year, Ashley's report can retrieve the sales figures already totaled by department and year from the cube in Analysis Services.

Analysis Services cubes and their supporting data are known as Multidimensional BI Semantic Models. These models are not built by the users of the data. Business intelligence professionals within the IT department work with the users to design and build these models. As a result, the method of creating Multidimensional BI Semantic Models resembles the traditional method for building business intelligence solutions more closely than it resembles the new, user-centric method.

To remedy this situation, Microsoft has enhanced Analysis Services to host a new type of structure known as a Tabular BI Semantic Model. As the name implies, the Tabular BI Semantic Model manages data in a tabular format similar to the way Excel and, more importantly, PowerPivot manage data. This model provides the architecture and optimization for a large number of users to access data in a format identical to the data storage method used by PowerPivot. Having Analysis Services host Tabular BI Semantic Models fills the need for the top level of scalability in this user-centric approach to business intelligence.

Tabular BI Semantic Models are built using a tool called SQL Server Data Tools that comes with Microsoft SQL Server. With this tool, a model can be created from scratch or a PowerPivot workbook can be imported to create the basis for the model. Once the model is complete, it is deployed to Analysis Services, which provides the infrastructure to make the model available to reporting tools and other client software.

The user-centric approach to business intelligence now functions in this manner:

► A business decision maker connects to existing data sources and loads the data into PowerPivot for Excel in order to begin analysis.

► As time passes, the decision maker determines the workbook would be beneficial to the entire department and deploys the PowerPivot workbook to a Microsoft SharePoint document library used by the department. The members of the department can use and enhance the workbook.

► Over time, the department members enhance the PowerPivot workbook, adding calculations and charts that would be useful to the entire company. The IT department imports the PowerPivot workbook from Microsoft SharePoint and uses it as the foundation for a Tabular BI Semantic Model. The IT department deploys the model to Analysis Services to make the data available to the entire company.

Our users now need a way to analyze and explore data in a Tabular BI Semantic Model deployed to Analysis Services. Power View fulfills that role.

Launching Power View

Now that you're familiar with a little of the history of Microsoft business intelligence, you're ready to get back to learning about Power View. In fact, it's time to start up Power View and take a look around.

Power View and Microsoft SharePoint

Microsoft Power View is not a stand-alone application like Microsoft Word or Microsoft Excel. You do not install Power View onto your PC to begin building and using reports. Much of the functionality of Power View depends upon the features built into Microsoft SharePoint and, as a result, Power View can be launched only from a SharePoint environment.

SharePoint Server was introduced by Microsoft in 2001 and was originally used as a document management and search tool. It provided the ability to upload documents and track document versions as they were being authored. Microsoft SharePoint Server also allowed users to find documents easily by searching both the names and the contents of the documents.

Microsoft SharePoint has changed a great deal since the original version in 2001. SharePoint is now used as a powerful tool for sharing information internally between employees and externally with customers and vendors. With Microsoft SharePoint 2010, companies can host employee blogs, share project and team information using many different site templates, provide business intelligence dashboards, build custom applications, and provide many social networking features to their employees and customers.

As a result, SharePoint is a natural fit for Power View. SharePoint is focused on collaboration and content sharing. Power View is a tool used to both visualize data and share it with others.

Required Software

In order to successfully create and run reports with Power View, certain software is required on your PC. Power View runs inside an Internet browser, but not all browsers will run the Power View interface. Power View will run in Internet Explorer 8 and Internet Explorer 9. Power View also runs in Firefox 4.

In addition to browser considerations, Microsoft Silverlight 5 also needs to be installed on your PC. Microsoft Silverlight provides a rich user experience in browser-based applications. It is Silverlight that makes possible many of the easy-to-use features in Power View.

Power View Data Sources

Microsoft Power View reports do not work like other reporting engines that access data directly from databases. The data for Power View reports needs to be placed in the proper model. Power View reports are generated using a BI Semantic Model. That BI Semantic Model can be a PowerPivot workbook or a Tabular BI Semantic Model created using SQL Server Data Tools. Although Power View cannot access other data sources directly, many different data sources can be used to load data into these PowerPivot workbooks and Tabular BI Semantic Models.

Launching Power View Using a PowerPivot Workbook

Once a PowerPivot workbook has been built and loaded with data, the workbook can be deployed to Microsoft SharePoint, either in a PowerPivot gallery or in a standard document library. The workbook in the gallery or library can then be used as the data source for Power View reports.

NOTE

If you have access to a physical learning environment hosting the Pan-Geo Hospitality and Travel data created according to the steps in Appendix A or if you have created a virtual learning environment using the steps in Appendix B, then you can use the Learn By Doing steps here to try launching Power View for yourself. If you do not have a learning environment available, please view the indicated video to watch as these steps are completed by one of the authors. Use this same approach for the Learn By Doing exercises in the remainder of this chapter and throughout the book.

Learn By Doing: Opening Power View Using a PowerPivot Workbook Connection

In this Learn By Doing exercise, we are simply going to launch Power View from a PowerPivot workbook and then return to the SharePoint library.

Video 1-1   **Launching Power View Using a PowerPivot Workbook**

1.   Open Internet Explorer and navigate to the home page of the SharePoint site hosting your learning environment.
2.   Click the PowerPivot Gallery link on the left side of the screen under Libraries, as shown in Figure 1-2.

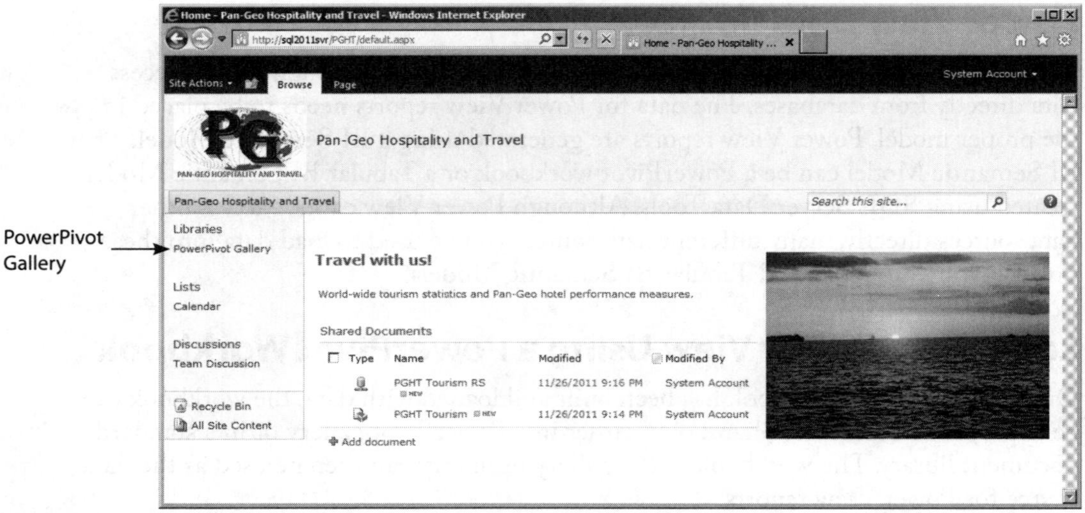

Figure 1-2   *PowerPivot Gallery link*

3.   This PowerPivot Gallery screen shows the list of PowerPivot workbooks that have been uploaded to SharePoint. Locate the entry for "PGHT Tourism PowerPivot Model." The upper-right corner of each PowerPivot gallery entry contains three icons, as shown in Figure 1-3. These icons appear faded, as if they were disabled, until you hover your mouse pointer over them. When you hover over the middle link, it displays a tooltip saying "Create Power View Report." Click the middle icon of the "PGHT Tourism PowerPivot Model" entry to launch Power View.

4.   Microsoft Power View will open with the tables from the PowerPivot workbook listed on the right. Your screen should look similar to Figure 1-4.

5.   Click your browser's Back button to return to the PowerPivot Gallery. If you made any changes to the Power View canvas, you will see a dialog box asking, "Are you sure you want to navigate away from this page?" If you see this dialog box, click OK.

6.   Click the browser's Back button a second time to return to the SharePoint site.

Launching Power View Using a Tabular BI Semantic Model

Tabular BI Semantic Models are not loaded into SharePoint in the same way PowerPivot workbooks are. The models are hosted within SQL Server Analysis Services. As a result, Microsoft Power View needs to know the location of the Tabular BI Semantic Model in

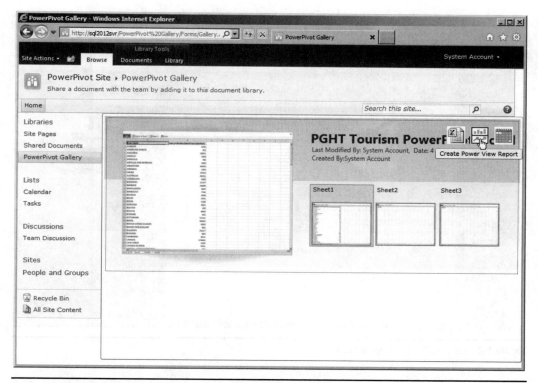

Figure 1-3   *Create Power View Report button for a PowerPivot Gallery entry*

order to load data into the reports. The location of the Tabular BI Semantic Model on an Analysis Services server is identified in one of two ways: using a BI Semantic Model connection file or using a Reporting Services data source. Both the connection file and the data source are essentially small files that contain the name of the server and database that hosts the Tabular BI Semantic Model.

NOTE

BI Semantic Model connection files and Reporting Services data sources can also be used to point to PowerPivot workbooks that have been uploaded to SharePoint.

Learn By Doing: Opening Power View Using Tabular BI Semantic Model Connections

In this Learn By Doing exercise, we are simply going to launch Power View using a BI Semantic Model connection file, return to the SharePoint library, and then do the same thing using a Reporting Services data source.

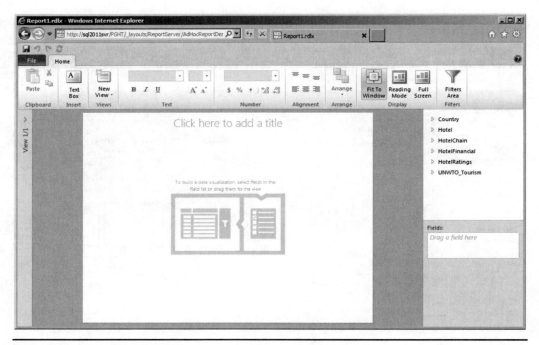

Figure 1-4 *Microsoft Power View main screen*

Video 1-2

Launching Power View Using a Tabular Model

1. Open Internet Explorer and navigate to the SharePoint document library hosting your learning environment, if you are not already there.

2. Hover your mouse over the PGHT Tourism item in the document library. A drop-down arrow appears.

3. Click the drop-down arrow and select Create Power View Report from the drop-down menu, as shown in Figure 1-5. Microsoft Power View opens, with the tables from the Tabular BI Semantic Model listed on the right.

4. Click your browser's Back button to return to the SharePoint site.

5. Hover your mouse over the PGHT Tourism RS item. A drop-down arrow appears.

6. Click the drop-down arrow and select Create Power View Report from the drop-down menu. Power View opens once again.

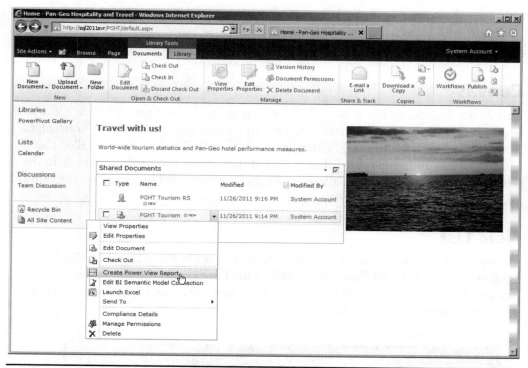

Figure 1-5   *Open Power View from a BI Semantic Model connection file.*

Notice the same steps are performed whether you are loading Power View using a BI Semantic Model connection file or a Reporting Services data source.

TIP

You can open Power View by simply clicking the BI Semantic Model connection file in the document library. This is not true for the Reporting Services data source. Clicking the Reporting Services data source opens the properties of the data source rather than opening Power View.

Microsoft Power View User Interface

When you open a Microsoft Office 2010 application such as Word to a new blank document, you see a fairly basic screen. There is lots of white space to start creating your document. The commands you may need are available on the various tabs of the ribbon.

This is true of Microsoft Power View as well. The interface in Power View has lots of white space, a ribbon, and a few additional elements. Let's take a tour through the important parts of the interface, as shown in Figure 1-6.

Canvas

One of the first things you notice when looking at the Power View interface is the lack of clutter. The screen is dominated by an empty section (except for a gray "watermark" in the center) with the heading "Click here to add a title." This section is called the *canvas* and is used to hold the different data visualizations and navigation tools in the report. All of the tables, charts, slicers, and other elements will be placed on the canvas and will display selected data from the data sources.

Field List

The upper-right side of the screen below the ribbon is the Field List. The Field List holds the tables in the BI Semantic Model or the PowerPivot workbook, and the fields contained within the tables. The list of fields for each table can be viewed by clicking the triangle next to the table name.

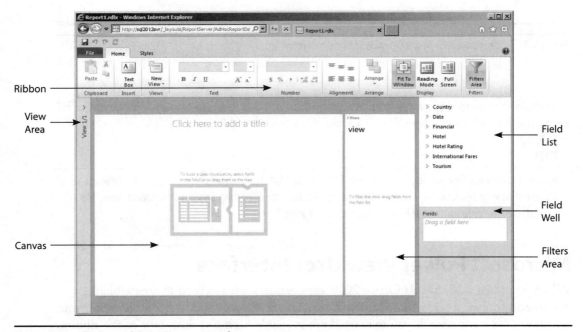

Figure 1-6 *The Microsoft Power View user interface*

Field Well

The Field Well resides in the bottom-right corner of the screen. It shows the fields selected from the model to appear on the canvas. It also provides access to properties and commands related to the object on the canvas that is currently selected. We use these properties and commands to control the appearance and behavior of the items on the canvas.

Filters Area

The Filters Area is used to restrict the amount of data displayed in a report. For example, we can use the Filters Area to restrict a report to show data only for the years 2005 to 2010. The Filters Area can be hidden or displayed by clicking the Filters Area button on the ribbon. It can also be minimized using the ">" toggle at the top of the Filters Area.

View Area

The View Area is used to track several states or views of the report for analyzing the state of your data at various points in time or as other values change. It can also be used to present several states of your data when you are presenting that data to others.

Ribbon

The ribbon spans the top of the screen and holds the commands that can be performed on the entire report or a selected object in the report. The ribbon is broken out into separate tabs that categorize and organize the commands.

File Tab

The label for the File tab has a green background for emphasis. Clicking this tab activates a drop-down menu that holds several key commands, including Save and Print.

Home Tab

The Home tab, which is shown in Figure 1-6, holds the basic formatting commands. In addition, the Home tab holds a button to show or hide the Filters Area.

Additional Tabs

Other tabs will appear in the ribbon as needed. These tabs will often be highlighted in the ribbon to make them stand out from the standard tabs.

Sample Data

This book guides you through the creation of a number of reports using Power View. To follow along, you need to have a set of data to work with. This data comes from our fictitious company, Pan-Geo Hospitality and Travel (PGHT). Throughout the book, you will be asked to assume different roles within the company and develop reports to meet the business needs of PGHT. If you do not have a learning environment available to you, you can watch the reports being developed in the accompanying videos.

A little bit about the company—PGHT owns and manages approximately 1,000 hotels around the world. The company has been working hard to bring together hotel performance and financial data so the leadership team can make informed business decisions about hotels that are underperforming and may be in need of improvement. In addition, the company has imported tourism data from the United Nations World Tourism Organization (UNWTO). This data can be used to identify tourism trends around the world. PGHT is looking to combine the tourism data with the hotel data to find where it should be building new hotels and where it may need to close hotels.

While you are creating reports with the PGHT data, you have our permission to occasionally daydream about a vacation to Fiji or a getaway to South America!

Wrap-Up

Now that you have an introduction to Microsoft Power View, it's time to get busy creating reports and taking advantage of all its great features. In the next chapter, you'll create your first tabular reports and explore the different ways to customize the presentation of the tabular data. The "table" is set!

Chapter 2

The Table Visualization

In This Chapter

The previous chapter introduced you to the Power View environment—the canvas, the Field List, and other aspects of the Power View window. In this chapter, you move beyond the blank canvas and create an actual report that delivers business information.

Visualizations

As you work with Power View, remember when you create a report, it isn't a typical report. It is an interactive view (or report; we will use these terms interchangeably throughout this book) in which the viewer analyzes data through a data model. Each building block of this interactive view provides a way to visualize the information. So we call these building blocks *visualizations*.

Power View reports consist of visualizations. A visualization can be a basic table, a multilevel table with row and column groupings, or a chart. When you place one or more visualizations on the Power View canvas, the visualization or the combination of visualizations becomes your report. They can be added, arranged and rearranged, modified, or removed in whatever manner will best tell the story behind the data. Visualizations communicate information.

The Lifecycle of a Report in Power View

Let's create our first Power View report. Each time we create a report, we will first examine the business reason for creating the report. In real life, a report is created to fulfill some business purpose. The same will be true of each report in this book. We will use scenarios from our fictitious company, Pan-Geo Hospitality and Travel (PGHT), described at the end of Chapter 1.

Jade, the Vice President of Marketing at PGHT, needs to compare total revenue generated by various hotel chains operated by PGHT. She needs to take into account local economic factors as she looks at the performance of each chain. She will use this information to allocate marketing and improvement dollars among the underperforming brands.

Now that we know the business reason behind the report, let's begin. We start by creating a blank report. This is actually as simple as launching Power View. Then we'll add some simple visualizations. The goal of these visualizations is to describe the financial performance of our various chains of Pan-Geo hotels.

NOTE

As mentioned in Chapter 1, if you have access to a physical learning environment hosting the Pan-Geo Hospitality and Travel data created according to the steps in Appendix A or if you have created a virtual environment using the steps in Appendix B, then you can try the Learn By Doing steps here. If you do not have a learning environment available, please view the indicated video to watch as these steps are completed by one of the authors.

Step 1: Launch Power View

To begin, we want a brand-new report canvas in front of us. If Power View is still active with a blank canvas from Chapter 1, you can skip this set of steps.

Learn By Doing: Opening Power View Using the Appropriate Model Connection

Video 2-1   **Creating a Table Visualization**

Try the following steps to create our first table visualization:

1. Open Internet Explorer and navigate to the SharePoint document library hosting your learning environment, if you are not already there.
2. Hover your mouse over the PGHT Tourism item in the document library. A drop-down arrow appears.
3. Click the drop-down arrow and select Create Power View Report from the drop-down menu.

The Power View application opens with a blank canvas on which to create your report. As you saw in Figure 1-6 in Chapter 1, the initial canvas consists of a watermark with some basic instructions and a single textbox with "Click here to add a title" as the text. Your initial view is the Home tab of the Power View ribbon—we'll look in more detail at the design features available on this ribbon tab in a moment.

Step 2: Design Your Report

Here is where the fun begins. To design our report, all we need to do is specify the report title and choose a couple of fields from the Field List.

Learn By Doing: Specifying the Report Title

Let's start by adding a report title:

1. Maximize your browser window to give yourself plenty of room to work.
2. Click the text that says "Click here to add a title," and then type **Revenue by Chain**.

We're going to report on total revenue for each chain operated by Pan-Geo Hospitality and Travel.

Learn By Doing: Selecting a Field

Now we add visualizations. Every visualization begins its life as a simple table. A table is the default layout for a visualization, so it is the automatic starting point for each new part of our report.

Let's add a field to our report canvas:

1. Click the arrow next to the Hotel table in the Field List. This will expand the Hotel table to show all the fields in this table.
2. Select the Chain Name check box.

In seconds, your first visualization will appear on the canvas as a simple table of chain names, as shown in Figure 2-1.

Next, let's examine the Field List again. Only related tables can be combined in a single visualization. Any table that is not related to the tables selected for the visualization will turn light gray and will not be available for inclusion in the visualization. In our model, all of the tables are related, so no tables appear in light gray.

Learn By Doing: Adding a Field to the Table Visualization

Let's continue by adding a field to the table visualization:

1. Click the table visualization on the canvas to make sure it is selected.
2. In the Field List, expand the Financial table. The Financial table includes Profit & Loss measures that we can add to our report.

   Measures are numerical amounts, percentages, counts, and similar data that help us to measure business performance. They have a calculator symbol to the left of the field name.
3. Select the Total Revenue check box. This adds a Total Revenue field to the table visualization, as shown in Figure 2-2.

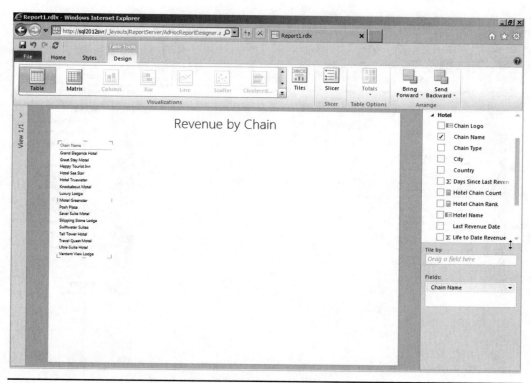

Figure 2-1   *A Power View report with a one-column table visualization*

And there it is! Selecting only two fields produces a useful report. Granted, we're seeing revenue across all years of operations around the entire world. In later Learn By Doing exercises, we'll focus in on smaller business units and time periods.

Before we add anything else to the table visualization, take a quick look at the Field Well. Notice that the fields you selected have been moved to the Fields box. We can add more related fields, including related measures, to the Field Well to expand our simple table.

TIP

Whenever you wish to add something to an existing visualization, be sure that visualization is the active selection on the canvas. To do so, click the visualization. Clicking an unused area of the canvas tells Power View you wish to create a new visualization.

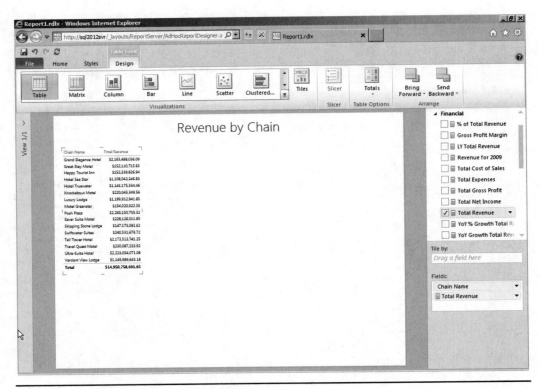

Figure 2-2 *A table visualization with two columns*

Learn By Doing: Adding More to the Table Visualization

Let's add the country name to our table visualization:

1. Click the table visualization on the canvas to make sure it is selected.
2. In the Field List, expand the Country table.
3. Drag the Country field down to the Field Well, to the Fields drop zone, and drop it between Chain Name and Total Revenue, as shown here.

Step 3: Enhance and Customize Visualizations

Perhaps you noticed when you selected the Total Revenue field (measure) or the Country field that the table resized itself to accommodate the additional columns in the table. Power View does a great job of keeping things organized on the canvas for you, which includes automatically placing and resizing visualizations. You do have liberty to put things wherever you want on the canvas and make them whatever size suits the needs of your report. For now, however, we'll let Power View do all the layout work.

Also, whenever you have a lot of rows in a table, more than you can see on the page at one time, you can use your mouse to scroll through the list. Power View briefly displays a wait indicator while it gets more rows from the data model. To ensure good performance, Power View only retrieves the visible data rather than getting them all the data at once. For this reason, Power View can work efficiently with a lot of data, and you never have to wait long for your results to appear!

Now let's add some features to our visualization to make it even more meaningful.

Learn By Doing: Accessing the Filters Area Using the Ribbon

First, let's narrow our report to a single fiscal year and to the countries of a single continent. To do so, we utilize the Filters Area.

Video 2-2   **Filtering Data in a Visualization**

1. Click the table visualization on the canvas to make sure it is selected.
2. Click the Home tab of the ribbon.
3. Click the Filters Area button.

   An area opens on the right side of the canvas. This is the Filters Area. It is used to tell Power View you wish to look at specific sets of your data rather than all of the data in the model.
4. Click the word "table" in the Filters Area.

The Filters Area now shows each of the fields and measures in the visualization and how each is currently being filtered, as shown in Figure 2-3. In our case, we have no filters applied, so all of the items show all of their data.

Learn By Doing: Accessing the Filters Area Using the Show Filters Icon

We can also view the filters for a given visualization by clicking the Show Filters icon associated with that visualization. In the next steps, we'll first hide the Filters Area, and then display it again.

1. Click an open area of the canvas to deselect the table visualization.
2. Click the Filters Area button in the ribbon to close the Filters Area.

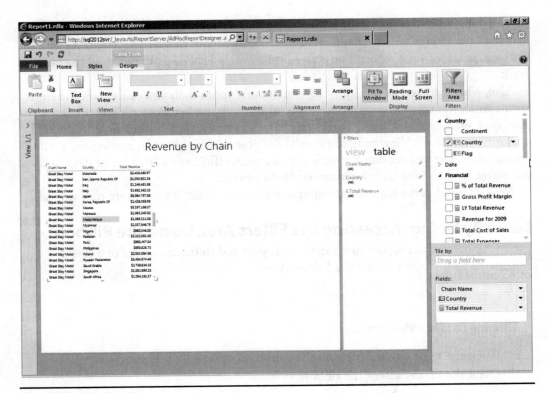

Figure 2-3 *The Filters Area*

3. Hover your mouse pointer over the table visualization. You will see two icons appear above the right side of the visualization.

4. Click the Show Filters icon, as shown here. The Filters Area will appear with the filters for the table visualization showing.

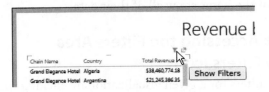

Learn By Doing: Adding Filters to a Visualization

In our current case, it will be helpful to see Total Revenue for a single year, and a single continent.

1. Expand the Date table.
2. Drag Year from the Date table in the Field List, and drop it onto the Filters Area. A year range slider appears, as shown here.

3. There is a slider handle above 1990 and another above 2020. Drag the slider handle above 1990 to the right until the text reads "is greater than or equal to 2011."
4. Drag the slider handle above 2020 to the left until the text reads "equals 2011," as shown here.

5. Drag Continent from the Country table in the Field List, and drop it onto the Filters Area.
6. Select the South America check box.

Notice that to the right of each choice in the selection area is a number—there are 13 members (or Countries in this case) in the data for the South America continent.

As you change the filter selections, the data in the table visualization changes accordingly.

Learn By Doing: Formatting the Title

Let's update the title of our report to reflect our filtering:

1. Select all of the text in the report title.
2. Change the font size from 28 to 20 using the font-size selector on the Home tab of the ribbon.
3. Add – **South America, 2011** to the end of the title.

Your report should appear as shown in Figure 2-4.

TIP

Power View lets you undo changes to your report. If at any time you think "Oops" as you're designing your report, you'll find the Undo and Redo buttons right above the ribbon.

Learn By Doing: Sizing a Visualization

Let's add more data to our visualization to provide a more complete financial picture of each chain. In the process, we will explore how visualizations can be sized automatically and manually.

Revenue by Chain – South America, 2011

Chain Name	Country	Total Revenue
Grand Elegance Hotel	Argentina	$4,628,662.63
Grand Elegance Hotel	Brazil	$25,073,836.33
Grand Elegance Hotel	Chile	$3,575,823.19
Grand Elegance Hotel	Colombia	$6,961,341.25
Grand Elegance Hotel	Peru	$4,313,008.72
Grand Elegance Hotel	Venezuela	$5,460,838.74
Great Stay Motel	Argentina	$43,695.59
Great Stay Motel	Brazil	$322,013.05
Great Stay Motel	Chile	$40,149.46
Great Stay Motel	Colombia	$104,284.96
Great Stay Motel	Peru	$41,561.28
Great Stay Motel	Venezuela	$62,244.96
Happy Tourist Inn	Argentina	$56,389.37
Happy Tourist Inn	Brazil	$360,347.78
Happy Tourist Inn	Chile	$46,404.26
Happy Tourist Inn	Colombia	$97,748.18
Happy Tourist Inn	Peru	$57,677.98
Happy Tourist Inn	Venezuela	$69,001.30
Hotel Sea Star	Argentina	$1,596,456.71

Figure 2-4 *The Revenue by Chain - South America, 2011 report*

Video 2-3

Sizing a Visualization

1. Make sure the table visualization is selected on the canvas.

2. Select the Total Cost Of Sales check box in the Financial table in the Field List to add the Total Cost Of Sales field to the table.

   As we have seen before, the table resizes to accommodate the new field. Let's see what happens if we manually resize the table, and then add a new field.

3. Hover your mouse pointer over the small gray line at the middle of the table's right edge. This is one of the sizing handles for the table. The mouse pointer will change to a double-headed arrow, as shown here.

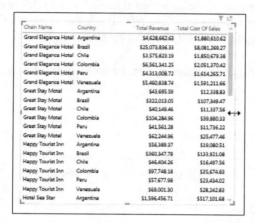

4. Drag the table a bit wider. We have now manually resized the table.

5. Select the check boxes for the following fields in the Financial table in the Field List to add them to the table:

   ▶ Total Gross Profit

   ▶ Total Expenses

   ▶ Total Net Income

   Notice the table no longer changes size as you add each new field. Instead, a horizontal scroll bar has been added and the content scrolls to the right to show each additional field. Once you manually size a visualization, you change its mode of operation from auto-size mode to manual-size mode. When in manual-size mode, a visualization will only change size when you drag one of the sizing handles as you did in step 4.

6. Double-click the sizing handle. The visualization returns to auto-size mode. At the same time, it grows wider to accommodate all of the new fields.

Learn By Doing: Using Tiles

One issue with the current layout of our table visualization is the fact that anyone viewing the report has to do a lot of scrolling to find the data for a particular country. We are going to remedy this issue by using the tiles feature.

Using Tiles

Video 2-4

1. From the Field Well, drag the Country field up and drop it in the Tile by box.

   The Country column disappears from the table visualization and instead the Country names appear on tabs across the top of the table, as shown in Figure 2-5. The data is split up across multiple *tiles*. Each tile contains the data for a single country. We navigate between the tiles by clicking the various tabs across the top of the visualization.

2. Try clicking several of the tabs in turn to move between the data for the various countries.

Revenue by Chain – South America, 2011

Argentina	Brazil	Chile	Colombia	Peru	Venezuela

Chain Name	Total Revenue	Total Cost Of Sales	Total Gross Profit	Total Expenses	Total Net Income
Grand Elegance Hotel	$4,628,662.65	$1,880,610.62	$2,748,052.01	$1,070,928.23	$1,677,123.78
Great Stay Motel	$43,695.59	$12,338.83	$31,356.76	$10,877.52	$20,479.24
Happy Tourist Inn	$56,389.37	$19,080.51	$37,108.86	$10,435.42	$26,873.44
Hotel Sea Star	$1,596,486.71	$517,101.68	$1,079,355.03	$317,686.04	$761,668.99
Hotel Truewater	$1,709,217.66	$639,718.71	$1,069,498.95	$301,267.29	$768,231.66
Knockabout Motel	$127,470.29	$43,132.20	$84,338.09	$23,589.96	$60,748.13
Luxury Lodge	$1,878,932.60	$608,598.02	$1,270,334.58	$373,888.98	$896,445.60
Motel Greenstar	$42,751.88	$12,072.37	$30,679.51	$10,642.66	$20,036.85
Posh Plaza	$3,118,393.93	$1,292,556.71	$1,825,837.22	$640,076.91	$1,185,760.31
Saver Suite Motel	$99,498.50	$35,373.56	$64,124.94	$21,866.91	$42,258.03
Skipping Stone Lodge	$43,685.37	$13,315.37	$30,370.00	$9,826.54	$20,543.46
Swiftwater Suites	$248,257.86	$82,904.61	$165,353.25	$40,604.37	$124,748.88
Tall Tower Hotel	$3,617,729.64	$1,102,691.74	$2,515,037.90	$813,754.59	$1,701,283.31
Travel Quest Motel	$106,371.63	$55,051.77	$51,319.86	$21,120.96	$30,198.91
Ultra-Suite Hotel	$2,718,692.34	$828,656.13	$1,890,036.21	$611,535.13	$1,278,501.08
Verdant View Lodge	$2,735,145.86	$1,016,254.85	$1,718,891.01	$493,725.87	$1,225,165.14
Total	**$22,771,351.86**	**$8,159,457.68**	**$14,611,894.18**	**$4,771,827.37**	**$9,840,066.81**

Figure 2-5   *Tiling the report by country*

3. When you click in the tabs area, the Tile Tools Design tab is displayed in the ribbon, as shown here.

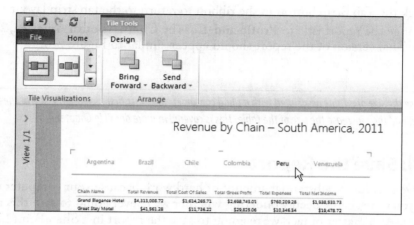

4. Click the Cover Flow button in the ribbon. The visualization changes from using the tab strip method for moving between tiles to using the cover flow method, as shown here.

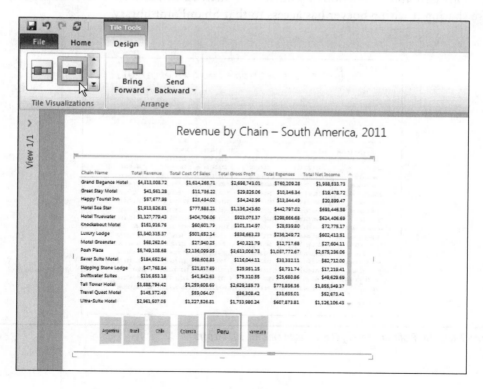

5. Try clicking several of the items in the cover flow to move between the data for various countries.
6. Click the Tab Strip button in the ribbon to return to the tab strip layout.
7. Change the report title to **Profit-and-Loss by Chain – South America, 2011**. The final version of the report should appear similar to Figure 2-6.

NOTE

To increase the size of a table associated with a tiling container, you must first increase the size of the tiling container, and then increase the size of the table. This is covered in more detail in Chapter 4.

Step 4: Save the Report

If you have ever lost a substantial amount of hard work because your computer suddenly crashed, you've probably been wondering whether we're ever going to save this report. Great idea! As a matter of fact, we're going to save the report in a SharePoint library right now. Power View reports cannot be saved to your PC; everything takes place in SharePoint. (Technically, there are ways to save Power View reports to your PC, but they don't have much functionality outside of SharePoint.) Once we save the report, we're sharing it with whoever has access to that SharePoint library.

Profit-and-Loss by Chain – South America, 2011

	Argentina	Brazil	Chile	Colombia	**Peru**	Venezuela

Chain Name	Total Revenue	Total Cost Of Sales	Total Gross Profit	Total Expenses	Total Net Income
Grand Elegance Hotel	$4,313,008.72	$1,614,265.71	$2,698,743.01	$760,209.28	$1,938,533.73
Great Stay Motel	$41,561.28	$11,736.22	$29,825.06	$10,346.34	$19,478.72
Happy Tourist Inn	$57,677.98	$23,434.02	$34,243.96	$13,344.49	$20,899.47
Hotel Sea Star	$1,913,826.81	$777,583.21	$1,136,243.60	$442,797.02	$693,446.58
Hotel Truewater	$1,327,779.43	$404,706.06	$923,073.37	$298,666.68	$624,406.69
Knockabout Motel	$161,916.76	$60,601.79	$101,314.97	$28,539.80	$72,775.17
Luxury Lodge	$1,340,315.37	$501,652.14	$838,663.23	$236,249.72	$602,413.51
Motel Greenstar	$68,262.04	$27,940.25	$40,321.79	$12,717.68	$27,604.11
Posh Plaza	$5,749,108.68	$2,136,099.96	$3,613,008.73	$1,037,772.67	$2,575,236.06
Saver Suite Motel	$184,652.94	$68,608.83	$116,044.11	$33,332.11	$82,712.00
Skipping Stone Lodge	$47,768.84	$21,817.69	$25,951.15	$8,731.74	$17,219.41
Swiftwater Suites	$116,853.18	$41,542.63	$75,310.55	$25,680.86	$49,629.69
Tall Tower Hotel	$3,888,794.42	$1,259,608.69	$2,629,185.73	$773,836.36	$1,855,349.37
Travel Quest Motel	$145,372.49	$59,064.07	$86,308.42	$33,635.01	$52,673.41
Ultra-Suite Hotel	$2,961,507.05	$1,227,526.81	$1,733,980.24	$607,873.81	$1,126,106.43
Verdant View Lodge	$3,481,858.79	$1,162,755.55	$2,319,103.24	$569,472.19	$1,749,631.05
Total	$25,800,264.78	$9,398,943.62	$16,401,321.16	$4,893,205.76	$11,508,115.40

Figure 2-6   *The Profit-and-Loss by Chain - South America, 2011 report*

TIP

Above the ribbon, next to Undo, is the Save button. Click this button whenever you wish to save your work on the current report.

Learn By Doing: Saving a Report

Let's save our report:

Video 2-5

Saving a Report

1. Click the Save button in the upper left of the screen. The Save As dialog box appears.
2. Navigate to the SharePoint document library where you created the PGHT Tourism connection files.
3. In the File name field, enter **Profit-and-Loss By Chain S. America 2011**. The Save As dialog box should appear as shown in Figure 2-7.

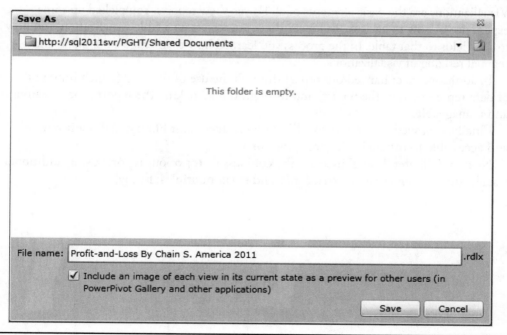

Figure 2-7   *The Save As dialog box*

4. Click Save. The report is saved. It may take a few seconds for the dialog box to disappear.

5. Click your browser's Back button to exit Power View and return to the SharePoint site.

6. Click your browser's Refresh button to refresh this page. Note the new entry in the document library for Profit-and-Loss By Chain S. America 2011.

7. Hover over the entry for our new report and click the drop-down arrow.

8. Select View Properties from the menu. The Properties dialog box appears.

   Notice the report file was saved in the document library with an .rdlx file extension. (You'll see this in the title at the top of the dialog box.) This designates the file as a Power View report.

9. Click Close to exit the Properties dialog box.

As you'll discover in the next chapter, you can always return to an existing report to view it or make changes to it by locating its RDLX file in the SharePoint library.

Wrap-Up

In this chapter, you learned how to create your first Power View report using a visualization. Visualizations are the basic elements of all Power View reports. You picked up some experience in how to navigate in Power View, how to create a table visualization, and how to add fields to that table. In the process you learned how to leverage auto-sizing and manual resizing of visualizations.

In addition, we enhanced our report through the use of filtering (which limited the set of data represented in the report) and through tiling, making the report more meaningful and manageable.

Finally, we saved our report to a SharePoint document library, making it reusable and accessible to others in the organization.

Next, in Chapter 3, we'll increase the coolness factor of our reports using additional visualizations, such as the matrix, cards, and small multiples. Enjoy!

Chapter 3

Additional Visualizations

In This Chapter

I n the previous chapter we created our first report. We enhanced that report to make it more useful. In this chapter we will continue to build upon this report and explore more visualization options that are available for us to use.

With our first report in Chapter 2, we created a table, which is the starting point for every visualization in Power View. We then expanded the table visualization to include additional columns. We filtered the data so only 2011 information for South American countries was displayed. We also used the tab strip layout to enable users to select which South American country they want to analyze in the report. Not bad for just a few clicks and a drag-and-drop or two.

This first report, however, just scratches the surface of the functionality that is available in Power View. In this chapter we look at more ways we can enhance our table visualization, employ advanced table layouts such as the matrix, and explore a new type of visualization—the card. Along the way, we utilize images that are made available through our BI Semantic Model.

So let's continue our journey into visualizations in Power View.

Setting the Table

With the Profit-and-Loss By Chain report we created in Chapter 2, we saw how easily we can add a data navigation feature with a tab strip. Our Vice President of Marketing at PGHT, Jade, found this report very useful. Now she has requested to have the hotel chain information on the report sorted by net income. That will enable Jade to easily determine which are the better performing chains and which are the underperforming chains.

Opening a Power View Report

To begin, we will need to open the report we created in Chapter 2.

Learn By Doing: Opening a Power View Report for Editing

Try the following:

Video 3-1   **Editing a Power View Report and Sorting a Table**

1. Open Internet Explorer and navigate to the SharePoint document libary hosting your learning environment, if you are not already there.
2. Click the Profit-and-Loss By Chain S. America 2011 item in the document library. Power View launches and the report opens in what is known as Reading Mode.

3. Click the Edit Report button in the upper left of the report area, as shown here. Power View changes to Editing Mode. We can now begin to modify and enhance our existing report.

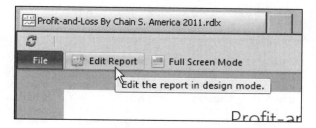

Editing the Profit-and-Loss Report

Let's sort the data in the table to meet Jade's requirement for the report:

Learn By Doing: Adding Sorting to the Table Visualization

1. Click the Total Net Income column heading in the table. When you first click this column, data sorts in ascending order, with the smallest values at the top. In our case, we would like the values to be listed in the opposite order.

2. Click the Total Net Income column heading a second time. Now the hotel chains are listed in descending order based on the Total Net Income column. The report should now look similar to Figure 3-1.

    To simplify the report and make it easier to read, we are going to modify the formatting of the values to remove the decimal places. Including the cents in these dollar amounts is really not beneficial.

3. Click a value in the Total Revenue column of the table.

4. On the Home tab of the ribbon, click the dollar sign ($) in the Number section. This sets the format of the values to Accounting Number Format.

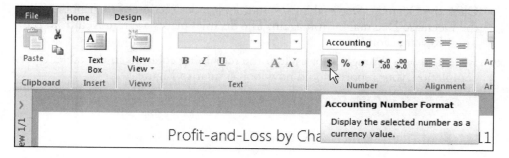

Profit-and-Loss by Chain - South America, 2011

Argentina   Brazil   Chile   Colombia   Peru   Venezuela

Chain Name	Total Revenue	Total Cost of Sales	Total Gross Profit	Total Expenses	Total Net Income ▾
Tall Tower Hotel	$3,617,729.64	$1,102,691.74	$2,515,037.90	$813,754.59	$1,701,283.31
Grand Elegance Hotel	$4,628,662.63	$1,880,610.62	$2,748,052.01	$1,070,928.23	$1,677,123.78
Ultra-Suite Hotel	$2,718,692.34	$828,656.13	$1,890,036.21	$611,535.13	$1,278,501.08
Verdant View Lodge	$2,735,145.86	$1,016,254.85	$1,718,891.01	$493,725.87	$1,225,165.14
Posh Plaza	$3,118,393.93	$1,292,556.71	$1,825,837.22	$640,076.91	$1,185,760.31
Luxury Lodge	$1,878,932.60	$608,598.02	$1,270,334.58	$373,888.98	$896,445.60
Hotel Truewater	$1,709,217.66	$639,718.71	$1,069,498.95	$301,267.29	$768,231.66
Hotel Sea Star	$1,596,456.71	$517,101.68	$1,079,355.03	$317,686.04	$761,668.99
Swiftwater Suites	$248,257.86	$82,904.61	$165,353.25	$40,604.37	$124,748.88
Knockabout Motel	$127,470.29	$43,132.20	$84,338.09	$23,589.96	$60,748.13
Saver Suite Motel	$99,498.50	$35,373.56	$64,124.94	$21,866.91	$42,258.03
Travel Quest Motel	$106,371.63	$55,051.77	$51,319.86	$21,120.95	$30,198.91
Happy Tourist Inn	$56,389.37	$19,080.51	$37,308.86	$10,435.42	$26,873.44
Skipping Stone Lodge	$43,685.37	$13,315.37	$30,370.00	$9,826.54	$20,543.46
Great Stay Motel	$43,695.59	$12,338.83	$31,356.76	$10,877.52	$20,479.24
Motel Greenstar	$42,751.88	$12,072.37	$30,679.51	$10,642.66	$20,036.85
Total	**$22,771,351.86**	**$8,159,457.68**	**$14,611,894.18**	**$4,771,827.37**	**$9,840,066.81**

Figure 3-1   *Profit-and-Loss by Chain report sorted by Total Net Income*

NOTE

The values in the PGHT Tourism model that are used in the Profit-and-Loss by Chain report were already formatted to currency, but if we were to simply decrease the number of decimals without first selecting the Accounting Number Format option, we would lose the currency format.

5. Click the Decrease Decimal button in the Number section of the ribbon. Click the Decrease Decimal button again. The decimal places are removed from the Total Revenue column.

6. Repeat steps 3 through 5 for each of the remaining columns in the table. Upon completion, your report should now look similar to Figure 3-2.

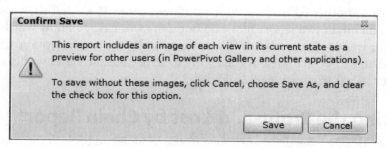

Profit-and-Loss by Chain - South America, 2011

Argentina   Brazil   Chile   Colombia   Peru   Venezuela

Chain Name	Total Revenue	Total Cost of Sales	Total Gross Profit	Total Expenses	Total Net Income ▾
Tall Tower Hotel	$3,617,730	$1,102,692	$2,515,038	$813,755	$1,701,283
Grand Elegance Hotel	$4,628,663	$1,880,611	$2,748,052	$1,070,928	$1,677,124
Ultra-Suite Hotel	$2,718,692	$828,656	$1,890,036	$611,535	$1,278,501
Verdant View Lodge	$2,735,146	$1,016,255	$1,718,891	$493,726	$1,225,165
Posh Plaza	$3,118,394	$1,292,557	$1,825,837	$640,077	$1,185,760
Luxury Lodge	$1,878,933	$608,598	$1,270,335	$373,889	$896,446
Hotel Truewater	$1,709,218	$639,719	$1,069,499	$301,267	$768,232
Hotel Sea Star	$1,596,457	$517,102	$1,079,355	$317,686	$761,669
Swiftwater Suites	$248,258	$82,905	$165,353	$40,604	$124,749
Knockabout Motel	$127,470	$43,132	$84,338	$23,590	$60,748
Saver Suite Motel	$99,499	$35,374	$64,125	$21,867	$42,258
Travel Quest Motel	$106,372	$55,052	$51,320	$21,121	$30,199
Happy Tourist Inn	$56,389	$19,081	$37,309	$10,435	$26,873
Skipping Stone Lodge	$43,685	$13,315	$30,370	$9,827	$20,543
Great Stay Motel	$43,696	$12,339	$31,357	$10,878	$20,479
Motel Greenstar	$42,752	$12,072	$30,680	$10,643	$20,037
Total	**$22,771,352**	**$8,159,458**	**$14,611,894**	**$4,771,827**	**$9,840,067**

Figure 3-2   *Profit-and-Loss by Chain report without decimal values*

7. Click the Save button in the upper left of the screen. You will be prompted with a dialog box to confirm the save operation, shown here. The dialog box states that saving the report will also update the preview images for this report. Click the Save button to confirm.

Confirm Save   ⊠

⚠ This report includes an image of each view in its current state as a preview for other users (in PowerPivot Gallery and other applications).

To save without these images, click Cancel, choose Save As, and clear the check box for this option.

Save   Cancel

NOTE

Preview images are saved with the reports to provide a visual representation of the view(s) available in the report file. These images are displayed in areas such as the PowerPivot Gallery and in storyboard mode which will be discussed later in this chapter.

We have now seen how to sort the data in a table visualization and how to override the formatting of the values. This helps to improve the usefulness of the table as well as reduce clutter and make the report easier to read. Now when we click each country in the tile tab strip, the data is refreshed to show us the hotel chains sorted by Total Net Income in descending order. The VP of Marketing can now easily determine which hotel chains need additional marketing dollars allocated to them.

Including Images

We have seen how quickly we can create a report in Power View, add filtering options, and include customizations. Now we are going to see how we can include some visual aids in the report design. One of the features available in our BI Semantic Model is the ability to include images. These images are exposed to the users of the model and can be included in the report design to provide a nice visual representation of what is being analyzed.

Jade has decided that she really likes the Profit-and-Loss by Chain report. She would like to start using this report in meeting presentations. One thing she would like to do is add some images so people can quickly determine what data is being displayed. She would like to maintain the existing report as is for printing purposes, and she would like a second version of the report that includes the visuals for presentation purposes.

To fulfill Jade's requirements, we will need to create a second copy of the Profit-and-Loss by Chain report. One way to do this is to perform a Save As while editing the report to create another RDLX file with a different name. If we do this, we will have to track and maintain two report files, and our users will have to know which report is to be used for which purpose. With Power View, we have a second option. One of the features available in Power View is the ability to have multiple views within a single RDLX report file. Let's see how this works.

Enhancing the Profit-and-Loss by Chain Report

If you do not already have the report open in the browser, go back to the previous Learn By Doing exercise and follow the steps to open a Power View report in Editing Mode.

Learn By Doing: Adding a View to a Report

Let's make a copy of our existing view so that we can make the necessary modifications as requested:

Video 3-2   **Adding a View to a Report**

1. Click the Home tab of the ribbon.
2. Click the drop-down list below the New View button and select Duplicate View, as shown in Figure 3-3. The View Area opens on the left side of the screen. An additional view is created and becomes the active view on the canvas. The screen should look similar to Figure 3-4.

Learn By Doing: Adding Images to a Report

Now that we have a copy of our report, we move to the next requirement—adding images.

1. Click anywhere in the table to select it.
2. Click the arrow next to the Country table in the Field List to expand it.

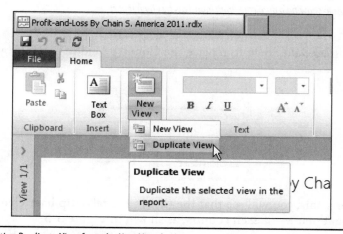

Figure 3-3   *Selecting Duplicate View from the New View button*

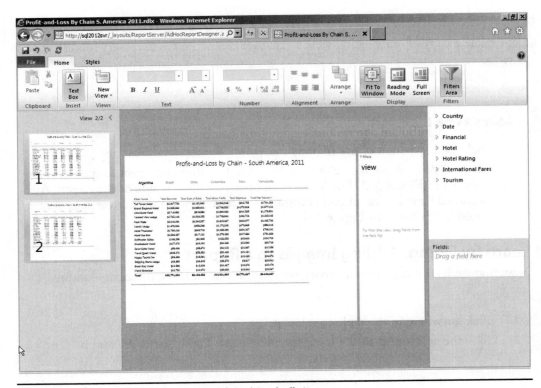

Figure 3-4   *View Area showing a duplicate Profit-and-Loss by Chain report*

3. Drag the Flag field down to replace the Country field in the Tile by section, as shown.

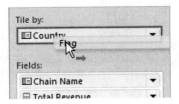

After doing this, you will see that the tiles in the tab strip have changed to include the flags and names of each country, as shown in Figure 3-5.

4. Use the sizing handles to adjust the size of the tile container so that you can see the entire table on the report.

5. Click the Save button in the upper left of the screen, and, if asked, confirm that you want to update the preview images by clicking Save again.

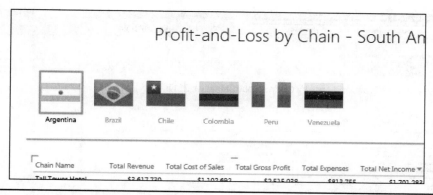

Figure 3-5   *Country flags and names in the tile tab strip*

You have now created a copy of the original Profit-and-Loss by Chain view and included images so that it is ready for Jade to present during her meetings.

NOTE

You will notice that, in tab strip mode, included with the country flag images are the names of the countries. As part of the BI Semantic Model design, which will be discussed in Part II of this book, a default label is defined in a table. When using a default image in the tab strip, the default label is also displayed. Without the default label defined, you will receive an error message when you try to include an image field as a tile.

Navigating the Profit-and-Loss by Chain Report

When Jade goes into her presentations, she has two views from which to choose in the Profit-and-Loss by Chain report. Let's take a closer look at how this works.

Let's go through an exercise on using these two navigation options.

Learn By Doing: Navigating a Power View Report

First let's use the view navigation option:

Video 3-3   **Navigating a Power View Report**

1.   Click the Reading Mode button on the Home tab of the ribbon (on the right side).

You will notice a couple of items in the lower left and right corners of the report as shown in Figure 3-6. The item in the lower left selects the storyboard mode. The item in the lower right is the view navigation option. These items enable us to navigate and display the different views within a report.

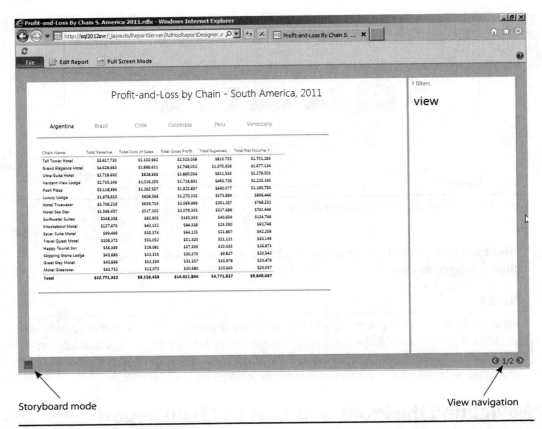

Storyboard mode

View navigation

Figure 3-6   *View navigation items*

2. Click the previous button in the view navigation in the lower right portion of the screen. The first view in the RDLX report file is loaded. This is the view without the images of the country flags. Click the next button to return to the view with the images of the country flags.

3. Click the storyboard mode option in the lower left portion of the screen. You are presented with a screen similar to Figure 3-7. This option displays a tab strip below the existing view with images of all the views included in the report.

4. Click the image of the first view in the tab strip. The first view is now the active view and the storyboard is closed.

5. Click the Full Screen Mode button at the top of the window. Your screen should now look similar to Figure 3-8. Full Screen Mode hides the browser and maximizes the view to fill the screen. The view navigation options are still available in Full Screen Mode.

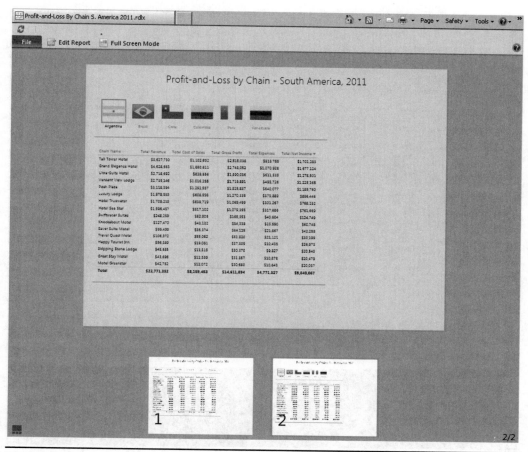

Figure 3-7   *Power View report in storyboard mode*

6. Press ESC to exit Full Screen Mode.
7. Click your browser's Back button to exit Power View.

Now that you have seen how to create a copy of a report to create a new view, how to include images in a report, and the different options for navigating and presenting the report, we are going to move on to exploring other visualizations, the matrix and the card, and we'll create a new report.

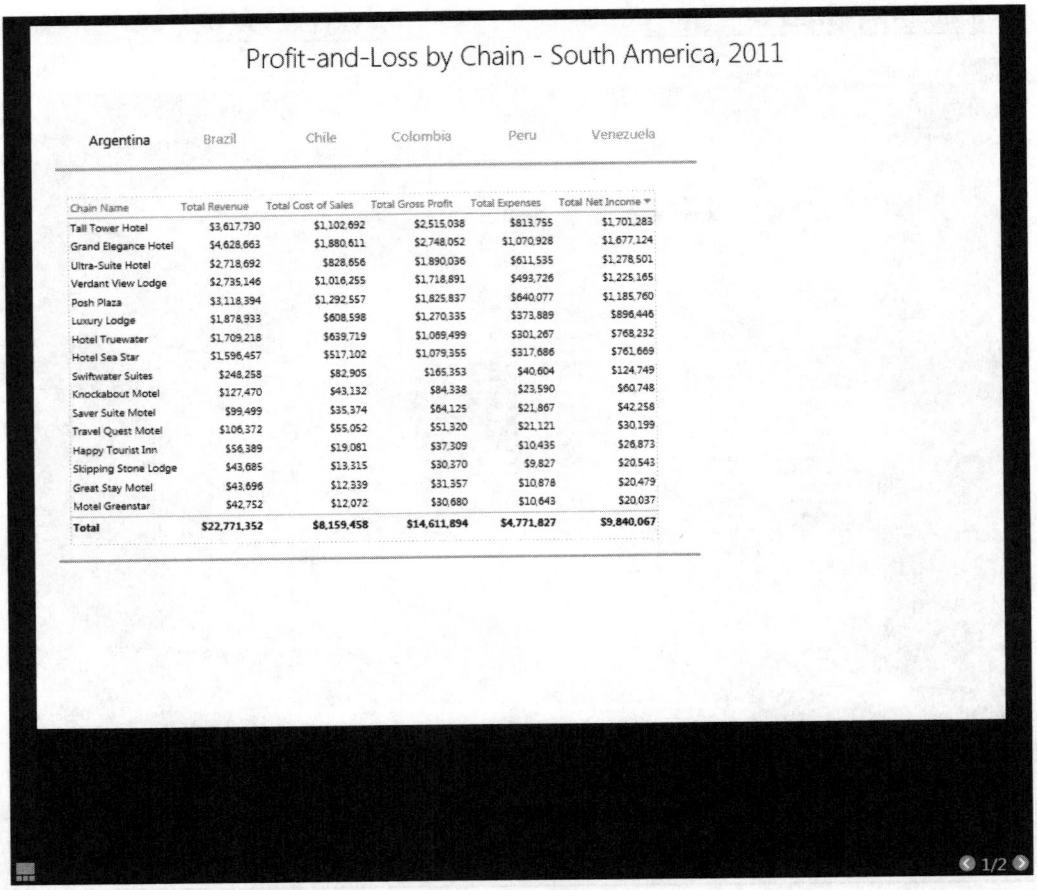

Figure 3-8   *Power View report in Full Screen Mode*

Entering the Matrix

The table is the starting point of all our visualizations in a report. A basic table contains rows of data and has column headers for each of the fields being displayed. Now we are going to take a look at another style of visualization that provides the ability to group the rows of data and also includes the option to group the columns. The visualization that will deliver this functionality is called a *matrix*.

Creating the Matrix

Jade has been using the Profit-and-Loss by Chain report to review the South America data for 2011 and has determined there are a few areas her team needs to focus on. Specifically, she feels Argentina, Chile, and Peru are countries for which they need to try to increase revenue. In order to verify her findings, she has asked Dennis, the Marketing Analyst for PGHT, to review the revenue growth in these areas. In particular, she would like to know which of the hotel chains requires the most attention.

In order to perform his analysis, Dennis decides to create a report filtered on the target countries and showing revenue growth over the past five years.

Learn By Doing: Creating a Matrix Report

In this exercise we will create a new report using the BI Semantic Model connection file for PGHT. Let's take a look at the steps needed to create this new report:

Video 3-4   **Creating a Matrix Report**

1. Open Internet Explorer and navigate to the SharePoint document libary, if you are not already there.
2. Click the PGHT Tourism connection file in the document library. Power View opens to create a new report.
3. In the empty report, click the Filters Area button on the Home tab of the ribbon. The Filters Area is displayed.
4. Click the arrow next to the Date table in the Field List to expand it.
5. Drag the Year field into the Filters Area.
6. Drag the sliders from both sides so that the Year filter reads "is between 2007 and 2011."
7. Expand the Country table in the Field List by clicking its arrow.
8. Drag the Country field into the Filters Area.
9. Select the check box next to Argentina.
10. Scroll down and select the check box next to Chile.

11. We use the filter search to find and select Peru. The filter search entry area is directly above the list of items, as shown here.

Filter search ⟶

Type **Peru** in the filter search entry area and press ENTER (or click the magnifying glass button). The list will be filtered to show only the values satisfying your search. In this case, only Peru will be showing, as shown.

12. Select the check box next to Peru.
13. Click the Country header in the Filters Area to collapse the Country entry.
14. Click the Filters Area button on the Home tab to hide this area. Now we are ready to build the report.
15. Click the arrow next to the Hotel table in the Field List to expand it.
16. Select the check boxes next to Chain Type and Chain Name. This will create a table visualization on the report.
17. Click the arrow next to the Financial table in the Field List to expand it.
18. Select the check box next to the YoY % Growth Total Revenue measure (YoY stands for Year-over-Year; this measure will show the percentage change in total revenue from one year to the next). We now have a table with three columns, but we want to add grouping using a matrix.

19. Click the Matrix button on the ribbon's Design tab (which is part of Table Tools), as shown.

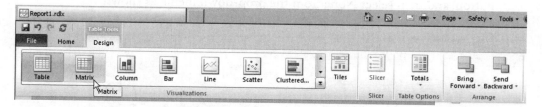

Grouping is now added to our visualization and the repeating values in the Chain Type column have disappeared, as shown in Figure 3-9. (You may need to expand the table a bit to see all of the data and the percent signs). You will also see that subtotals (Total rows) have been added for each of the Chain Types. In the Field Well, note that the matrix has three sections—Values, Row Groups, and Column Groups.

Chain Type	Chain Name	YoY % Growth Total Revenue
Hotel	Grand Elegance Hotel	26.25 %
	Hotel Sea Star	20.10 %
	Hotel Truewater	19.20 %
	Tall Tower Hotel	25.40 %
	Ultra-Suite Hotel	22.50 %
	Total	**23.67 %**
Lodge	Luxury Lodge	19.05 %
	Skipping Stone Lodge	-5.82 %
	Verdant View Lodge	19.28 %
	Total	**18.69 %**
Motel	Great Stay Motel	-5.58 %
	Knockabout Motel	0.52 %
	Motel Greenstar	-6.16 %
	Saver Suite Motel	-0.38 %
	Travel Quest Motel	0.63 %
	Total	**-1.22 %**
Other	Happy Tourist Inn	-5.91 %
	Posh Plaza	26.40 %
	Swiftwater Suites	0.20 %
	Total	**24.45 %**
Total		**22.14 %**

Figure 3-9   *Initial view of the matrix visualization*

20. In our report, the subtotals and totals are not going to be used with the percentage values. On the ribbon's Design tab (which is part of Matrix Tools), click the Totals button, and then select None from the drop-down menu, as shown.

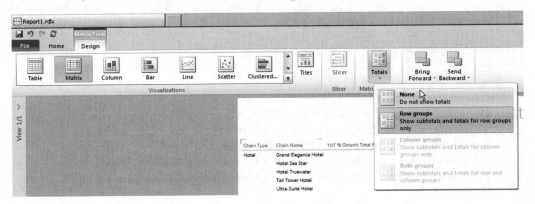

21. With the matrix visualization still selected, drag the Country field from the Country table in the Field List into the Column Groups portion of the Field Well.
22. Drag the Year field from the Date table in the Field List below the Country field in the Column Groups.
23. Click in the "Click here to add a title" section at the top of the report and replace this text with **YoY Revenue Growth Analysis - South America**.
24. Resize the table so you can see all the columns of data.
25. Click the Save button in the upper left.
26. In the Save As dialog box, enter **YoY Revenue Growth Analysis S. America** in the File Name field.
27. Click Save. The report is saved in the SharePoint document library.
28. Click your browser's Back button to exit Power View.

NOTE

Remember to refresh your browser in order to see the new report in the SharePoint document library.

Dennis can now use the report to focus in on the underperforming hotel chains in Argentina, Chile, and Peru. Based on the year-over-year revenue growth in numbers, he sees that Skipping Stone Lodge, Great Stay Motel, Motel Greenstar, and Happy Tourist Inn have had the largest negative revenue growth the past five years. He notifies Jade that these chains should be the target of their marketing efforts to move these numbers in a positive direction.

Calling All Cards

The next visualization we want to look at is the *card* visualization. This visualization takes a set of data and displays it in a layout resembling an index card. Jade has decided she would like a report showing all the hotels available for a selected country. This will be a hotel inventory report. She would like to see some visual aids as part of the design to make it a bit more colorful.

Creating the Cards

As we create the cards in the following Learn By Doing exercise, we will take advantage of a feature of the Tabular BI Semantic Model called the *default field set*. A default field set can be defined for any table in the model. Instead of selecting individual fields from a table, as we have done so far, we can select an entire table by using a default field set. When we do this, all of the fields in the default field set are placed on the canvas at the same time.

We don't have to keep all of the fields in the default field set in our visualization. These fields simply serve as a convenient starting point when we need most of the basic fields from a given table in our visualization. We can remove one or more of these fields or add other fields to the Field Well as needed.

Learn By Doing: Creating a Hotel Inventory Report

In this exercise we use the card visualization to create an inventory of all the hotels in a selected country. Let's take a look at the steps needed to create this new report requested by Jade:

Video 3-5   **Creating a Card Style Report**

1. Open Internet Explorer and navigate to the home page of the Pan-Geo Hospitality and Travel SharePoint site, if you are not already there.
2. Click the PGHT Tourism connection file in the document library to create a new Power View report.
3. Click the Hotel table name in the Field List (click the name of the table this time, not the arrow). You will see that this creates a new table visualization on the canvas with several fields that include Chain Logo, Hotel Name, and Number of Employees. Pretty cool, right?
4. Click the drop-down arrow on the Design tab of the ribbon to view all of the visualizations available, as shown in Figure 3-10.

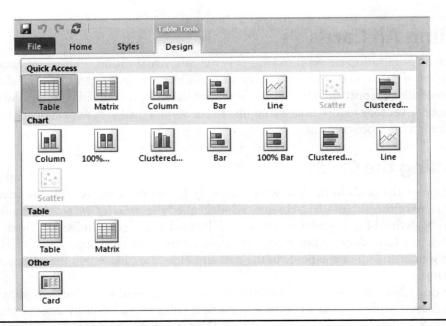

Figure 3-10   *Full list of the Power View visualizations*

5. In the Other category, click the Card visualization. You now see your table transformed into a card. The card includes a heading, an image, and additional information about the item, in this case hotels. Your report should look similar to Figure 3-11.

6. Click the arrow next to the Country table in the Field List to expand it.

7. Drag the Flag field down to the Tile by area in the Field Well. This adds a tile tab strip filter area around the card visualization. The tab strip provides the ability to display cards for hotels from a selected country.

8. Click the arrow next to the Hotel table in the Field List to expand it.

9. Select the check box next to Life to Date Revenue. This field is added to each card.

10. Click the arrow next to the Financial table in the Field List to expand it.

11. Select the check boxes next to Total Revenue and LY Total Revenue. The two fields are added to each card.

12. Select the Life to Date Revenue field in the Field Well.

13. Click the Home tab in the ribbon.

14. Click the dollar sign ($) in the Number section to change the formatting of the value to Accounting Number format.

Figure 3-11   *Power View report with card visualization*

15. Click twice on the Decrease Decimal option in the Number section of the Home tab to remove the decimal places from the Life to Date Revenue values.

16. Repeat steps 14 and 15 for the Total Revenue and LY Total Revenue fields. Right now all three revenue fields are the same, which is not too useful. The reason these values are the same is we have no Date context applied to the report. Let's make an adjustment to the report to fix this by displaying the data for a single year.

17. Click the Filters Area button on the Home tab of the ribbon.

18. Click one of the flags in the tile strip. This will select the tiling container and will deselect the card visualization within the tiling container. We will add our filter at the tiling container level.

19. Click the arrow next to the Date table in the Field List to expand it.

20. Drag the Year field into the Filters Area.

21. Click the Advanced filter mode button in the Year filter.

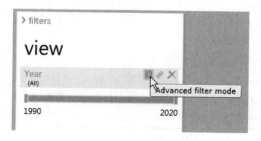

22. Below the section that says "Show items for which the value," select **is** from the drop-down list.

23. In the next box down, enter **2011**.

24. Click the Apply Filter option at the bottom of the Filters Area. You will see that the values for Total Revenue and LY Total Revenue have changed to display information based on the year filter we just applied. Total Revenue is displayed for 2011 and LY Total Revenue is displayed for 2010.

25. Click the Filters Area button on the Home tab of the ribbon to hide this area.

26. Click in the "Click here to add a title" section at the top of the report and replace this text with **Hotel Inventory by Country - 2011**.

27. Resize the items and move them around so that they look similar to Figure 3-12.

28. Click the Save button in the upper left of the screen.

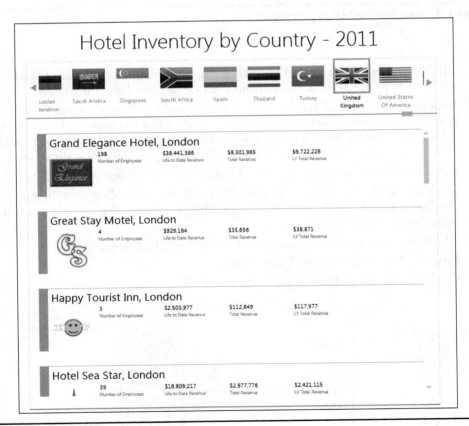

Figure 3-12   *Hotel Inventory by Country – 2011 report*

29. In the File name field, enter **Hotel Inventory by Country 2011**.
30. Click Save. The report is saved in the SharePoint document library.
31. Click your browser's Back button to exit Power View.

We have now created a report that provides a list of hotels available within a selected country. We included images and added revenue numbers to go along with the hotel information. We did all of this very quickly, with minimal effort and just a few clicks, thanks to Power View and our BI Semantic Model. Jade is once again very pleased with the results.

Wrap-Up

This chapter introduced you to two report visualizations, the matrix and the card. You also learned how to include images in your design and how to create multiple views within a single report file. As you saw, you can easily navigate among these views when in Reading Mode or Full Screen Mode. You also encountered the storyboarding feature that allows you to see a thumbnail of the views included within a Power View report.

We are now ready to dive into the world of charting. Charting provides very useful visualizations and ways to explore our data. As you will see in Chapter 4, the chart comes in many flavors—bar, column, line, and scatter, just to name a few. So dig in, and happy charting!

Chapter 4

Charting

In This Chapter

▶ **The Charting Advantage**
▶ **Chart Types**
▶ **Wrap-Up**

A s you saw in Chapter 2 and Chapter 3, Microsoft Power View provides an easy way to create reports. Once a connection to a data model is in place, creating a report can be as easy as placing a check mark by a few fields. This creates a basic table visualization that can then be enhanced using filters, formatting, and tiles. Even with these enhancements, tables don't make it easy to view trends in data or quickly compare the magnitude of several numbers. For this, we need charting.

The Charting Advantage

Consider the example shown in Figure 4-1. You can see that the gross profit and total revenue of the company are increasing over the years. A few questions come to mind right away. Is the growth accelerating or staying steady over the years? Is revenue growing more than gross profit or are they growing at the same rate?

By converting the table into a chart, as shown in Figure 4-2, it is much easier to answer those questions. The growth of both numbers is accelerating (that's a good thing!) and the growth in revenue is proportional to the growth in gross profit.

The good news is that, in Power View, converting a table visualization into an interactive chart requires only a few additional steps. Let's enter into uncharted territory!

Year	Total Gross Profit	Total Revenue
1997	$165,184,715.03	$255,841,761.0
1998	$183,300,006.87	$283,778,568.0
1999	$206,521,469.48	$319,610,534.1
2000	$235,920,305.33	$364,938,473.8
2001	$272,901,006.25	$421,918,148.6
2002	$319,229,012.90	$493,275,390.9
2003	$377,514,727.05	$583,047,626.2
2004	$450,709,300.43	$695,701,014.6
2005	$541,929,899.96	$836,043,209.3
2006	$655,551,826.39	$1,010,783,807.1
2007	$799,308,860.11	$1,231,764,154.7
2008	$978,657,316.60	$1,507,452,340.5
2009	$1,202,221,985.66	$1,851,111,674.4
2010	$1,480,859,005.92	$2,279,864,143.7
2011	$1,829,404,193.52	$2,815,627,843.9
Total	**$9,699,213,631.50**	**$14,950,758,691.6**

Figure 4-1   *Table visualization of financials*

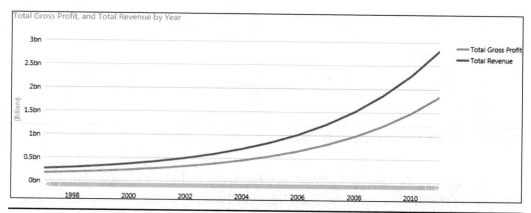

Figure 4-2   *Chart visualization of financials*

Creating a Chart

All visualizations in Power View start out as tabular data—there is no way to add data to a report and have it initially display as a chart. Once the table visualization has been added to the report, it can then be easily converted into a chart. Let's create our first chart and see just how easy it is.

Tom, the Vice President of Sales at PGHT, wants to analyze the United Nations tourism statistics to determine the tourism spending habits in countries around the world. Armed with this information, he can then compare the spending habits with hotel revenue and see where opportunities to grow the business are being missed.

Learn By Doing: Creating a Chart

Video 4-1   **Creating a Chart**

1. Open Internet Explorer and navigate to the SharePoint library hosting your learning environment.
2. Click the PGHT Tourism connection file in the document library to open Power View.
3. Click the Fit to Window button to turn off the Fit to Window feature. This will make the visualizations in the report larger and easier to read.

Total Inbound Travel Spending	Continent
325,324	Africa
1,793,257	Asia
4,195,897	Europe
2,001,749	North America
276,397	Oceania
168,212	South America
8,760,836	

Figure 4-3   *Total Inbound Travel Spending by Continent*

4. Click the arrow next to the Tourism table in the Field List to expand it.

5. Select the check box for the Total Inbound Travel Spending field to add it to the report.

6. Expand the Country table and select the check box for the Continent field. You should now have a table on your report that breaks out the Total Inbound Travel Spending by Continent, as shown in Figure 4-3.

    The columns in the table are in the same order as they were added to the table. What if you want to see the Continent column first and then the Total Inbound Travel Spending column second? Do you have to remove the Total Inbound Travel Spending column and then add it back again? No. You can drag the fields in the Field Well to make them appear in the desired order within the table.

7. Drag the Total Inbound Travel Spending field below the Continent field in the Field Well, and the columns will rearrange in the table.

8. Convert the table into a column chart by clicking the Column button on the Design tab of the ribbon.

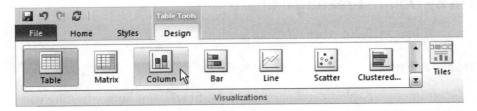

    The table changes to a column chart, as shown in Figure 4-4. The chart is very small right now. Let's make it larger so it is easier to read.

9. Click the background of the chart to select it, and move the mouse pointer to the edge of the chart. A dotted line should surround the chart, with solid lines (called *handles*) appearing at each corner and the middle of each side of the chart.

Figure 4-4   *Column chart*

10. When the mouse pointer is placed over the dotted line, as shown in Figure 4-5, the mouse pointer appears as a hand icon. To move the chart to a new location on the report, click and drag the mouse while the mouse pointer is on the dotted line. Feel free to move the chart to a new location and then place it back in the top-left corner of the report.

11. When the mouse pointer is placed over one of the handles of the border, the mouse pointer appears as a two-headed arrow, as shown in Figure 4-6. The handles on the top, bottom, and sides of the chart allow you to resize the chart either vertically or horizontally. To resize the chart in both directions at the same time, use the handles in the corners of the chart. Resize the chart to fill most of the report.

Components of a Chart

Before we add any enhancements to this simple chart, let's identify the components of a chart and the purpose for each component. Figure 4-7 shows a sample chart with the components labeled, each of which is described in Table 4-1.

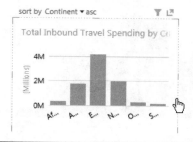

Figure 4-5   *The chart border*

Figure 4-6   *Resizing a chart*

In general, a chart visually displays calculated values by grouping the data. The primary grouping creates the categories in the chart, and the secondary grouping creates series in the chart. Power View allows only one level of grouping for the categories and one level of grouping for the series.

Enhancing the Chart

Now that we have a basic chart in the report, let's enhance that chart to make it more useful for our users. In this section, we'll add new data values to the chart. At the same time, we'll explore features that make the chart easier to read even as it becomes more complex with the additional content.

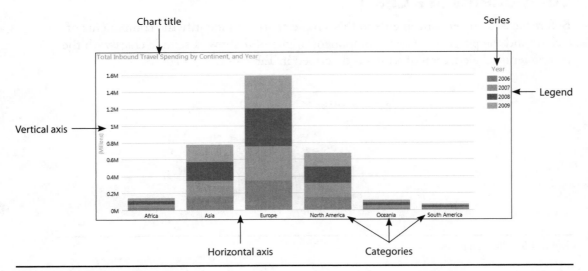

Figure 4-7   *Chart components*

Component	Purpose
Chart title	Describes the contents of the chart using a brief phrase.
Categories	The primary way data is grouped in the chart.
Series	An additional method for grouping data in the chart.
Vertical axis	The axis that usually portrays the range of values in the chart.
Horizontal axis	The axis that usually portrays the range of categories in the chart.
Legend	Displays the names of the data values in the chart if there are multiple data values being charted. Also displays the series values if a series is used in the chart.

Table 4-1   *Chart Component Table*

Learn By Doing: Charting with Multiple Values

We begin by adding data to the chart:

Video 4-2

Enhancing a Chart

1. Let's add the Total Outbound Travel Spending to the chart so we can compare the figures to the Total Inbound Travel Spending. With the chart selected, select the Total Outbound Travel Spending field in the Tourism table.

2. The Total Outbound Travel Spending appears stacked on top of the Total Inbound Travel Spending, as shown in Figure 4-8. Notice that the chart now has a legend indicating which value is represented by which color. By default, the legend does not appear when only one value appears in the chart. Once a second value is added, the legend appears automatically.

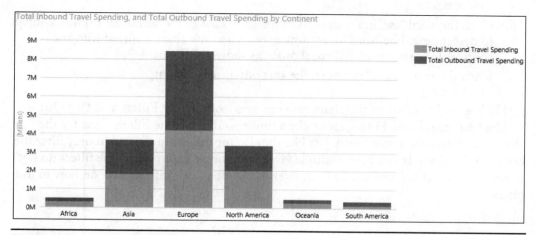

Figure 4-8   *Total Inbound and Outbound Travel Spending*

The stacked column chart does not do a very good job of allowing us to compare the inbound versus the outbound travel spending. We will resolve this issue a little later in the chapter.

Chart Icons

As you place your mouse pointer over the chart, icons appear in the top-left and top-right corners of the chart. These icons allow you to modify the appearance of the chart. They disappear when you move the mouse pointer away from the chart.

In the top-left corner, the current sort order for the chart categories is displayed. The sort order currently reads "sort by Continent asc." The sort order allows you to sort the columns by either the categories or the values in the chart and allows you to sort the chart in either ascending or descending order.

Learn By Doing: Changing the Sort Order in a Chart

Let's change the sort order within our chart:

1. Place your mouse pointer over the chart so that the sort order appears in the upper-left corner.
2. Click the drop-down arrow next to "sort by Continent."
3. Select Total Inbound Travel Spending from the drop-down menu. The chart is now sorted by Total Inbound Travel Spending—smallest amount on the left, largest amount on the right.
4. Click the words "Total Inbound Travel Spending" that are part of the sort order icon in the upper-left corner of the chart. The selected sort order advances to the next entry that you saw previously in the drop-down list. The chart is now sorted by Total Outbound Travel Spending. Click once again and the sort order returns to Continent.
5. Click the word "asc" in the upper-left corner to change the sort order from ascending to descending. The word "desc" now appears and the chart is sorted with the continents in reverse alphabetical order, as shown in Figure 4-9.
6. Click the word "desc" to return the sort order to ascending.

The top-right corner of the chart contains two icons, Show Filters and Pop Out.

The first icon, Show Filters, looks like a funnel and opens the Filters Area for the chart. The filters for a chart work just like they do for the entire report but only filter the values in the chart. If you have multiple visualizations on your page, these filters do not affect the other visualizations. You can refer to Chapter 2 for information on how to use filters.

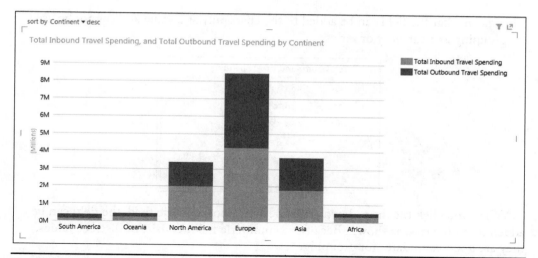

Figure 4-9   *Sorting the continents in descending order*

NOTE

The Show Filters command opens the Filters Area but does not close it. To close the Filters Area, click the Filters Area button on the Home tab of the ribbon.

The second icon, Pop Out, looks like an arrow. Pop Out causes the chart to fill the entire report similar to the way the Maximize command fills the entire screen in Microsoft Windows. It is a nice way to enlarge the chart without having to drag the edges of the chart around the canvas. Pop Out works like a toggle switch, so you can click the icon to "pop out" the chart and click it again to "pop in" the chart back to its original size.

Add to Chart Drop-down Menu

Hovering your mouse pointer over the Total Inbound Travel Spending field in the Tourism table in the Field List activates a drop-down menu. You can use this drop-down menu to see a list of ways to add the field to the chart. The options differ for numeric fields and nonnumeric fields.

When you click the drop-down arrow next to a numeric field (containing a calculator or a sigma next to the value), every option is disabled except Add to Values as shown.

This means that the field can be added to the chart only as a value and cannot be used for grouping as a category or series.

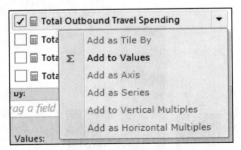

When you click the drop-down arrow next to a nonnumeric field, the field can be added in more ways, as shown. Because nonnumeric fields consist of discreet values, they are good candidates for grouping.

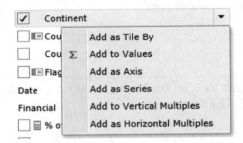

Table 4-2 describes how the Add to Chart options work when a nonnumeric field is selected. If a field already exists in one of these roles within the chart (except for the Values role), the selected field will replace the existing field in that role.

Option	Description
Add as Tile By	Adds the field to be used for tiling the data similar to the way tiling works with tables.
Add to Values	Adds the field as a count of values to the chart. This option is only available if the field being added is in the same table as the field used for the categories axis. Otherwise, this option is not available.
Add as Axis	Adds the field to the axis of the chart and is used to define the categories in the chart.
Add as Series	Adds the field as a series in the chart.
Add to Vertical Multiples	Adds the field to be used to create multiple versions of the chart broken out by the values within the field. The fields are stacked vertically from top to bottom on the screen.
Add as Horizontal Multiples	Adds the field to be used to create multiple versions of the chart broken out by the values within the field. The fields are stacked horizontally from left to right on the screen.

Table 4-2   *Add to Chart Menu Table*

Learn By Doing: Using the Add to Chart Drop-down Menu

Let's try using the Add to Chart drop-down menu:

1. Remove the Total Outbound Travel Spending field from the chart. This can be accomplished either by clearing the check box next to the field name in the Field List or by selecting the Remove Field command from the drop-down list for the Total Outbound Travel Spending field in the Values area of the Field Well.

2. Expand the Date table.

3. Hover the mouse pointer over the Year field and click the drop-down arrow.

4. Select Add as Series from the drop-down menu. The chart should appear similar to Figure 4-10. The series has provided an additional grouping to the chart in the form of different-colored bars.

It is important to note that charts in Power View can have multiple values displayed, similar to the way Total Inbound Travel Spending and the Total Outbound Travel Spending were displayed on the same chart. Charts can also be grouped using a series similar to the way the chart is now grouped by Year to produce different-colored bars.

NOTE

Power View charts cannot display both multiple values and a series at the same time. If the chart has a series and another value is added to the chart, Power View will remove the series and add the value. If the chart has multiple values, you cannot add a series until one of the values is removed.

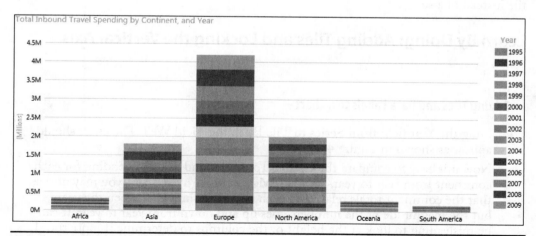

Figure 4-10   *Total Inbound Travel Spending by Continent and Year*

Chart Title

At this point, you may have noticed that the title of the chart changes as fields are added to or removed from the chart. If the report is only going to contain the chart, you could use either the chart title or the report title, but you probably don't need both. You can remove the chart title by clicking the Chart Title command located on the Chart Tools Layout tab of the ribbon, as shown here. You have the option to select either None, to remove the chart title, or Above Chart, to place a title at the top of the chart.

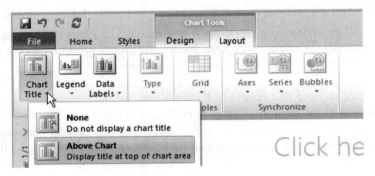

Tiles

The chart is now fairly cluttered. Each column is composed of many colored bars. It is very difficult to see how the Total Inbound Travel Spending compares between continents for any specific year. To better display this data, let's use the Year field as a tile instead of a series.

Learn By Doing: Adding Tiles and Locking the Vertical Axis

Video 4-3   **Adding Tiles and Data Labels to a Chart**

1. Drag the Year field from Series to Tile By in the Field Well. The chart should appear as shown in Figure 4-11.

   Now it is easy to compare the relative Total Inbound Travel Spending for each continent from year to year. As you navigate through the years, you may notice that the continent totals relative to each other are similar between the years but the magnitude of the numbers goes up and down from year to year. It can be misleading to look at the height of the columns to determine if more travel occurred in one year than in another. For example, the columns are higher in 2005 than they are in 2006, but the total travel spending was higher in 2006. The reason for this discrepancy is the vertical axis automatically adjusts between the years.

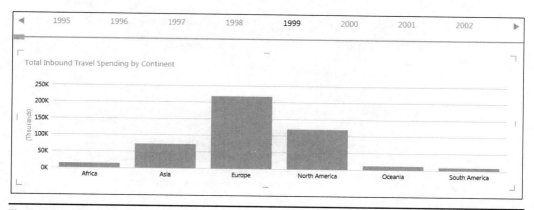

Figure 4-11   *Tiled chart*

In 2005, the maximum scale on the vertical axis is 350K, and in 2006, the maximum is 400K. Let's lock in the vertical axis scale so the chart is easier to read when tiling from one year to the next.

The Chart Tools menu contains two submenus—Design and Layout. The Design menu holds the commands to change the type of chart and to change the layout of the chart element on the report. The Layout menu holds the commands to adjust the contents of the chart itself. In order to lock in the vertical axis, we are going to use the Layout menu.

2. Select the main body of the chart.

3. Select the Layout tab under Chart Tools on the ribbon.

4. Click the Axes button on the ribbon to view the drop-down menu.

5. Within the Vertical Axis section, select "Same across all tiles," as shown in Figure 4-12.

   Power View calculates the maximum value across all tiles and adjusts the vertical axis based on that maximum value to stay the same for all of the tiles. Now it is much easier to get an idea of how the travel spending compares from year to year.

   When the Year tile was added to the chart, the body of the chart became shorter in order to make room for the tile. Let's make more room for the body of the chart.

6. Use the sizing handle in the center of the bottom edge of the blue line to make the tile container taller. (Remember to use the sizing handle and not the dotted line.) You will find that the chart itself does not enlarge.

7. To enlarge the chart itself, click the background of the chart between the bars, and a border will appear around the chart as shown in Figure 4-13. Drag the bottom edge of the chart to enlarge the chart itself. You cannot enlarge the chart to be bigger than the tile container.

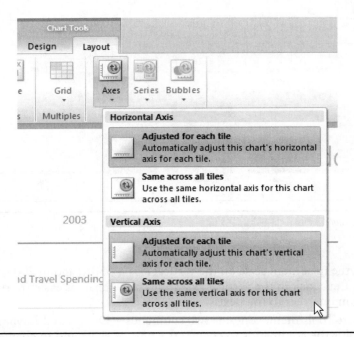

Figure 4-12 *Same across all tiles command*

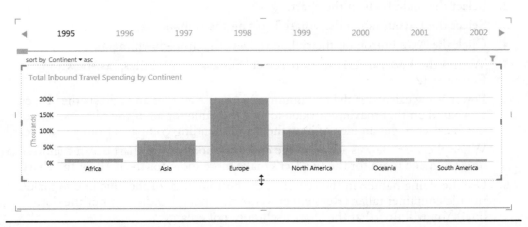

Figure 4-13 *Enlarging a chart with a tile*

When you clicked the background of the chart, if you happened to click one column, that column became highlighted compared to the rest of the columns. This feature can be used to highlight the data in the chart or to slice the data in tables or other charts within the report. This subject will be covered in more detail in Chapter 5. Click the background of the chart so all of the columns are highlighted again.

Data Labels

Up to this point, we have been focusing on the relative size of the columns between the continents and years. We have not considered what the actual values are for each of the columns. Of course, you could determine the value by comparing the height of the column to the gridlines in the chart. If you want to know how much money was spent on inbound travel in Europe for 2009, for example, you can see that the column is just below the 0.4M line, so the total is around $375,000.

There are a few ways to determine the exact values for each of the data points in Power View charts. First, if you place your mouse pointer over the column in the chart, a tooltip appears showing the exact value and what categories and/or series the value fits into. If you place your mouse over the Europe column in the 2009 tile, the tooltip tells you that Total Inbound Travel Spending was $382,067 in Europe that year.

Learn By Doing: Adding Data Labels

Another way to view the exact values in the chart is to turn on data labels for each data point. You can adjust the location of the data labels to appear either inside or outside the columns on the chart—depending on the type of chart being displayed.

1. Click the background of the chart to make sure the chart is selected.
2. Select the Layout tab under Chart Tools on the ribbon.
3. Click the Data Labels button on the ribbon to view the drop-down menu.
4. Select Show from the drop-down menu. The chart should appear as displayed in Figure 4-14.

   It is now easy to determine the dollars spent for each continent in each year. You will notice that Power View automatically identifies the best format to use to display the data labels, so no manual adjustment of formats is necessary. In fact, Power View uses different formats for different values on the same chart. For example, the data label for Asia in 2009 is 0.21M and for Africa in the same year it is 36.95K.

   You can control the location of the data labels in relation to the columns for certain types of charts. The column chart is not one of the charts that allow you to change the location of the data labels. You can either show or hide the data labels for a column chart.

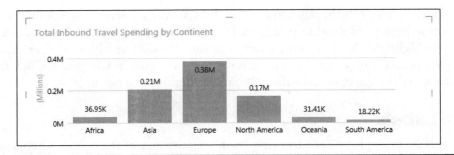

Figure 4-14   *Data labels*

Another chart that is similar to the column chart is the clustered column chart. Let's convert our chart to a clustered column chart and see if it better suits our purposes.

5. Select the Design tab under Chart Tools on the ribbon.

6. Expand the Visualizations section of the Design menu and click the Clustered Column item.

   Do you notice the difference between the two charts? No? That's because there is none! A clustered column chart is useful for comparing multiple values with one another. Since our chart contains only one value, Total Inbound Travel Spending, the charts look identical. There is one difference in the way the charts work.

7. Select the Layout tab under Chart Tools on the ribbon.

8. Click the Data Labels button on the ribbon to view the drop-down menu.

9. Now we can control the location of the data labels in relation to the column. Select Inside Base. The chart appears as shown in Figure 4-15.

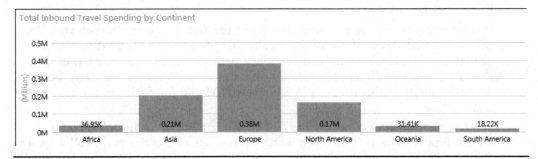

Figure 4-15   *Inside Base data labels*

Chart Types

We just changed our first chart into a different chart type. Each chart type has different strengths and purposes. The first chart type we worked with, the column chart, does a good job of displaying a single value broken out by categories and/or series. Once a second value is added to the chart, the new value appears stacked on top of the initial value, which makes it hard to compare the values. The column chart also only allows the data labels to be located above the columns.

Clustered Column Chart

The clustered column chart enables us to move the data labels to one of several positions in relation to each column. In addition, the clustered column chart places the columns for multiple values next to each other for easy comparison.

Learn By Doing: Adding a Second Value
to a Clustered Column Chart

Let's add the Total Outbound Travel Spending value back to the chart and see what it looks like:

Video 4-4   **Chart Types**

1. Make sure the chart is selected on the report canvas.
2. Select the check box next to the Total Outbound Travel Spending field in the Tourism table.
3. Select the Layout tab under Chart Tools on the ribbon.
4. Click the Data Labels button on the ribbon to view the drop-down menu.
5. Select Inside End. This change will separate the labels from one another and make them easier to read. The chart should look similar to the one shown in Figure 4-16.

100% Stacked Column Chart

The other type of column chart is the 100% stacked column chart. This type of chart is useful for displaying the ratio of multiple values in relation to one another. The chart shown in Figure 4-17 is the clustered column chart converted into a 100% stacked column chart. This chart allows you to get a good feel for which continents have more

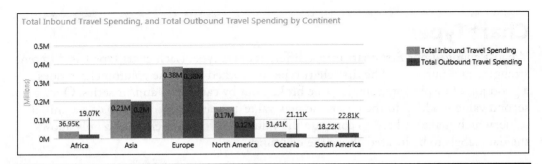

Figure 4-16   *Clustered Column chart*

inbound travel spending than outbound travel spending. As you can see, people going to Africa spend more on travel than Africans spend traveling abroad. Notice that the vertical axis has changed from displaying dollars to displaying a percentage.

Bar Chart

Bar charts are very similar to column charts. In fact, they are essentially column charts turned 90 degrees. Figure 4-18 shows the 100% stacked column chart from Figure 4-17 converted into a 100% Stacked Bar chart.

Line Chart

Line charts are especially good at showing trends in data over time.

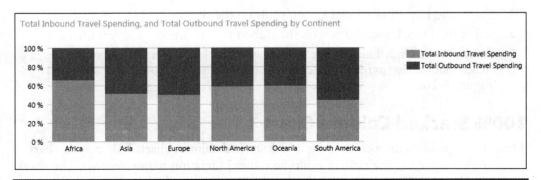

Figure 4-17   *100% Stacked Column chart*

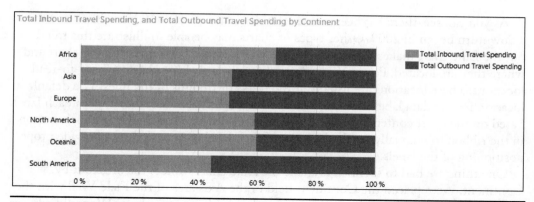

Figure 4-18   *100% Stacked Bar chart*

Learn By Doing: Manipulating a Line Chart

Let's convert our chart into a line chart to see the trends in travel through the years:

1. Select the Design tab under Chart Tools on the ribbon.
2. Expand the Visualizations section of the Design menu and select the Line item.
3. Drag the Year field from Tile By in the Field Well to Axis in the Field Well to make the chart display the spending by year. The chart appears similar to Figure 4-19.

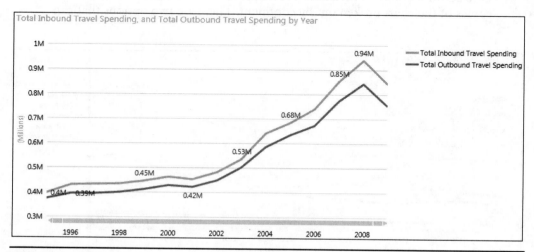

Figure 4-19   *Line chart*

As you can see, there has been a dramatic rise in travel from 1995 to 2008, and then a downturn began in 2009. Other types of charts may be able to illustrate this trend, but the Line chart makes it obvious. Notice which data labels appear on the chart and where they are located. Power View places data labels on Line charts in easy-to-read locations. These locations are usually at the peaks or troughs of the lines. The default location for the data labels is Auto—Power View selects the best location for each label based on the chart contents surrounding the label. You can use the Data Labels button in the ribbon to manually set the location of each label if Auto does not provide proper positioning of the labels.

One thing we had to sacrifice to make the Line chart work is the breakout by Continent. We replaced the Continent field in the Axis area of the Field Well with the Year field. How could we add the Continent data back into the chart? We could add the Continent back in as a tile or as a series. If we add the Continent as a series, we will have to remove one of the two measures because Power View does not allow multiple values and a series to be used in the same chart.

To add Continent as a series:

1. Activate the drop-down menu for Total Outbound Travel Spending in the Values Field Well.
2. Select Remove Field from the drop-down menu.
3. Drag the Continent field from the Country table in the Field List to the Series Field Well. The Line chart will produce one line per continent, as shown in Figure 4-20, to make it easy to compare Inbound Travel Spending between continents over the years.

   One additional way to break out the line chart by continent is to create multiple copies of the chart broken out by continent. There are two options that can

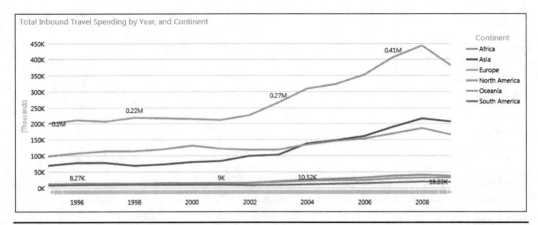

Figure 4-20   *Line chart broken out by continent*

be used to create these multiple charts—Vertical Multiples and Horizontal Multiples. The Vertical Multiples option lays out the charts on the screen so vertical scrolling is required to see all of the charts. The Horizontal Multiples option requires horizontal scrolling to see all of the charts. The advantage to using multiples is that we can add the Total Outbound Travel Spending back in the chart. Let's multiply our chart!

4. Drag the Continent field from Series to Horizontal Multiples in the Field Well.

5. Select the check box next to Total Outbound Travel Spending in the Tourism table to add it to the charts. You should now see multiple charts—one for each continent—spanning from left to right.

6. You can control how many charts appear on the screen at a time by using the Grid command. On the Layout tab of the ribbon, click the Grid button to expand the grid options. Since we are using Horizontal Multiples, we only have the option of laying out the charts using the first row of the grid.

7. Select 1×1 Charts. This causes the report to display one chart at a time—similar to tiling. This makes the charts easy to read, but it is hard to compare values.

8. Use the Grid button again to switch the grid to 2×1 Charts. Now two charts appear on the screen at a time. This is better, but it's still hard to compare all of the continents.

9. Use the Grid button again to switch the grid to 6×1 Charts, since we have six continents. Now all of the charts fit on the screen. The charts are fairly small, but it is easy to compare the Inbound and Outbound Travel Spending across all of the continents.

10. One way we can enlarge the charts is to move the legend to a different position. Let's place it below the chart instead of next to the chart. Click the Legend button on the Layout tab and select Show Legend At Bottom. Now the charts spread out nicely to fill in the report. Your report should look similar to Figure 4-21.

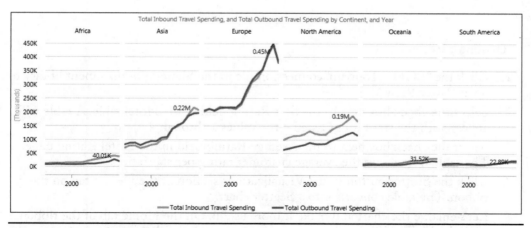

Figure 4-21 *Horizontal multiples*

NOTE

As the charts get narrower, they display a limited number of year labels along the horizontal axis. However, the data for all of the years is still being displayed in the chart.

11. Let's add a title to the report and save it. Change the report title to **Travel Spending**.
12. Click the Save button to save the report. We will leave the default location as the SharePoint document library. Enter **Travel Spending** in the File Name field and click Save.
13. Click the Back button in Internet Explorer to return to SharePoint.

Scatter Chart

The last type of chart we are going to create is the Scatter chart. A Scatter chart enables us to compare multiple numeric and category values to see which factors influence one another. We are going to create a scatter chart to analyze the average rating provided by our customers, using the star rating of each of our facilities, to see if there is a correlation between how nice the facility is (a one-star facility versus a four-star facility) and the customer ratings it receives. We will also look at the type of facility (hotel, motel, lodge, other) and see which types of facilities are the most successful in our company.

Learn By Doing: Creating a Scatter Chart

Let's create our last chart type, the scatter chart:

Creating a Scatter Chart

1. Click the "PGHT Tourism" connection file in the SharePoint document library to open Power View.
2. Select the check box next to the Star Rating field in the Hotel table. A table will appear with the star ratings listed—the values 1 through 4.
3. Select the check box next to the Average Rating field in the Hotel Rating table. The table now shows the average customer rating per star rating.
4. Click the Scatter button in the Visualizations section of the Design tab on the ribbon. The table converts into a Scatter chart.
5. Let's enlarge the chart and make it more useful. On the Home tab of the ribbon, click the Fit To Window button to enlarge our view of the report.
6. Drag the edges of the chart to fill the visible part of the report.

7. The Star Rating field was placed in Details in the Field Well. Let's move the Star Rating to the Y Value in the Field Well so we can chart the star rating vs. the average rating. Your chart should look similar to Figure 4-22.

8. There are several problems with this chart. First, the star rating is a sum, so the value 4000 appears on the Y axis. We want the average star rating. The Average Rating field came directly from the model (the value is an average of all customer ratings that was created in the model by the designer), but the model does not contain an Average Star Rating field. We can calculate the average in the report itself to make up for the missing field. Click the drop-down list next to Star Rating in the Y Value in the Field Well and select Average. We now have a single data point showing the average rating and average star rating.

9. To create more data points, we are going to break out the data by chain type. We use Color in the Field Well for this purpose. Color works similarly to Series in column charts. Drag the Chain Type field from the Hotel table into Color in the Field Well.

   Now we are getting somewhere! We can start to see that hotels have both the highest average star ratings and average ratings while motels have the lowest of both values. Figure 4-23 shows the Scatter chart broken out by chain type.

   What about revenue? Where does our company make the most money? We would hope that it would be in the most successful chain type, but we don't know at this point. Let's add the Total Revenue field to the Scatter chart to find out.

   How best can we represent the total revenue in the chart? The Scatter chart provides an additional way to portray data by allowing us to control the size of the points based on the magnitude of a number. By using total revenue, the size of each data point will reflect the total revenue for that data point.

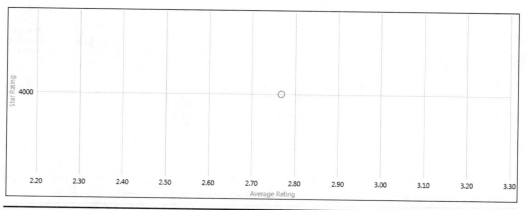

Figure 4-22   *Initial Scatter chart*

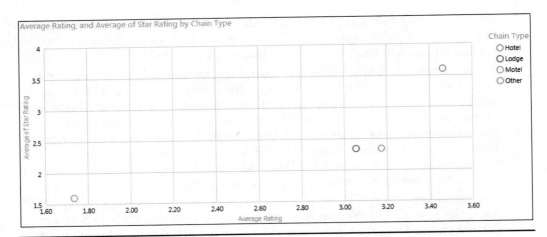

Figure 4-23   *Scatter chart broken out by chain type*

10. Drag the Total Revenue field from the Financial table into Size in the Field Well. As illustrated in Figure 4-24, the Scatter chart now shows that we get the most revenue from hotel business and the least revenue from motel business. When you place your mouse pointer over the data points, the Total Revenue is also displayed in the tooltip.

11. Change the report title to **Performance by Chain Type**.

12. Click the Save button and save the report as **Performance by Chain Type**.

13. Click your browser's Back button to exit Power View.

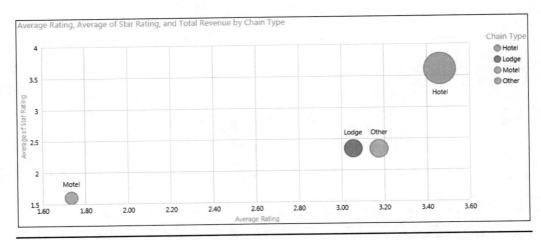

Figure 4-24   *Scatter chart including Total Revenue*

We have gleaned some very interesting information from the Scatter chart. We know that the hotel business is doing well but the motel business is struggling. We also know that our lower-rated facilities may need some improvements in order to have better customer satisfaction. There is no reason a 2 star motel can't get a 5 point rating by our customers. We can now make important decisions based on a chart that took us only a few minutes to create.

Wrap-Up

As we have seen in this chapter, charting in Power View provides powerful data analysis capabilities. There are several different types of charts and many features within each chart to present the data in an easy-to-read format.

The next chapter focuses on user interactivity. Power View reports not only can present data to our users but also can provide an environment for the users to make discoveries on their own. Let's bring the spark of life to our reports!

Chapter 5

Bringing Your Data to Life

In This Chapter

▶ **Interactivity**
▶ **Wrap-Up**

The previous three chapters familiarized you with many of the report design features of Power View. You learned how to assemble table, matrix, card, and chart visualizations in a manner that makes an impact. Visualizing data has never been easier! But it is still possible, using Power View, to have an even greater business impact by providing views of data that respond to user interaction and inquiry. Often, when we view a chart, we want to know more. We want to be able to click a data point or series to find out something more specific—to go deeper.

Interactivity

The discussion and exercises that follow build on what you have learned thus far. We look at how to use the play axis to make it easier to see our data's progress through time. We examine the use of slicers as a means of filtering data. We see how multiple visualizations on a single report work together. We continue to utilize tiles to divide the data into more manageable segments. We examine Power View's ability to highlight report elements to clarify business insight. And, finally, we see how easy it is to zoom in on individual visualizations to bring them into clearer focus for analysis, design, and discussion.

And with each of the tools just mentioned, Power View provides enhanced capabilities for interactive inquiry. You will find that Power View makes *interpreting* the data easy through interactive navigation. When users can interact with the data, the data responds. Power View helps bring the data to life!

Push Play

One of the most dynamic features of Power View is the play axis. The play axis is used with scatter and bubble charts. It enables us to animate the chart and witness the data's behavior over time or across a range of values, as shown here.

Far from merely being a means to impress, the play axis is a very useful tool for telling a more in-depth story. The data in our visualization alone does tell a story; but if a picture is worth a thousand words, a moving picture adds many thousands more. The play axis helps us easily compare the state of our data at different points along an axis. Most commonly, a time field is used for the play axis, allowing us to easily visualize the progress in data across a time period; however, any category field (a field that is not a measure) can be used with the play axis.

Learn By Doing: Adding a Play Axis

To set up our next exercise, let's consider a new business need. We have received very positive feedback for our Performance by Chain Type report. In fact, Juno, the Marketing Manager for Hotels, has given a thumbs-up concerning many of the reports that various users have created since Power View became available. She would like us to put together a composite view of hotel performance related to other factors and present it as a performance dashboard. We'll begin by spicing up the Performance by Chain Type report using the play axis.

Video 5-1   **Adding a Play Axis**

1. Return to the document library where you saved the last report in Chapter 4—Performance by Chain Type. Click the name of the report to see it in Reading Mode.

2. Click Edit Report to switch to Edit Mode. See Figure 5-1 to recall what the report looked like at the end of Chapter 4.

   We're going to need to make a few changes to the existing visualization in order to incorporate a play axis that works across Quarter Name. The Date table isn't available to us because of the chart's existing fields. Let's start by creating a new view that is a duplicate of the current view. Then, we'll change the chart so that we're comparing revenue against gross profit.

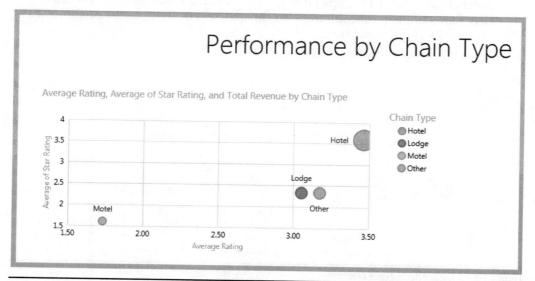

Figure 5-1   *Performance by Chain Type report*

3. Click the New View button on the Home tab of the ribbon. A drop-down menu appears.

4. Select Duplicate View from the drop-down menu. A new view appears, View 2, and becomes the currently active view.

5. Click the scatter chart, and then in the Field List, expand the Financial table.

    Because we're going to replace some fields in the scatter chart, manually selecting the chart location in which to place the new fields is more efficient than selecting the check box next to the field names.

6. Click the drop-down arrow for the Total Revenue measure and select Add as X Value. (This measure will be in the chart in two places until Step 8.)

7. Click the drop-down arrow for Total Gross Profit and select Add as Y Value.

8. Click the drop-down arrow for YoY Growth Total Revenue and select Add as Size.

9. Expand the Date table and select the check box next to Quarter Name to create the play axis. Figure 5-2 shows the resulting chart.

10. Click the play button in the new play axis to see the change in revenue performance over time.

11. Resize the scatter chart so that it only takes up the top-left quarter of the report. We'll need the rest of the space for additional visualizations.

    Now it is possible to see the correlation between revenue and gross profit by chain type. The growth in year-over-year revenue can also be seen as an increase in the size of the bubbles. It's also important to note that the measures are trending in the right direction, showing a healthy gross profit margin, particularly for the hotel chains. Now let's supplement our performance chart with another chart that shows tourism expenditures over time, to help us see how our performance is affected by global travel trends.

12. Click an empty part of the canvas.

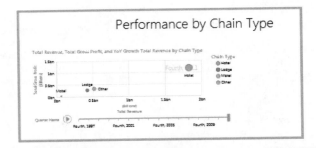

Figure 5-2   *Revenue performance over time*

13. In the Field List, expand the Tourism table and select the check box for Total Tourism Spending Abroad. A new table appears with the single column in the table.

14. Select the check box by Total Tourism Spending In-Country to add a second measure to the table.

15. Expand the Date table and select the check box for Year.

16. From the visualizations on the Design tab of the ribbon, select Line to convert the table to a line chart.

17. Drag the chart to the bottom-left corner of the canvas and resize it to match the width and horizontal placement of the scatter chart.

18. Go to the Layout tab of the ribbon and click Legend.

19. Select Show Legend at Top from the drop-down menu. This improves the layout of the chart. The result appears similar to the report shown in Figure 5-3.

So far, there's nothing particularly lively about the pair of charts on this report. They don't interact because they're based on different measures, and they don't have much in common other than they show trend information. However, what if we put these charts in the context of location? It will be helpful to slice the information by continent in order to more easily compare performance of our chain types between global centers.

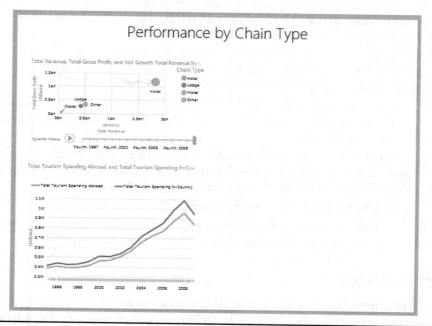

Figure 5-3   *Travel trends compared to revenue performance*

The Slicer

A slicer works a lot like tiles, which we have used in preceding chapters. However, a slicer is a single object on your report with which a user can filter all visualizations at once, not just those within the tiling container (the area beneath the tiles).

Learn By Doing: Interactive Filtering Using a Slicer

Let's apply a continent slicer to our existing report:

Video 5-2   **Adding a Slicer**

1. Click an empty part of the canvas.
2. In the Field List, expand the Country table and select the check box for Continent. This creates a simple table of continents.
3. On the Design tab of the ribbon, click Slicer.
4. Move the new slicer to the top-right corner of the report.

   The table is converted to a slicer. Slicers must be limited to one field, an image or text. If you click an item in the slicer, all of the visualizations on the report based on tables related to the slicer will be filtered by the value you select. Any visualization with unrelated data will not be affected.

   If you hover your mouse pointer over the slicer, you will also see a Clear Filter icon in the top-right corner—clicking this icon clears the slicer's filtering.

5. Click South America in the slicer. All of the visualizations adjust to display data for South America only. Click Europe—now all of the visualizations adjust to display data for Europe.
6. Click South America again. Now, holding down CTRL, click North America so that both North America and South America are selected. The entire report now represents data for both North America and South America.
7. Click the Clear Filter icon to return to an unfiltered view.
8. Click the Save icon to save the changes you have made so far. If you're prompted with a warning that you'll update preview images, click Save again.

Chart as Slicer

Now we'll take interactivity a step further. We're going to see that multiple visualizations on a report can interact with each other. In Chapter 4, you observed that a chart element changes color when you click it. This is called *highlighting* and is one of the more powerful interactivity features of Power View. Highlighting provides a dynamic filtering experience, helping report users narrow in on the answers they need. We take full advantage of highlighting in the next exercise.

Learn By Doing: Using Highlighting to Slice Information

One of the dashboard components that Juno, the PGHT Marketing Manager for Hotels, requested is a visualization that interactively shows more tourism detail by country, and that also allows us to see how PGHT hotels in each city have been rated by guests, on average. To keep the report from becoming too overwhelming with the vast number of cities where PGHT has properties, we are going to provide this information in a highly interactive format.

Video 5-3

Using Highlighting to Slice Information

1. Click again on an empty portion of the canvas.
2. Expand the Country table and select the check box for the Flag field. A new table that consists of country flags is created on the canvas.
3. In the Visualizations box on the Design tab of the ribbon, click Card to convert the table to a card visualization.
4. Let's add more data for each country in the card visualization. In the Field List, select the check boxes for the following fields:
   ▶ In the Hotel Rating table, check Average Rating.
   ▶ In the Tourism table, check Total Hotel Check-Ins and Total Tourist Arrivals.
5. Rearrange the new table and the continent slicer on the canvas so that the visualizations appear as shown in Figure 5-4.
6. Click the Country card visualization, and click the Tiles button on the Design tab of the ribbon.
   Now we have a banded card visualization that lets us view country tourism details.
7. Click the empty space under the card for the selected country, within the tiling container. You may expand the size of the tiling container, if it is too small, by dragging its borders.
8. In the Field List, from the Hotel table, select the check box for City. A new table is created within the tiling container.
9. From the Hotel Rating table, select the check box for Average Rating.
10. On the Design tab of the ribbon, click a chart type of Bar.
11. Edit the title at the top of the report to read **Hotel Performance Dashboard**.
12. Resize the new chart to occupy the entire space beneath the card for the selected country so we can see the list of cities better.

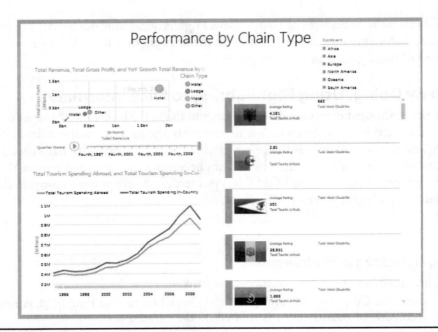

Figure 5-4   *Addition of country cards to the report*

This places a bar chart showing average hotel rating by city within the banding container for the country flag. Figure 5-5 shows the resulting layout with North America chosen in the slicer, and the United States selected among the tiles.

To see how charts behave like mutual slicers throughout the report, try the following:

13. Click the Hotel bubble within the scatter chart. If you need the scatter chart to be larger, return to the Home tab of the ribbon and click Fit To Window to turn off this setting. The scatter chart changes to show the track taken by the Hotel chain type over time.

14. Click the play button of the play axis. You can observe the tracking of the hotel's plot points over time.

    Notice also that the Average Rating by City bar chart changes to highlight the average rating pertaining to the Hotel chain type. Not only can you see the data pertinent to hotels highlighted on the chart, but you're also still able to see the overall average for all chain types at

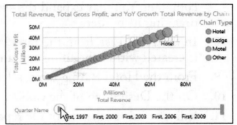

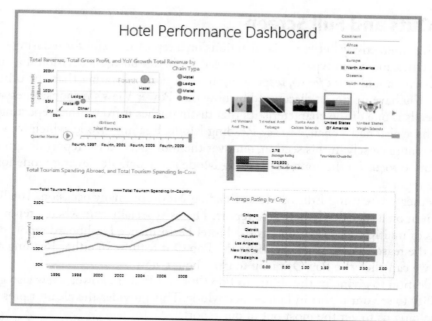

Figure 5-5   *The Hotel Performance Dashboard*

the same time for comparison purposes. The overall average rating values appear as gray bars above and below the highlighted values.

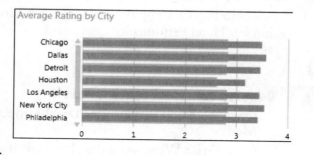

15. Click between the bubbles on the scatter chart to remove the highlighting. Now we're able to see data for all chain types again.

16. Click the bar pertaining to one of the cities in the Average Rating by City bar chart. The scatter chart changes to highlight the portion of revenue relevant to the chosen city. Click the chart right next to, but not on any of, the bars to remove the highlighting of the individual city.

    Let's save our work. We are going to use Save As to rename the report to better reflect its broad functionality.

17. Click File | Save As from the main menu. The Save As dialog box appears.

18. Change the File name to **Hotel Performance Dashboard** and then click Save.

Pop Outs and Full Screen

All of this interactivity between visualizations on a report is useful for focusing in on specific cities and chain types, which is needed for better business decision making. Our reports should work *for* us, responding to our questions, rather than the other way around. You have no doubt discovered by now that Power View's responsiveness to users' needs is one of the characteristics that distinguishes it from other reporting tools.

You have also had a chance to see Reading Mode. Reading Mode, which we will examine more closely in this section, removes the tools needed for report design and helps you to focus on the content. Reading Mode is the default viewing mode for existing reports.

Whether you're using Edit Mode or Reading Mode, on many occasions you'll need to zoom in on a specific element of a report. This is especially true when a report consists of multiple visualizations, as the Hotel Performance Dashboard report does. This is the reason Power View provides the Pop Out feature. In either Reading or Edit Mode, we can click the Pop Out icon to get a better view.

In addition to giving us the ability to Pop Out and Pop In, Power View also gives us the ability to see our report in Full Screen Mode. This provides the clearest presentation view, helping us to get the most out of our reports.

Learn By Doing: Using Pop Out and Full Screen to Focus In

To see both Pop Out/Pop In and Full Screen Mode at work, let's put them to use within our Hotel Performance Dashboard.

Video 5-4

Using Pop Out and Full Screen to Focus In

1. Open the Hotel Performance Dashboard report (if you closed it) and go to Edit Mode.
2. Click Fit To Window on the Home tab, if you turned it off earlier.
3. Select Europe from the continent slicer.
4. Hover your mouse pointer over the upper-right corner of the scatter chart and click the Pop Out icon.

   Observe how much easier it is to see the relative measure of the chain types within the scatter chart. Also, notice that you still are able to access the Field List and Field Well in order to make changes to the scatter chart if needed. Figure 5-6 shows the scatter chart after we have used Pop Out to zoom in.
5. Click the Pop In icon to return the chart to its normal position.
6. Switch to the Home tab of the ribbon and click Full Screen.

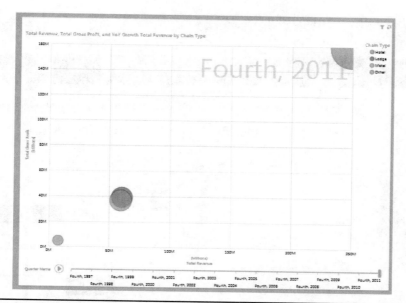

Figure 5-6   *The scatter chart with Pop Out*

You will remember Full Screen Mode from Chapter 3. In Full Screen Mode, you have navigation features that let you move between multiple report views. All of the interactivity features we have discussed in this chapter also work in Full Screen Mode, including Pop Out.

7. Click Pop Out and Pop In for either of the charts on the left half of the report.

NOTE

Pop Out only works for visualizations, tables, or charts, which stand alone on the report outside of a banding container.

8. Press ESC to exit Full Screen Mode.

9. Navigate to the Home tab of the ribbon again, and click the Reading Mode button.

   Reading Mode has the same navigation capabilities as Full Screen Mode. You can slice, zoom, and perform all of the same filtering and navigation actions as you can in Edit Mode or in Full Screen Mode. Included is the ability to go directly from Reading Mode to Full Screen Mode. The only things missing in Reading Mode are the design tools.

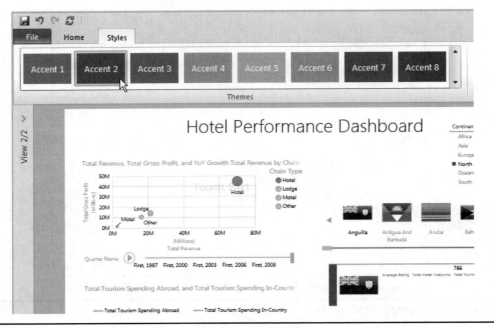

Figure 5-7   *Selecting a report color scheme using the Styles tab of the ribbon*

Report Color Style

Power View provides us with the ability to modify and coordinate the colors used in the visualizations on our reports. This is done using the Styles tab of the ribbon. The styles tab enables you to select from a number of predefined color pallets as shown in Figure 5-7. Selecting a color pallet from the Style tab of the ribbon will change the colors on all of the visualizations in a view. Each view within a report can have its own style.

Wrap-Up

You can take it from here! Add additional filters and visualizations, and familiarize yourself with the interactivity and navigation features Power View provides. Then continue reading. Now that we have our business intelligence in clear, easy-to-understand, fully interactive form, it is time to put it into action by sharing it with others in our organization. Chapter 6 shows you powerful techniques for exporting, printing, and presenting information contained in Power View reports.

Chapter 6

Sharing Reports

In This Chapter

- ▶ **Saving Reports in SharePoint**
- ▶ **Security**
- ▶ **Printing Reports**

- ▶ **Exporting Reports to PowerPoint**
- ▶ **Wrap-Up**

I n the preceding chapters, we have created a number of reports using Power View, ranging from basic tabular data listings to a dynamic interactive dashboard. Each of the reports provides valuable business intelligence to the individuals that requested the reports. Because Power View is designed to be used by the consumers of the data, there is a good chance that many of the people who requested the reports actually created the reports themselves.

Once the reports were designed to meet the stated business needs, we saved them to a document library in SharePoint. With these reports deployed in SharePoint, users can run them anytime using a web browser.

You can probably imagine what happens next. Other employees see these great reports in a meeting or presentation and want to use them to meet their own business intelligence requirements. What started as a report to provide information to an individual becomes an asset to an entire department or to the entire organization.

This chapter covers the different ways that Power View reports can be shared among multiple users. We explore ways to make sure the reports are available to the users who need them. We also look at ways to restrict access to only those users who should be able to run a given report. Finally, we examine ways to output the contents of the reports by printing reports and exporting them to PowerPoint.

Saving Reports in SharePoint

As you saw in previous chapters, deploying Power View reports is as easy as saving them to a document library in SharePoint. Power View reports can be saved in any document library. In our examples, we created the Power View reports from data sources within a document library and then saved the reports to that same document library. We could easily have saved the reports to a different document library and they would have worked just the same.

As Figure 6-1 shows, our document library contains not only the reports we have created but also the PGHT Tourism RS data source and the PGHT Tourism BISM connection used to create those reports. Even if a report is created from this document library and saved to a different document library (maybe a library called Production Reports), we do not need to save the data source to that same library. The report in the Production Reports document library will simply refer to the data source in the original document library.

The data source for a report can be changed by clicking the drop-down arrow for a report and selecting Manage Data Sources. This displays the Manage Data Sources page with an entry called EntityDataSource. Clicking EntityDataSource reveals the properties for this data source, as shown in Figure 6-2. The connection string contains a string similar to the following:

```
Data Source="http://{servername}/{documentlibraryname}/PGHT Tourism.bism"
```

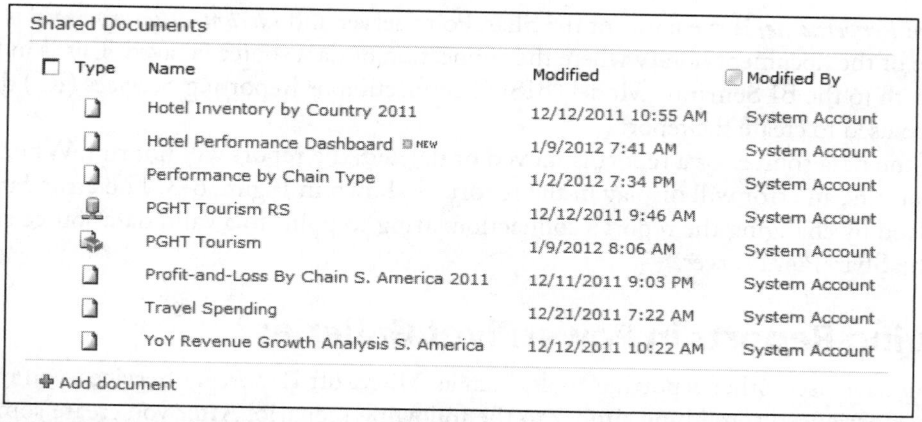

Shared Documents			
☐ Type	Name	Modified	☐ Modified By
🗋	Hotel Inventory by Country 2011	12/12/2011 10:55 AM	System Account
🗋	Hotel Performance Dashboard 🗆 NEW	1/9/2012 7:41 AM	System Account
🗋	Performance by Chain Type	1/2/2012 7:34 PM	System Account
🖳	PGHT Tourism RS	12/12/2011 9:46 AM	System Account
🖼	PGHT Tourism	1/9/2012 8:06 AM	System Account
🗋	Profit-and-Loss By Chain S. America 2011	12/11/2011 9:03 PM	System Account
🗋	Travel Spending	12/21/2011 7:22 AM	System Account
🗋	YoY Revenue Growth Analysis S. America	12/12/2011 10:22 AM	System Account
✚ Add document			

Figure 6-1   *A document library with reports and data sources*

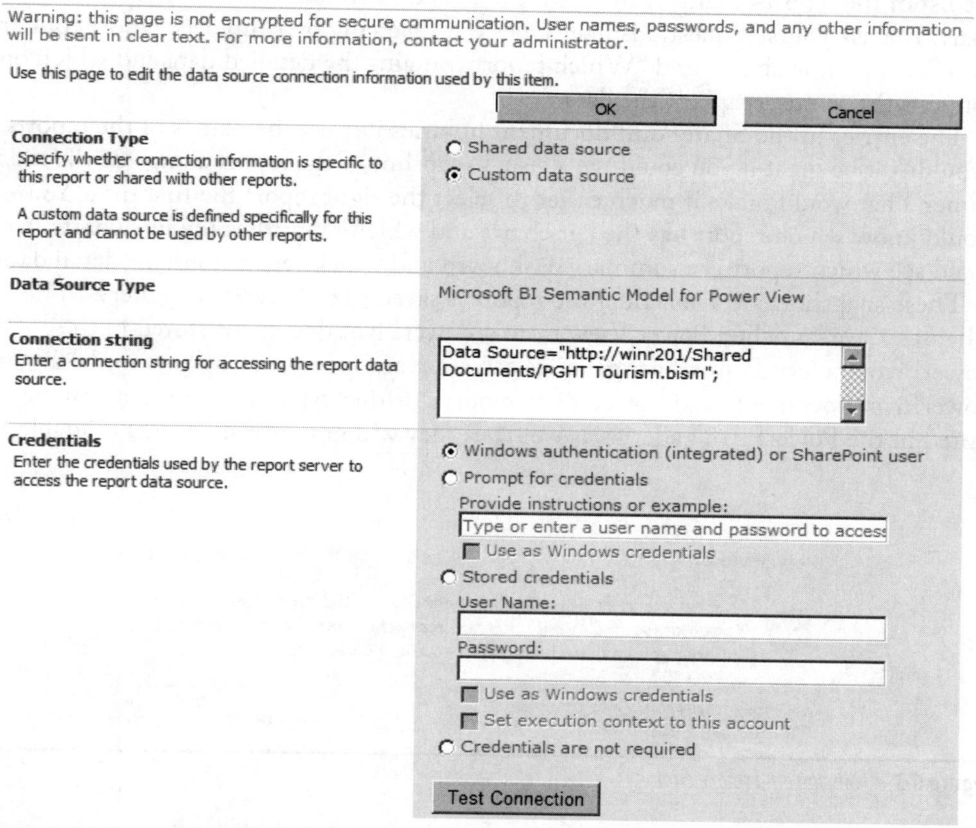

Warning: this page is not encrypted for secure communication. User names, passwords, and any other information will be sent in clear text. For more information, contact your administrator.

Use this page to edit the data source connection information used by this item.

[OK]   [Cancel]

Connection Type
Specify whether connection information is specific to this report or shared with other reports.

A custom data source is defined specifically for this report and cannot be used by other reports.

○ Shared data source
◉ Custom data source

Data Source Type

Microsoft BI Semantic Model for Power View

Connection string
Enter a connection string for accessing the report data source.

```
Data Source="http://winr201/Shared
Documents/PGHT Tourism.bism";
```

Credentials
Enter the credentials used by the report server to access the report data source.

◉ Windows authentication (integrated) or SharePoint user
○ Prompt for credentials
    Provide instructions or example:
    [Type or enter a user name and password to access]
    ☐ Use as Windows credentials
○ Stored credentials
    User Name:
    [ ]
    Password:
    [ ]
    ☐ Use as Windows credentials
    ☐ Set execution context to this account
○ Credentials are not required

[Test Connection]

Figure 6-2   *The Data Source Properties page*

where *{servername}* is the name of the SharePoint server and *{documentlibraryname}* is the name of the document library where the connection or data source is saved. This is in fact the path to the BI Semantic Model (BISM) connection or Reporting Services (RS) data source used to create the report.

If the data source for a report is moved or deleted, the report will not run. When this occurs, an error will display in the report, as shown in Figure 6-3. The error can be resolved by changing the report's connection string to point to a valid data source stored on the SharePoint server.

Saving Reports in PowerPivot Galleries

If you have used other reporting tools, such as Microsoft Reporting Services, you may have experienced something similar to the following scenario: After you create some really useful reports, your coworkers request additional reports similar to those you have made. In a short period of time, you have created 20 or 30 reports. When you look at the list of the reports, many of them start to sound so similar that you can't tell them apart. You ask yourself questions like "Does the Invoicing by Employee report contain a bar chart or a line chart?" and "Which report contains the detailed data and which one contains the scatter graph of the data?"

The entries in the SharePoint document libraries just list the names of the reports. Wouldn't it be great if you could see a visual snapshot of the report alongside the report name? That would make it much easier to select the right report the first time. You would know which report has the bar charts and which report has the line charts. You could see which report is a summary dashboard and which report contains detail data.

These snapshots are available if the report is saved to a PowerPivot gallery. In Chapter 1, we launched Power View from a PowerPivot document stored in the PowerPivot gallery. PowerPivot galleries can store and provide snapshots for both PowerPivot documents and Power View reports. (Other types of documents can be stored in the PowerPivot galleries as well, but they will not have snapshots available.)

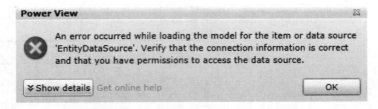

Figure 6-3   *Missing data source error*

Learn By Doing: Saving a Power View Report to a PowerPivot Gallery

Let's save a Power View report into a PowerPivot gallery and see how it appears in the gallery:

Video 6-1

Saving a Power View Report to a PowerPivot Gallery

1. Return to the SharePoint document library where your Power View reports are saved.
2. Click the drop-down arrow next to the Hotel Performance Dashboard report and select the Edit in Power View command.
3. Select the File tab of the ribbon and click Save As.
4. The Save As dialog box that appears points to a document library. Navigate up one level either by clicking the drop-down list box that displays the library path and selecting the root of the site or by clicking the Up Folder button next to the drop-down list box, as shown in Figure 6-4.

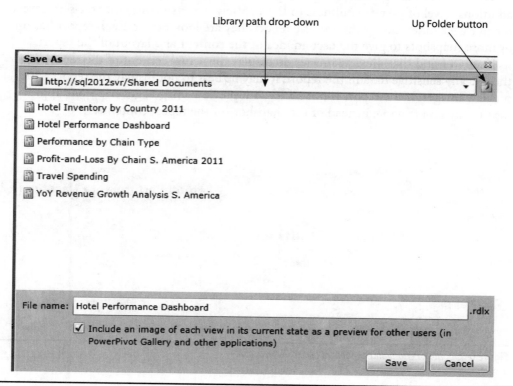

Figure 6-4   *Navigation options in the Save As dialog box*

5. Select the PowerPivot Gallery folder to navigate into that folder.

6. Make sure the "Include an image…" check box is checked.

7. Click Save to save the report in the PowerPivot gallery. The Save As dialog box closes.

8. Click your browser's Back button to exit Power View. You will return to the document library.

9. Click the PowerPivot Gallery link on the left side of the page.

10. The PowerPivot gallery now contains the Hotel Performance Dashboard report along with any PowerPivot documents that have been deployed to the gallery. Figure 6-5 shows the report in the PowerPivot gallery.

11. Notice that the Hotel Performance Dashboard has two snapshots associated with the report. Those two snapshots coincide with the two views that we created in the report. Click the second view that contains the multiple charts. Power View opens to that view of the report in Reading Mode.

12. Click your browser's Back button to exit Power View.

When saved with preview images, reports in PowerPivot galleries can provide an additional level of user-friendliness to Power View reports management. Users have a much easier time finding the specific report they are looking for. Each report has one or more snapshots to give the user an idea of the content and layout of the report.

Keep in mind that preview images do display the actual content of the report. If there is any sensitive data in the report, it may be best to not display the report with preview images. If the report is not saved with preview images, generic icons appear next to the report name instead of the snapshots of the report contents.

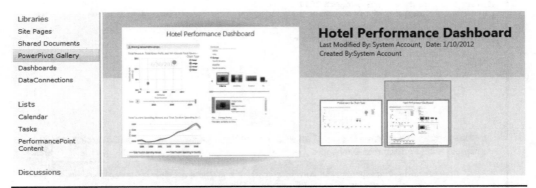

Figure 6-5   *Hotel Performance Dashboard in a PowerPivot gallery*

Opening Reports in Reading Mode vs. Edit Mode

Power View reports can be opened in Full Screen Mode, Reading Mode, and Edit Mode. Reading Mode is the default mode and is used by end users to "run" the report. When a user clicks the name of a report in a document library, the report opens in Reading Mode.

The interactive features described in Chapter 5 are available in Reading Mode. The user cannot, however, change the layout of the report or the appearance of the visualizations in Reading Mode. Edit Mode provides the full feature set of Power View and is the primary mode we have been working in throughout the book.

As we have seen, there are two ways to open a report in Edit Mode. You can open the report in Reading Mode by clicking the report name, and then click the Edit Report button. Alternatively, you can click the drop-down arrow next to the report name and select Edit in Power View. This latter method will take you directly to Editing Mode.

Security

Securing access to Power View reports, connections, and data sources is important. These Power View items provide access to sensitive information such as employee salaries or company financials. It is important to control access to these items so only authorized users are able to utilize them. In addition, some users will be considered report authors and will be authorized to change or create new reports, but other users will just be consumers of the reports and should only be able to run the reports and print or export them.

Securing Reports

The security of Power View reports is managed by the security settings in the SharePoint document libraries that hold the reports. As a report author, you might be expected to configure this security, or it might be the responsibility of a network or SharePoint administrator. In either case, it is helpful to have an understanding of how security works with regard to your reports.

SharePoint consists of sites that contain document libraries. These document libraries consist of items such as Power View reports. To simplify security, SharePoint uses a hierarchical security model. This means you can set security at the site level and have the same settings inherited at the next level, the document library, and the subsequent level, the items in the library. For example, if Amy has the rights to be a designer (someone who can edit content) of a SharePoint site, by default she is a designer for each of the document libraries within the site and a designer for each of the documents within the libraries.

Of course, the real world does not work that simply. In the example, Amy may be a designer of all content within a site *except* one Power View report that contains salaries. The administrator of the site can make an exception to the security model by "breaking the inheritance" for the Power View salary report. Once inheritance is broken for the report, the security can be set specifically for that report by not allowing Amy access to the report. Breaking inheritance can be reversed at any time if there is any reason to revert to the default state.

A user who attempts to access a Power View report (assuming the user has access to the site and document library holding the report) will come across one of three security scenarios:

▶ **No access**   The user has no rights to the Power View report and can't even see it in the document library.

▶ **Viewer rights**   The user has only View access to the report, which enables the user to run the report and even edit the report but does not allow the user to save any changes to the document library.

▶ **Full Control**   The user has Full Control access to the report, which enables the user to run the report, edit the report, and overwrite the report with those changes.

Figure 6-6 shows the Power View report drop-down menu for a user with Viewer rights. There are very limited options available. The user can open the report by clicking the link for the report but cannot use a menu command to edit in Power View.

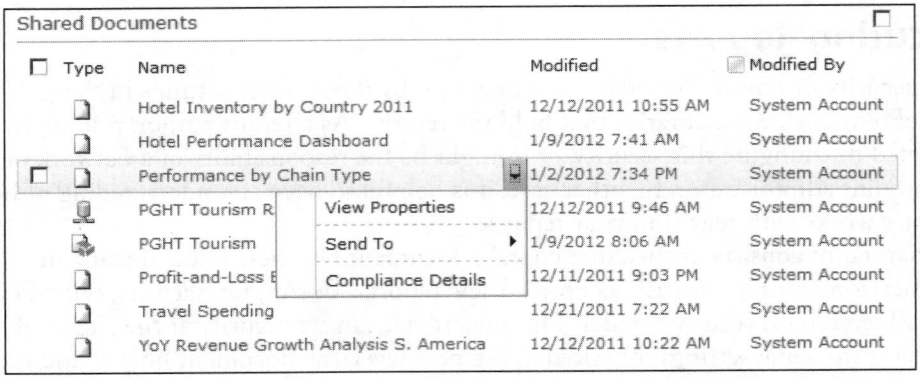

Figure 6-6   *Power View report menu for Viewer rights*

A user with Viewer rights can run reports and even edit existing reports, but the user cannot save the reports to the document library. Users with Viewer rights can also create Power View reports using a Reporting Services data source or a BI Semantic Model connection file, but those users cannot save these new reports to the document library. Figure 6-7 illustrates the error message a user with Viewer rights receives when trying to save to the document library.

Table 6-1 lists the features available in Power View and shows which of those features are supported by Viewer rights and which are supported with Full Control.

Securing Data Sources and Data Connections

Reporting Services data sources and BI Semantic Model connection files are very important to the functionality of the Power View reports and should be secured more tightly than the Power View reports. There are several reasons they should have extra security. First, these files may contain sensitive information, such as usernames and passwords, that could compromise the security of the source data. In addition, a user could accidentally edit or delete a data source, thereby breaking any number of Power View reports that rely on this data source.

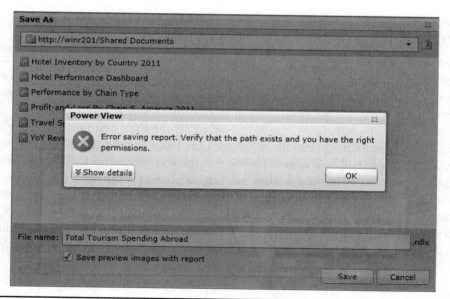

Figure 6-7   *Viewer rights save error*

Feature	Viewer Rights	Full Control
View existing visualizations	X	X
Interactive features: tiling, slicers, highlighting	X	X
Pop Out and Pop In	X	X
Edit filters	X	X
Print reports	X	X
Export reports to PowerPoint	X	X
Save reports		X
Create visualizations		X
Move and resize visualizations		X
Create views		X

Table 6-1   *Features Available in Reading Mode and Editing Mode by Viewer Rights and Full Control*

It is recommended that only administrators be given Full Control rights to Reporting Services data sources or BI Semantic Model connection files. All other users should have Viewer rights to the data sources.

Printing Reports

Power View is a reporting tool. When many people think of the word "report," they picture a piece of paper they can hold in their hand. Reports have become more of an electronic medium, but people still like to have a paper copy of their report to carry to a meeting or to look at when they aren't in possession of an electronic device.

Printing a Power View report is as easy as selecting the Print command on the File tab of the ribbon. Power View prints the report as if the visible report canvas was the paper. The report on paper will look almost identical to the way the canvas looks on the screen.

On the screen, if any of the visualizations are too large for the report or for the space allocated to them on the report, navigation arrows appear so you can navigate through the content of the visualization. For example, Figure 6-8 shows the arrows on the country tile from the Hotel Performance Dashboard. Since the size of the tile is fairly small, the countries don't all fit on the screen. The navigation arrows allow you to switch

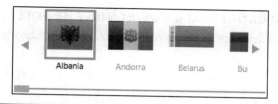

Figure 6-8   *Tiling navigation arrows*

from one country to another for all of the countries in Europe despite the fact that three or four countries are visible.

When a report is printed, the report displays the navigation arrows exactly as they appear on the screen. In addition, if you have scrolled to a specific location in the visualization, the report prints the visualization in that same location. For example, if you scrolled in the country tile so only half of the French flag displayed on the screen, the printout would display only half of the French flag.

If a report has multiple views, such as the Hotel Performance Dashboard, the Print command prints only the view that is visible on the screen. To print all views, you need to navigate to each view and click Print. Alternatively, you can export the report to PowerPoint and print the slide show...which leads us to exporting reports for use in slide presentations with PowerPoint.

Exporting Reports to PowerPoint

Power View is much more of a presentation tool than most other reporting environments. Many reporting environments focus primarily on the paper layout of reports and provide few, if any, interactive features. Because their focus is on page layout, they place an emphasis on page breaks, landscape versus portrait orientation, and headers and footers.

Power View's emphasis is on providing interactive features for users working on a computer or other electronic device. Power View allows reports to be printed, but printing is not the focus of the tool. You will find no settings for page breaks or page headers and footers in Power View reports.

As a result, exporting Power View reports to PowerPoint makes perfect sense as a way to distribute report results. Power View and PowerPoint are both presentation tools and are built to share data in a presentation format.

Learn By Doing: Exporting a Power View Report to PowerPoint

Let's export a Power View report to PowerPoint and explore the options for sharing our results:

| Video 6-2 | **Exporting a Power View Report to PowerPoint** |

NOTE

This Learn By Doing exercise assumes you are using PowerPoint installed on the same computer where you have been authoring your Power View reports. See the explanation following the steps of this Learn By Doing exercise.

1. Return to the SharePoint document library where your Power View reports are saved.
2. Click the drop-down arrow next to the Hotel Performance Dashboard report and select Edit in Power View. Reports can be exported to PowerPoint from either Edit Mode or Reading Mode.
3. Select the File tab of the ribbon and click Export to PowerPoint. A dialog box appears stating the PowerPoint export is complete.
4. Click Save. The Save As dialog box appears.
5. Navigate to an appropriate location for the PowerPoint file.
6. Enter **Hotel Performance** in the File name field.
7. Click Save.
8. Power View exports the report and returns you to your original view of the report.
9. Open the PowerPoint file that was exported by Power View.
10. When you open PowerPoint, you may be prompted with a security warning, as shown here. Click the Enable Content button.

The PowerPoint document contains two slides—one for each view of the report. The document opens in Normal view, which displays the contents of the report as an image in each slide. The image is actually the preview image that was saved with the report. If no image was saved with the report, an icon placeholder will display on each slide.

This isn't very exciting so far. Export to PowerPoint behaves almost exactly the same as the Print command described in the previous section. The exciting part comes when you make the slide show interactive.

11. In the bottom-right corner of the screen is a set of buttons to control the current view of the PowerPoint document. These buttons are identified in Figure 6-9. To use the interactive features, switch to Slide Show or Reading View. For this exercise, click the Slide Show button to enter Slide Show view.

12. Once in Slide Show view, move your mouse pointer to the bottom-right corner of the slide and click the "click to interact" button.

The images are replaced with content that behaves just like a Power View report in Reading Mode. This feature is very powerful in presentations as you manipulate the report within the slide in response to attendee questions. For example, if your slide shows the average hotel rating and tourism trends for North America and one of the attendees would like to see the same numbers for Europe, you can use the slicer to select Europe, and the charts on the slide will automatically change just as they do when you are using Power View. You have answered the attendee's question with one click of the mouse!

There is one stipulation when using these PowerPoint documents exported from Power View. In order for the interactive features to work, the computer running PowerPoint must be connected to the same network or domain as the server that runs Power View. This makes sense because it would be impossible for PowerPoint to update the content of the report slides without access to the Power View reporting engine and the source data for the report.

The Power Point slides actually interact directly with the reporting server while you are manipulating the data in PowerPoint. This means any changes to the report in Power View will appear in PowerPoint when you switch to interactive mode in the PowerPoint document. These PowerPoint slides behave almost like a window peering into the Power View environment—a window that allows you to run the report without having to open SharePoint.

NOTE

The static views of the reports are still visible in PowerPoint even when no connection is available back to the server. In this case, however, the click to interact features are not available.

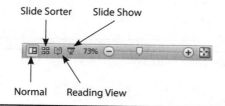

Figure 6-9 *PowerPoint views*

When we exported the report to PowerPoint, the slides opened as blank white slides with the report displayed in the middle, as shown in Figure 6-10. These slides can be visually enhanced either before exporting by changing the default slide template or after exporting using themes, images, and drawing tools.

Figure 6-11 shows the report after it has been enhanced with some of these design features. Notice the background of the report is still the same as it is in Power View and did not adapt to the color scheme of the slide. The Power View contents in a slide really are a window directly to Power View from the PowerPoint slide.

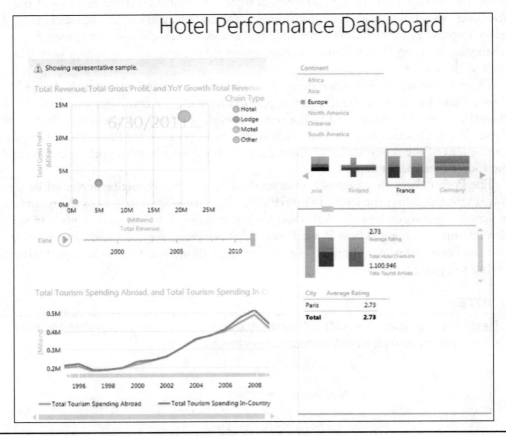

Figure 6-10   *PowerPoint slide before enhancement*

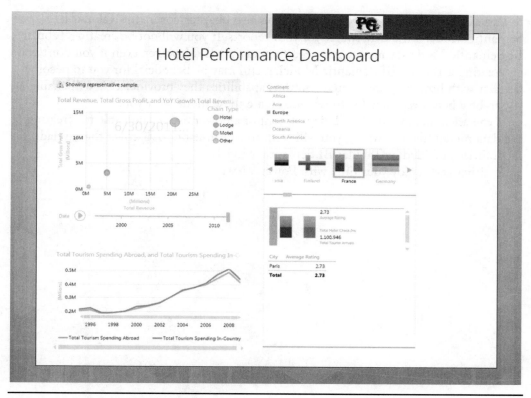

Figure 6-11   *PowerPoint slide after enhancement*

Wrap-Up

Power View provides a powerful, easy-to-use environment to create rich, interactive reports and to share those reports with others. In the past, business users employed many different static reports or dashboards to try to obtain the data necessary for informed business decisions. Oftentimes, these reports and dashboards were created by technical individuals that did not fully understand the business or the current business needs. Now those same decisions and many more can be made using a much smaller number of interactive Power View reports created by an organization's subject matter experts. These business users can quickly create and share reports. They can modify those reports as important facts and trends make themselves known.

Part II of the book, which begins with the next chapter, covers the Tabular BI Semantic Model—the data source for your reports. If you will not be creating Tabular BI Semantic Models, you may not need to read Part II. However, even if you don't end up creating a Tabular BI Semantic Model, it still may be beneficial for you to become familiar with how they are created and the capabilities they provide. This will enable you to be a better resource for those who create these models for you.

If you are a member of the IT department or a power user responsible for creating the data model (data steward), you will want to continue on to discover the myriad capabilities provided by Tabular BI Semantic Models.

In either case, enjoy your time with Power View!

Part II

Creating a BI Semantic Model (BISM)

Chapter 7

BISM: Getting Started

In This Chapter

▶ The BI Semantic Model
▶ Requirements for Developing Tabular BI Semantic Models
▶ Tabular BI Semantic Model Deployment Requirements
▶ Tabular Environment Server Configurations
▶ Additional SharePoint Setup Items
▶ Wrap-Up

In the first part of this book we looked at leveraging the new Microsoft report authoring tool called Power View. We went over the requirements for Power View, looked at the various ways to launch the tool, became familiar with the design surface, and explored the different reporting capabilities. In the process, we created some very interactive reports by simply clicking data items in the user interface. But the question remains, where did that data come from?

In this second part of the book, we take a closer look at the back-end portion of the environment that allowed us to create the reports: the BI Semantic Model (previously outlined in the introduction to the book). It is the heart and soul of what allowed us to perform the tasks in the first part of the book.

In this chapter, in addition to discussing the BI Semantic Model, we will go over the requirements for building models, discuss how to deploy those models, and gain some insight into the setup and configuration of the software and servers. We will not be diving into the setup of SharePoint, but we will discuss extending the SharePoint environment to provide the BI Semantic Model support needed for Power View report authoring.

| Video 7-1 | **Introduction to Part II** |

The BI Semantic Model

The BI Semantic Model is a descriptive layer that provides a single source, one model, which can be leveraged for reporting, dashboarding, analysis, and predictive analytics. This is the core piece that ties data together to provide insight into what is going on in your organization.

The model is where we pull in data from disparate systems. We can then define relationships between items in the model. This is where we scrub the data elements for presentation purposes and set up the necessary metrics. When the model is ready, we deploy that model so that it can be consumed by the end-user client tools, as depicted in Figure 7-1.

You need to be aware that there are a few different versions of the BI Semantic Model. Let's take a quick look at the different options:

▶ **Multidimensional** This format has been available in SQL Server since OLAP Services 7.0 and provides us with dimensions, hierarchies, measures, measure groups, key performance indicators (KPIs), partitioning, security, and cubes. This model is deployed to an Analysis Services Multidimensional server instance.

▶ **Tabular** This form of the BI Semantic Model is a scalable version of PowerPivot that has now been brought to the server level. The Tabular model leverages the

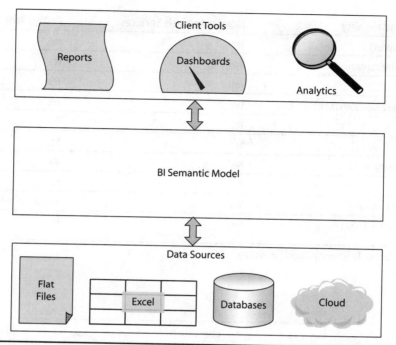

Figure 7-1   *BI Semantic Model—single model*

xVelocity in-memory analytics and keeps data in memory to improve processing speed. This model provides us with tables, hierarchies, measures, KPIs, partitioning, and role-based security. This model is deployed to an Analysis Services Tabular server instance.

▶ **PowerPivot**   This form of the Tabular model is available through an add-in to Excel 2010 and is intended for individual use and team use when deployed to a SharePoint 2010 environment. This model provides the same core functionality as the Tabular model with the exception of partitioning and role-based security. This model can be used on its own or can be deployed to a SharePoint library.

If we enhance Figure 7-1 to incorporate the different model types (keeping in mind that the PowerPivot model is a special form of the Tabular model), we end up with Figure 7-2. As this figure shows, both models can incorporate data from many of the same data sources. Both models also can be utilized by many of the same client tools.

This book focuses on the Tabular model because, at its initial release, Power View requires a Tabular model as the source for its data. Microsoft plans to have Power View also support the Multidimensional model at some point in the future.

Table 7-1 shows some of the key differences between the two different flavors of the Tabular model.

Feature/Functionality	Tabular Analysis Services	PowerPivot
Import data support	Yes	Yes
Excel linked table support	No	Yes
Hierarchies	Yes	Yes
Key performance indicators (KPIs)	Yes	Yes
Perspectives	Yes	Yes
Drillthrough	Yes	Yes
Row-level security	Yes	No
Partitioning	Yes	No
Scheduled data refreshes	Yes	Yes (via SharePoint)
Incremental data refreshes	Yes	No

Table 7-1 *Tabular BI Semantic Model Comparison*

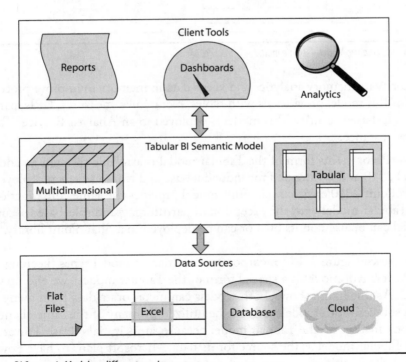

Figure 7-2 *BI Semantic Model—different versions*

NOTE

Not all features will necessarily be supported by all client tools, so it is very important to make sure the functionality you are looking for will be supported by your tool of choice.

Looking at Figure 7-2, we see that a Tabular model can incorporate data from various types of data sources such as flat files, Excel spreadsheets, relational databases (such as Microsoft Access and Microsoft SQL Server), and cloud-based services. We can import this data into our model, define relationships, and set up calculations in a short amount of time, so we can start building our reports very quickly. This ability to quickly combine data from disparate sources is one of the main advantages of the Tabular model.

Let's look at what we need to have in place to begin creating Tabular BI Semantic Models.

Requirements for Developing Tabular BI Semantic Models

Developing Tabular models can be done in two different environments:

- ▶ PowerPivot
- ▶ SQL Server Data Tools

Depending on the functionality you need (refer to Table 7-1), you can leverage either option. Keep in mind, your choice of model will determine which tool you use to create the model and which method you use for deployment.

Requirements for PowerPivot

First, we take a look at the PowerPivot development requirements.

Hardware Requirements

The following are the minimum hardware requirements:

- ▶ **Processor**   500 MHz, 32 bit or 64 bit
- ▶ **RAM**   2GB to 4GB
- ▶ **Disk space**   100MB

Software Requirements

The following are the minimum software requirements:

- **Operating system**   Windows XP SP3 (32 bit only), Windows Vista SP2, Windows 7, Windows Server 2003 R2 (32 bit only), Windows Server 2008 SP2, or Windows Server 2008 R2 (64 bit only)

- **.NET Framework**   Microsoft .NET Framework 4.0

- **Excel version**   Excel 2010, 32 bit or 64 bit

- **Office features**   Office Shared Features, .NET Programmability Support in Microsoft Excel, and Visual Studio 2010 Tools for Office Runtime

- **Excel add-in**   PowerPivot add-in for Excel 2010, 32 bit or 64 bit depending on the version of Excel 2010 installed

NOTE

The 32-bit version of PowerPivot supports up to approximately 2GB of data in memory (some overhead is needed within the 2GB for Excel). The 64-bit version supports up to 4GB of data in memory. Because of data compression applied when saving to disk, the maximum disk file size supported by each environment differs from the maximum in-memory data size. The 64-bit version supports PowerPivot files up to 2GB in size. The 32-bit version supports files up to a maximum of 500MB to 700MB. Take these constraints into account when selecting the appropriate platform for modeling.

Requirements for Tabular Analysis Services Projects

Now let's look at the requirements for creating Tabular Analysis Services projects using SQL Server Data Tools

Hardware Requirements

The following are the minimum hardware requirements:

- **Processor**   1 GHz or higher

- **RAM**   2GB to 4GB

- **Disk space**   2200MB (for SQL Server Data Tools)

Software Requirements

The following are the minimum software requirements:

▶ **Operating system**   Windows Vista SP2, Windows Server 2008 SP2, Windows 7 SP1, or Windows Server 2008 R2 SP1

▶ **.NET Framework**   Microsoft .NET Framework 4.0 (.NET 3.5 SP1 is a requirement before installing any SQL Server components)

▶ **Internet software**   Microsoft Internet Explorer 7 or higher

▶ **Development environment**   SQL Server Data Tools

Installation of SQL Server Data Tools installs .NET Framework 4.0 along with Microsoft Visual Studio Tools for Applications 3.0 and the Microsoft Visual Studio 2010 Shell.

The Development Environment

As you have seen, the requirements for these two development options are similar. The main difference is the software environment actually used for the creation of the model. With PowerPivot, that environment is Excel 2010. With a Tabular Analysis Services project, that environment is SQL Server Data Tools.

Excel 2010 is, of course, installed as part of Microsoft Office 2010. SQL Server Data Tools is installed as part of a SQL Server client installation. To install SQL Server Data Tools, you will need the SQL Server installation media and the appropriate product keys.

NOTE

SQL Server Data Tools is actually the Visual Studio 2010 development environment operating under a different name. If you already have Visual Studio 2010 installed on your computer, you still need to run the SQL Server client installation to obtain the business intelligence project types.

Next we will take a look at what is needed on the server side once you have a model created and are ready to deploy and share it.

Tabular BI Semantic Model Deployment Requirements

In this book, we are dealing with Tabular models in a multiuser environment. In order for a model to be used by multiple individuals, it must be moved from the computer where it is developed to a server that can be accessed by the users. This process of moving the model from the development environment to a server environment is called *deployment*.

So, where do we deploy our Tabular BI Semantic Models to make them more widely available? We have a few different options. If we have created a PowerPivot model, we want to deploy that model to PowerPivot configured on a SharePoint 2010 Enterprise Edition server. If we have created a Tabular Analysis Services model, we want to deploy that model to a Tabular instance of SQL Server Analysis Services.

PowerPivot Deployment

This section lists the requirements for deploying PowerPivot on a SharePoint 2010 Enterprise Edition server.

Hardware Requirements

The following are the minimum hardware requirements:

▶ **Processor**   3 GHz, 64 bit, dual core

▶ **RAM**   8GB

▶ **Disk space**   80GB

Software Requirements

The following are the minimum software requirements:

▶ **Operating system**   Windows Server 2008 SP2 (64 bit) or Windows Server 2008 R2

▶ **SharePoint version**   SharePoint 2010 Enterprise Edition with SP1 (with Excel Services, Secure Store Service, and Claims to Windows Token Service configured in the same farm) set up as a Server Farm install

▶ **PowerPivot for SharePoint**   PowerPivot instance of Analysis Services set up in PowerPivot mode for use in SharePoint

To set up PowerPivot for SharePoint, you choose the SQL Server PowerPivot for SharePoint option while doing a SQL Server installation, as shown in Figure 7-3. You can install the SQL Server relational database engine as part of this same installation, if desired. To do so, select the "Add SQL Server Database Relational Engine Services to this installation" check box. If you do not wish to install the SQL Server relational database engine, clear this check box.

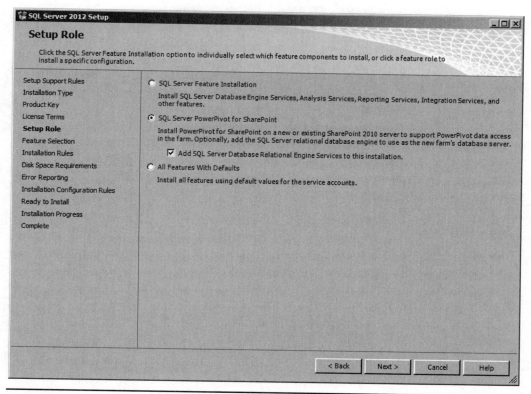

Figure 7-3   *PowerPivot for SharePoint installation option*

NOTE

When completing the PowerPivot for SharePoint setup, you must configure this as a named instance and you must use "PowerPivot" as the name of that instance. Also, because a named instance of SQL Server is required, the SQL Server Browser service must be installed and running on your server.

Tabular Analysis Services Deployment

If you create a Tabular Analysis Services model, you will need a Tabular instance of SQL Server Analysis Services. A Tabular instance of SQL Server Analysis Services can be installed using the SQL Server installation, as shown in Figure 7-4. In most cases, it is desirable to install this Tabular instance of SQL Server Analysis Services on a separate server, so it is not running on a computer where transactional processing is taking place.

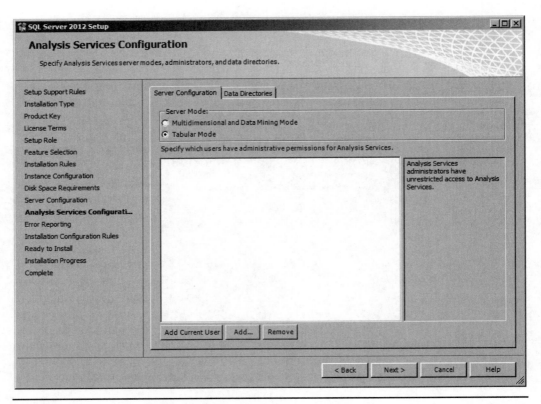

Figure 7-4   *Tabular Analysis Services installation option*

NOTE

When designing and building a Tabular BI Semantic Model in SQL Server Data Tools, you will need to have a Tabular instance of SQL Server Analysis Services running to serve as your workspace server. This workspace server is utilized by the development environment as a temporary working environment.

Hardware and Software Requirements

The minimum hardware and operating system requirements for a Tabular instance of SQL Server Analysis Services are the same as those listed in the previous section for a PowerPivot deployment.

Tabular Environment Server Configurations

Now that we have identified the pieces required for development and deployment of a Tabular BI Semantic Model, let's take a look at a few of the different options for setting up our environment.

The Single-Server Environment

The most basic configuration is a stand-alone environment consisting of a single server. In other words, all the server components are installed on one computer, as shown in Figure 7-5. The server in this figure includes the items for both types of Tabular models, PowerPivot and Tabular Analysis Services. This type of installation works well for evaluating software, for development, and for testing. For this reason, we will call this a *sandbox* server.

NOTE

Even though this is called a stand-alone, single-server configuration, performing a Server Farm install of SharePoint is a requirement. The PowerPivot for SharePoint option will not work on an instance of SharePoint installed with the Standalone setup option.

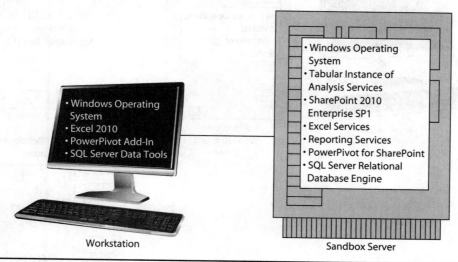

Figure 7-5   *Single-server environment configuration*

Having everything on one server makes it very easy to install and configure. However, to obtain an acceptable level of performance, you will need to have a decent hardware platform. Also, this type of environment won't scale well for heavy usage. Therefore, this environment is not recommended for a production environment. For recommendations on production deployments, check out the next section on the multiserver farm environment.

The Multiserver Farm Environment

In a multiserver farm environment, the components are distributed among several servers, as shown in Figure 7-6. There are three servers in the multiserver configuration

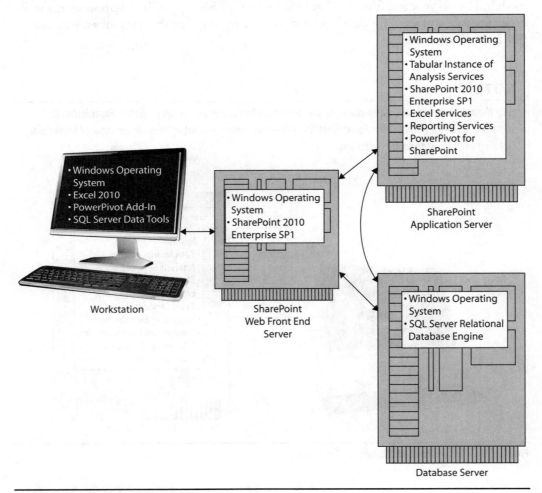

Figure 7-6 *Multiserver farm environment configuration*

shown here. The first is used for the SharePoint Web Front End (WFE) server. The second server functions as the SharePoint application server. This server also includes a Tabular instance of SQL Server Analysis Services. Having the Tabular instance on this server is not required. It could be split off to a fourth server to spread out the processing load even further. The third server is a separate database server containing the relational databases for SharePoint.

Handling end-user credentials can be somewhat tricky in a multiserver environment. The user enters their credentials on the workstation. The credentials are then passed from one server to another. In cases where the credentials will need to make more than one "hop" between servers, you need to configure your environment with impersonation and delegation features for Windows Authentication. This means you need to set up Kerberos and associate service principal names (SPNs) with domain accounts running the Windows services on the server. Configuring Kerberos is outside the scope of this book, but for a reference you can search the Internet for "SharePoint 2010 Kerberos White Paper." Another option to resolve this issue is to use stored credentials in your connections and leverage unattended service accounts in SharePoint.

Now that we have reviewed some of the different options for configuring your environment, we can take a look at a few additional setup items you need to be aware of on the SharePoint side of things.

Additional SharePoint Setup Items

After you install the Tabular environment in your SharePoint farm, you need to complete a couple of additional configuration items.

PowerPivot Configuration Tool

If you installed PowerPivot for SharePoint, you need to run the PowerPivot Configuration Tool. You do this after you have completed the SharePoint setup and installed the PowerPivot instance. The PowerPivot Configuration Tool is part of the SQL Server installation software, as shown in Figure 7-7. When the prerequisite items are installed and running, this option will be enabled in the SQL Server Installation Center menu.

The PowerPivot Configuration Tool allows you to complete the PowerPivot for SharePoint configuration. This tool performs validations on your environment to ensure the appropriate steps have been taken to set up a SharePoint web application and site collection, and to configure service accounts. It also ensures that all necessary Windows and SharePoint services and applications are set up and running, as shown in Figure 7-8.

This tool can also be used to remove features, services, applications, and solutions.

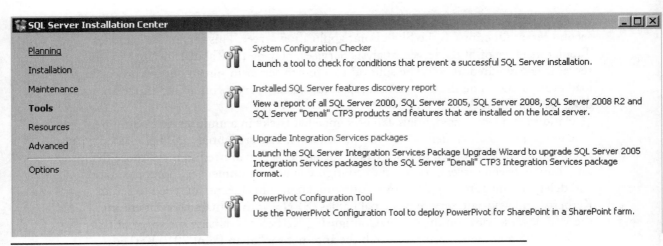

Figure 7-7 *PowerPivot Configuration Tool item in the Installation Center menu*

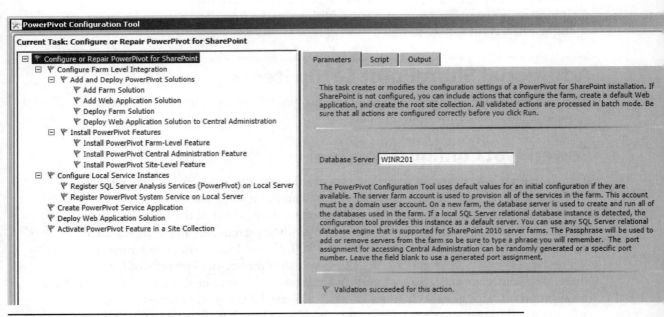

Figure 7-8 *PowerPivot Configuration Tool setup*

SQL Server Reporting Services SharePoint Integrated Mode

In addition to ensuring that Tabular model support is set up properly in your environment, you also need to have SQL Server Reporting Services (SSRS) installed in SharePoint Integrated Mode. This is why Reporting Services is included in Figure 7-5 and Figure 7-6. The SharePoint Integrated Mode installation of Reporting Services is required to enable the Power View reporting option in SharePoint.

Reporting Services must be installed on your SharePoint application server. To do this, you use the SQL Server installation software. When running a SQL Server installation, you will notice two Reporting Services feature options, one for performing a SharePoint install and another for installing the Add-in for SharePoint Products, as shown in Figure 7-9.

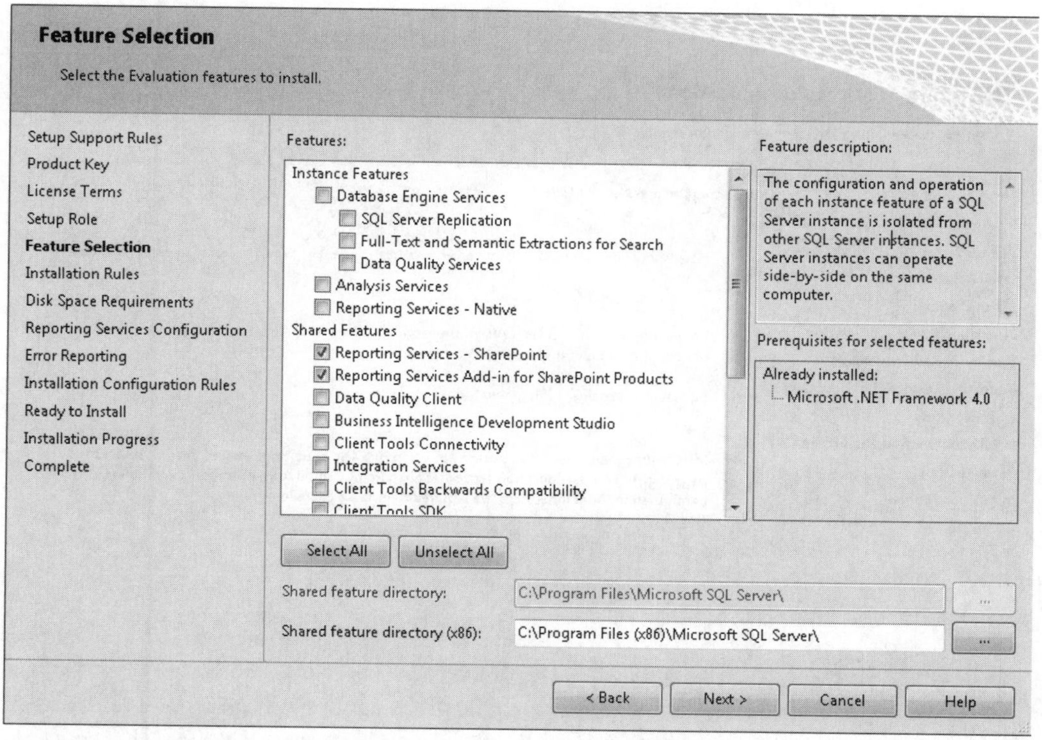

Figure 7-9   *Reporting Services SharePoint features*

NOTE

The Reporting Services SharePoint Integration Mode setup has completely changed in this version of SQL Server. You no longer use the Reporting Services Configuration Manager to perform this configuration. The setup and configuration for SharePoint Integration Mode is now done in SharePoint Central Administration (CA). You can also leverage PowerShell scripts to complete this configuration, if desired. The Reporting Services Windows service is no longer installed as part of a Reporting Services Integrated Mode installation. Instead, it is an application that runs within SharePoint, just like Excel Services and PerformancePoint Services.

The options available on the Reporting Services Configuration page of the installation depend on what you selected on the installation Feature Selection page shown in Figure 7-9. Figure 7-10 shows the Reporting Services Configuration page when the two SharePoint options were the only items selected. In this case, the sole option available is Install Only.

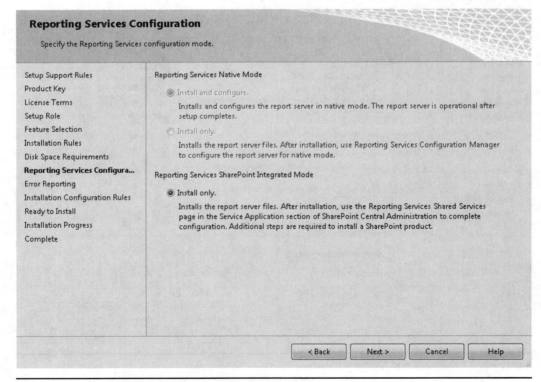

Figure 7-10 *Reporting Services SharePoint Integrated Mode configuration*

If you perform the Reporting Services SharePoint Integrated Mode installation after you have already installed and set up SharePoint, the rest of the process is fairly straightforward. You do the next step through SharePoint Central Administration, where you go into the SharePoint SQL Server Reporting Services Service Application that was just created and set up the database, credentials, and web application with which the application should be associated.

If, by some chance, you did all of the SQL Server feature installation prior to getting SharePoint set up, you will need to take some additional steps to complete the Reporting Services Integration. Once you have SharePoint set up and available, you must complete these steps using PowerShell and Central Administration as follows:

1. Run the Microsoft SharePoint 2010 Management Shell as Administrator.
2. Type the following PowerShell command:

   ```
   Install-SPRSService
   ```

3. To start the service, type the following PowerShell command:

   ```
   get-spserviceinstance -all |where {$_.TypeName -like "SQL Server
   Reporting*"} | Start-SPServiceInstance
   ```

4. In SharePoint Central Administration, select Application Management | Service Applications | Manage Service Applications.
5. Create a new SQL Server Reporting Services service application.
6. Go into the application and complete the process by specifying a name for the application, creating a new application pool, and specifying the database server name. Further down the page you also need to select the web application with which to associate this application, along with the database authentication type.

Wrap-Up

In this chapter, we discussed the environment that is necessary for hosting Tabular BI Semantic Models. Notes were provided on things to watch out for and things to consider when getting started with BI Semantic Models. At the end of the chapter, we covered the process required to configure the SharePoint environment so we are able to not only support our Tabular BI Semantic Models, but also create fabulous reports with Power View.

Next, in Chapter 8, we dive into designing and creating your very first BI Semantic Model.

Chapter 8

Basic BI Semantic Model Design

In This Chapter

► **Creating a BI Semantic Model from the Ground Up**
► **Bringing Additional Data into the BI Semantic Model**
► **Making the Model Work**
► **Wrap-Up**

In the previous chapter, we looked at the requirements for the environments in which to create and deploy BI Semantic Models for your Power View report authors. With these environments in place, you are now ready to design and create models. In fact, you're probably eager to apply business sense to a vast array of data sources to provide crisp, focused business metrics. You plan to deliver a nice, neat package—a BI Semantic Model—to insulate the report author from complex relational and multidimensional database structures.

This chapter helps you to do just that. We look at basic BI Semantic Model design and recommended practices for modeling data. You learn the specific steps involved in creating a BI Semantic Model for the business report author, using the tools we discussed in Chapter 7.

So, do you have the tools in place to actually begin creating models? Let's go over the requirements again:

▶ You have a workstation on which Microsoft Excel 2010, along with the PowerPivot add-in, is installed. From that workstation you can connect to the data, at its source, that your users are going to need. With these pieces in place, you have the ability to create Tabular BI Semantic Models with PowerPivot in Excel.

▶ You installed the Microsoft SQL Server client tools onto your workstation, including SQL Server Data Tools along with its templates for creating a BI Semantic Model for Analysis Services. You also set up a Tabular instance of Microsoft SQL Server Analysis Services.

With the necessary components in place, you're ready to use *either* PowerPivot or Analysis Services to create and share Tabular BI Semantic Models. Remember, as we discussed in the last chapter, you can choose to use either PowerPivot *or* Analysis Services to host a BI Semantic Model, the choice depending on whether your models are intended for individual, team, or enterprise use.

In this chapter we work with both PowerPivot (in Microsoft Excel) and Analysis Services (using SQL Server Data Tools). We begin by building a model in PowerPivot, and then use that model as the starting point to build a model in SQL Server Data Tools. We spend the remainder of this chapter, and indeed the remainder of the book, working in SQL Server Data Tools. As we saw in Chapter 7, the vast majority of the features available in PowerPivot are also available in the Tabular Analysis Services model built in SQL Server Data Tools, and vice versa.

Creating a BI Semantic Model from the Ground Up

As you will find in the exercises to follow, whether you are using PowerPivot in Excel or SQL Server Data Tools (two very different development environments), assembling the pieces in a BI Semantic Model is nearly the same. However, the process of initially creating that model is very different between the two environments. We're going to start by creating a PowerPivot model in Microsoft Excel. Then we'll set that model aside and create an Analysis Services Tabular project using SQL Server Data Tools.

Creating a BI Semantic Model Using PowerPivot in Excel

We begin by creating a model using PowerPivot for Excel. First, let's look at what we're trying to accomplish.

The Business Objective

Pan-Geo Hospitality and Travel needs a data model that provides tourism statistics by country for the continents of Europe and Asia. This model will be used by the marketing department to track foreign travel spending trends. The statistics must be classified by global region—in this case, Europe and Asia. Only arrivals to countries within these regions should be included, so we'll eliminate the other statistics.

Learn By Doing: Creating a BI Semantic Model Using PowerPivot

Video 8-1 **Creating a BI Semantic Model Using PowerPivot**

Launch the PowerPivot Environment
1. Start Microsoft Excel.
2. Select the PowerPivot tab of the ribbon.
3. Click the PowerPivot Window button, as shown in Figure 8-1, to open the PowerPivot Tabular model designer.

The PowerPivot Tablular model design window, shown in Figure 8-2, interacts with Microsoft Excel. Everything we do in the PowerPivot window is stored in the existing Excel workbook. As you'll see in a moment, when we're done managing data in PowerPivot, we return to Excel to work with that data.

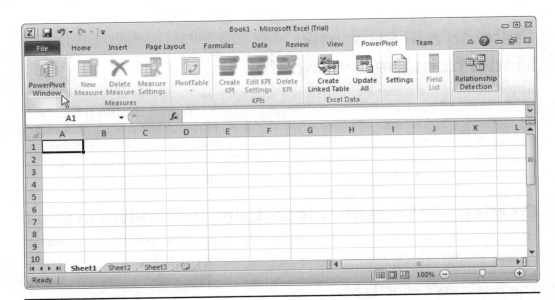

Figure 8-1 *The PowerPivot tab of the ribbon*

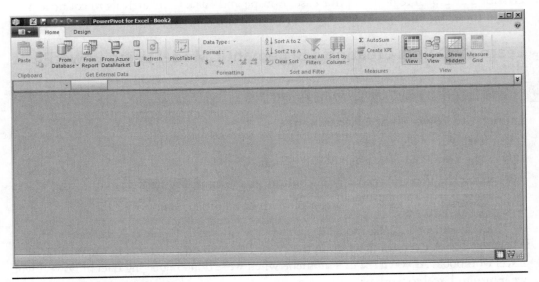

Figure 8-2 *The PowerPivot Window*

Import Data into the Model   Let's import data from Microsoft SQL Server into a PowerPivot Tabular model:

1. Click the From Database button in the ribbon and choose From SQL Server from the drop-down list, as shown here.

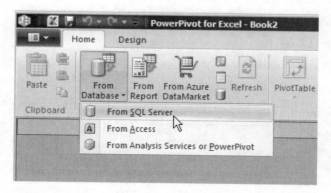

2. The Table Import Wizard opens, displaying the Connect to a Microsoft SQL Server Database page. Leave the Friendly connection name field as is. It will change as we choose other options.

3. For Server name, enter the name of the SQL Server instance where the PGHT_Tourism database was restored.

4. Enter the appropriate credentials for connecting to this server or use Windows Authentication, as appropriate.

5. Select PGHT_Tourism from the Database name drop-down list. The Connect to a Microsoft SQL Server Database page of the wizard should appear similar to Figure 8-3.

6. Click Next. The Choose How to Import the Data page of the Table Import Wizard appears.

   The default option allows us to import all of the data from one or more tables and views in the database. The other option available on this page of the wizard allows us to specify a query and import the result set of that query into the model. We'll be importing data from three tables in the PGHT_Tourism database—Country, Date, and UNWTO_Tourism—so we will stick with the default option.

7. Click Next to move to the Select Tables and Views page of the Table Import Wizard.

8. Select the check boxes next to the Country, Date, and UNWTO_Tourism source tables.

9. By default, the name in the Friendly Name column is the same as the Source Table name. The friendly name is the name the end users see. Replace UNWTO_Tourism with **Tourism** in the Friendly Name column for the UNWTO_Tourism table. The Select Tables and Views page of the wizard will appear as shown in Figure 8-4.

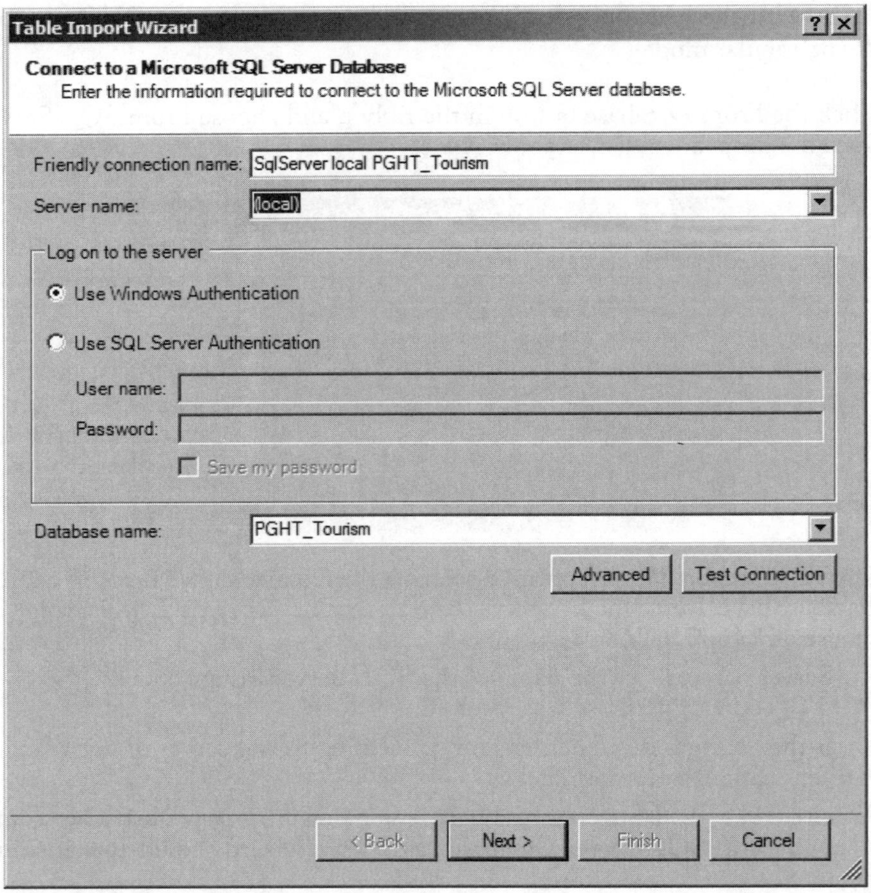

Figure 8-3 *The Connect to a Microsoft SQL Server Database page of the PowerPivot Table Import Wizard*

In many cases, there will be tables related to one or more of the selected tables by foreign key constraints in the source database. If we want to add these related tables to the model, we can click the Select Related Tables button. This will automatically check any related tables. This can save time if the database has dozens or hundreds of tables. For now, leave the Table Import Wizard open to the Select Tables and Views page, as we will continue from that point in the next section.

Preview and Filter Data   We can also filter the data coming from a selected table and take a look at that data by clicking the Preview & Filter button. This allows us to limit the data to only those rows and columns we want the users to see in the model.

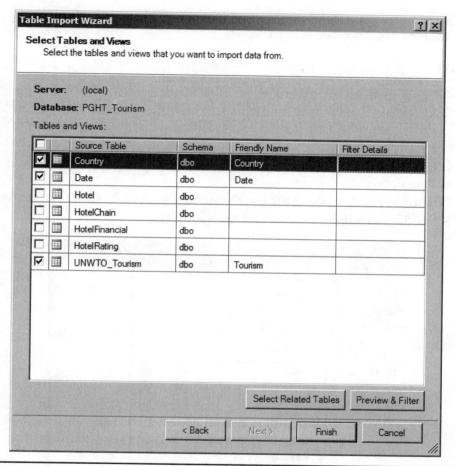

Figure 8-4   *The Select Table and Views page of the PowerPivot Tables Import Wizard*

This is a very useful capability of the BI Semantic Model. We use it here to narrow the scope of data coming into our model to include only Europe and Asia, as specified in the business objective.

1. Select the row for the Country source table by clicking anywhere in the row other than the check box.

2. Click the Preview & Filter button. The Preview Selected Table dialog box opens and shows the rows and columns from the Country table.

    We will import all fields from the Country table except the CountryID field, which has no significance for users of the model. Also, we will only import the rows for countries in the continents of Asia and Europe.

3. Deselect the check box in the CountryID column heading so this column is not included when the data is imported.

NOTE

The CountryCode column does not have significance to our business users. However, it is required in our model to create a link between the Country table and the UNWTO_Tourism table. The United Nations tourism data in the UNWTO_Tourism table uses this country code to identify each country. We discuss this in more detail when we enhance the model later in the chapter.

4. Click the drop-down arrow in the Continent column heading. The sort and filter options appear.
5. Deselect the (Select All) check box to clear all the check boxes for the continents.
6. Select the check boxes for Asia and Europe.

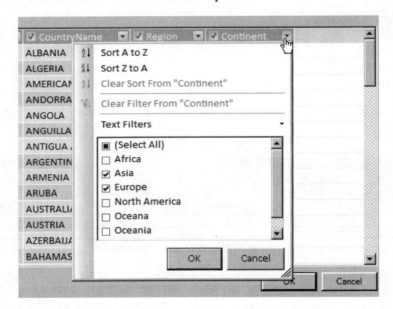

7. Click OK. Notice the filter icon that appears in the Continent column heading. Also, the data in the grid has changed to include only countries in Europe and Asia, as shown in Figure 8-5.
8. Click OK to exit the Preview Selected Table dialog box.
9. Next, let's filter the Date table. Select the row for the Date source table.
10. Click the Preview & Filter button to open the Preview Selected Table dialog box.
11. Deselect the check box in the upper-left corner of the grid to uncheck all columns.
12. Click the check boxes for the ID column and for the Year column. (The UNWTO_ Tourism table provides data at the year level, so we don't need the month level in this model.)

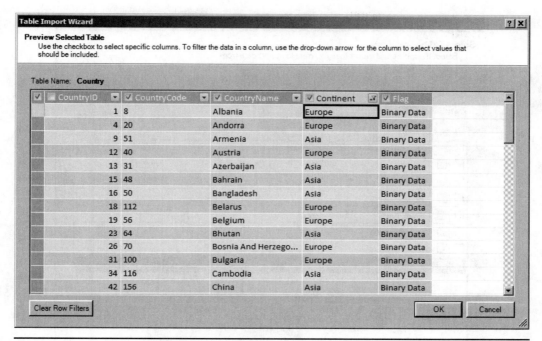

Figure 8-5   *The Preview Selected Table page of the PowerPivot Table Import Wizard*

13. Click OK to exit the Preview Selected Table dialog box.

    Now, we want to preview and filter the tourism data. We want the tourism data to contain only what is needed to determine in-country analysis. That is to say, we'll ignore outbound tourism data for this model.

14. Select the row for the UNWTO_Tourism source table.

15. Click the Preview & Filter button to open the Preview Selected Table dialog box.

16. Deselect the check box in the upper-left corner of the grid to uncheck all columns.

17. Select the check boxes for the following columns:

    CountryCode
    TravelYear
    NonResidentTouristArrivals
    NonResidentTouristHotelCheckins
    IBTravelExpenditures
    TourismExpenditureInCountry

18. Click OK to exit the Preview Selected Table dialog box. The Select Tables and Views page of the Table Import Wizard should now appear as shown in Figure 8-6, indicating that filters have been applied.

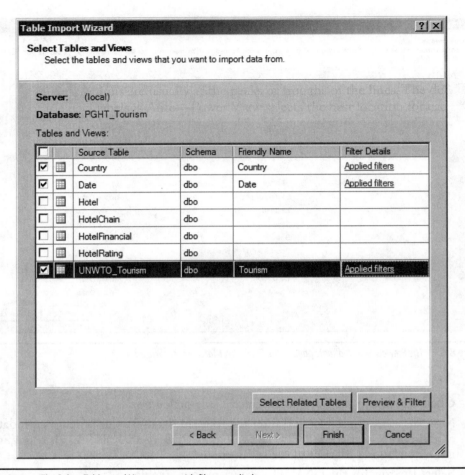

Figure 8-6   *The Select Tables and Views page with filters applied*

Finish Loading the Data into the Model

1. Click Finish to complete the Table Import Wizard.

   PowerPivot will now load data into each of the tables in the model from the tables in the data source. The status of the import of each table's data is shown on the Importing page of the Table Import Wizard, seen in Figure 8-7. If any problems occur while importing data, you see a link in the Message column. You can click that link to read a message to help you diagnose and correct the problem.

2. When the import process is complete, click Close to return to the PowerPivot window.

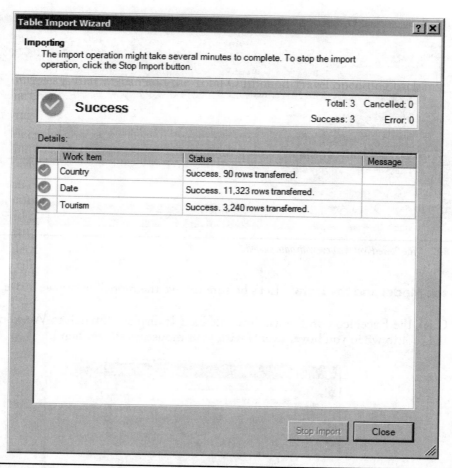

Figure 8-7 *The Importing page of the PowerPivot Table Import Wizard*

There you have it. You have completed the most important step in creating a basic BI Semantic Model using PowerPivot—loading data into the model. Our model now consists of three tables: Country, Date, and Tourism, each with its own tab at the bottom of the design area. This is shown in the PowerPivot Window in Figure 8-8.

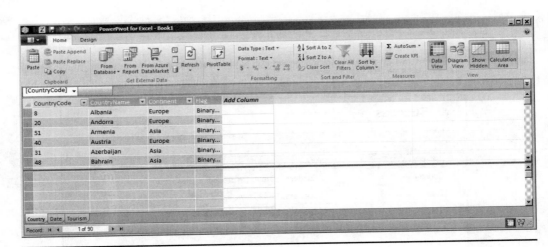

Figure 8-8   *The PowerPivot Window with data loaded*

Save the Model and the Data   Let's be sure to save the model before we move on.

1.   Click the Excel icon on the window title bar.(It displays "Switch to Workbook" in the tooltip when you hover over it with your mouse, as shown here).

2.   Click the Save button in the Quick Access Toolbar, as shown here, or select the File tab of the ribbon and click Save As.

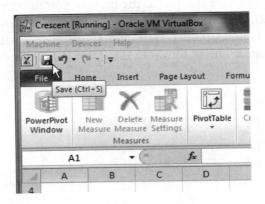

3. Navigate to the folder where you would like to save this Excel file.
4. Enter **Pan-Geo Tourism by Country** for File name.
5. Click Save.
6. Exit Microsoft Excel.

When we save our model, PowerPivot also saves the data that was imported into that model. When we're finished, we then have a high-performance and very flexible cache of data. In the example just completed, we have a model built specifically for analyzing statistics on European and Asian tourism.

Creating an Analysis Services Tabular BI Semantic Model in SQL Server Data Tools

We are going to move now to creating a BI Semantic Model that will be hosted by a Tabular instance of SQL Server Analysis Services. Unlike the PowerPivot example we just saw, this isn't something that is typically done by a business user who is savvy in Microsoft Excel. Most people in your organization are not likely to have SQL Server Data Tools—the tool necessary for this type of model creation—installed on their computers. It is normally in the hands of select individuals in an IT department. As we saw in the previous chapter, SQL Server Data Tools isn't installed with Microsoft Office. It is included as a component with the installation of the Microsoft SQL Server client tools.

The Business Objective

This data model is for the entire Pan-Geo Hospitality and Travel marketing department. The finished product won't be incredibly large, but it will support the entire company rather than just a few users who need a limited number of measures, as in the PowerPivot model. So, let's bring more data into the model to fulfill these requirements.

Learn By Doing: Getting Started with SQL Server Data Tools

Video 8-2   **Setting Defaults in SQL Server Data Tools**

First, let's launch, and get acquainted with, the development environment in which we'll build the new model.

Launch SQL Server Data Tools   To launch SQL Server Data Tools:
1. In Windows, click Start | All Programs.
2. Click the Microsoft SQL Server 2012 folder.
3. Click SQL Server Data Tools.

As we proceed through the following exercises, we assume you have some familiarity with the various parts of Microsoft Visual Studio or SQL Server Data Tools.

Set the Default Workspace Server Whenever SQL Server Data Tools is working with a Tabular model, it is in constant communication with a Tabular instance of SQL Server Analysis Services. The development environment creates a workspace database on this Analysis Services server. This workspace database hosts the data in the model to give us a real-time view of the model as we create it.

The location and behavior of the workspace database is controlled by three properties of the Tabular model:

- ► Workspace Server
- ► Workspace Retention
- ► Data Backup

Because the values found in these properties are used to create the workspace database as soon as we create or open a Tabular model, we must provide meaningful default values for these items.

The default values for these properties come from the following three SQL Server Data Tools option settings, shown in Figure 8-9 (we'll choose the specific settings following the list):

- ► **Default workspace server** The server name in this list box is assigned to the model's Workspace Server property, and a workspace database is immediately created on that server. This must be a Tabular instance of SQL Server 2012 Analysis Services. For optimum performance, it is recommended that you run this Tabular instance on the same computer on which you are executing SQL Server Data Tools.

- ► **Workspace database retention after the model is closed** The selection made for this option is assigned to the model's Workspace Retention property. This determines what happens to the workspace database when the model project is closed in SQL Server Data Tools. The options are

  - ► **Keep workspace in memory (recommended for local workspaces)** This option keeps the workspace database loaded in the Analysis Services memory space. The model is still available for querying and browsing through the server.

  - ► **Keep workspace databases on disk but unload from memory (recommended for remote workspaces)** This option (which is the default) unloads the workspace database from the Analysis Services memory space. However, it

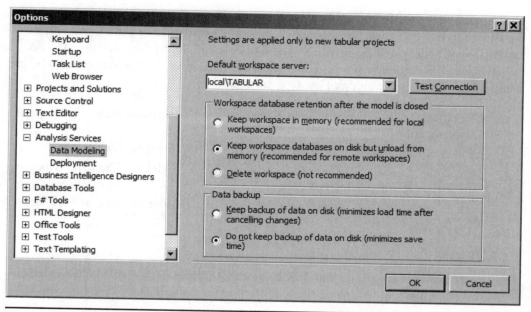

Figure 8-9   *The Data Modeling page of the Options dialog box*

persists a copy of the database on disk. This allows the database to be quickly reloaded into the Analysis Services memory space the next time the model project is opened, without having to reload the data from the data sources.

▶ **Delete workspace (not recommended)**   This option unloads the workspace database from the Analysis Services memory space and does not persist the database on disk. The next time the model project is opened, the workspace database is re-created and its data is reloaded from the data sources.

▶ **Data backup**   Specifies whether the data is backed up to disk (to an ABF file—Analysis Services backup file) each time the model definition is saved. This data backup is used if you cancel the changes made to the model. Therefore, having the backup of the data on disk will make canceling changes go faster. However, creating the backup of the data on disk will increase the time required each time the model is saved. Options are

   ▶ Keep backup of data on disk (minimizes load time after cancelling changes)

   ▶ Do not keep backup of data on disk (minimizes save time)—default setting

Remember, the SQL Server Data Tools option settings provide the default values for these model properties. For this reason, it makes sense to leave the second and third options, Workspace database retention and Data backup, set to their defaults. We do, however, need to ensure we have the Default workspace server option set correctly before creating our first Tabular model. The steps are as follows:

1. Select Tools | Options from the SQL Server Data Tools main menu. The Options dialog box appears.
2. Scroll down the left column until you see the section for Analysis Services.
3. Expand the Analysis Services entry and select Data Modeling. The Data Modeling page of the Options dialog box appears.
4. For Default workspace server, enter the name of a Tabular instance of SQL Server 2012 Analysis Services.

 CAUTION

Do not use a production server for the Learn By Doing exercises in this book.

5. Click Test Connection. A test result dialog box will appear.
6. If the test is successful, click OK. If the test is not successful, verify the server name is entered correctly.
7. The completed Data Modeling page should appear similar to Figure 8-9. Click OK to exit the Options dialog box.

These settings are the defaults that are applied to new models when they are created. You can change any of these settings later through the Properties windows for the model (bim file) in SQL Server Data Tools.

Review the Tabular Model Project Types   SQL Server Data Tools comes with project templates to get us started with our development tasks. There are several types of Analysis Services templates.

▶ You can create a Multidimensional BI Semantic Model either from scratch, by choosing Analysis Services Multidimensional and Data Mining Project, or from a model that already exists on an Analysis Services server, by choosing Import from Server (Multidimensional and Data Mining).

▶ For Tabular models, you can either create a new Tabular model, by choosing Analysis Services Tabular Project, or create a Tabular model from an existing model, by choosing Import from Server (Tabular).

▶ You can also create a new Analysis Services Tabular project by importing a Tabular model from PowerPivot, by choosing Import from PowerPivot. Importing a model from PowerPivot makes it possible to take advantage of tried-and-true aspects of a model that was previously created in Excel and used by a small group of people. And it's the fastest way to get started—why reinvent the wheel? Once we import the PowerPivot model we can extend and change it according to the needs of the larger organization.

Learn By Doing: Creating a BI Semantic Model by Importing from PowerPivot

We create our first model for Analysis Services by importing a model from PowerPivot.

Video 8-3   **Creating a BI Semantic Model by Importing from PowerPivot**

1. Click the New Project link on the Start tab or the New Project button in the toolbar. The New Project dialog box appears.
2. Under Installed Templates, expand Business Intelligence and select Analysis Services.
3. Click Import from PowerPivot.
4. Enter **Pan-Geo Tourism by Country** for Name. The completed New Project dialog box should appear similar to Figure 8-10.
5. Click OK. The Open dialog box appears, allowing you to select a Microsoft Excel workbook containing a PowerPivot model. We're going to select the workbook that holds the PowerPivot model we created earlier in the chapter. (Make sure the Excel file has been closed before attempting the import.)
6. Navigate to the folder where you saved the Pan-Geo Tourism by Country Excel file. Select the file and click Open. The PowerPivot model is imported into the model in SQL Server Data Tools. The model is displayed in the model design tab as shown in Figure 8-11.

   Before we make any more changes to this new BI Semantic Model, let's change the name. This will help us to better track our model throughout its development.
7. In the Solution Explorer window, click the Model.bim file to display its properties in the Properties window.
8. In the Properties window, change the File Name property to **Pan-Geo Marketing.bim**.

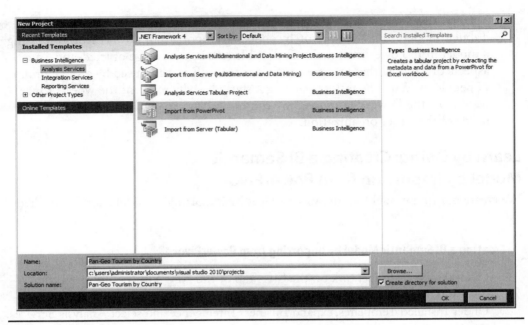

Figure 8-10   *The New Project dialog box*

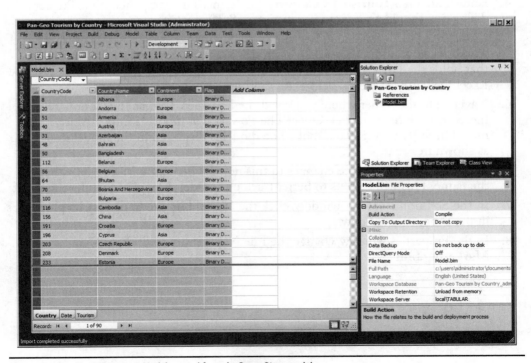

Figure 8-11   *The BI Semantic Model created from the PowerPivot model*

Bringing Additional Data into the BI Semantic Model

Thus far in this chapter, all of the data in our models has come from Microsoft SQL Server database tables. We can, however, bring data into the model from a wide variety of data sources. We can even bring in data from another BI Semantic Model in PowerPivot or Analysis Services. To demonstrate this diversity of data source types, we'll first import data from a new source and then add data using an existing connection.

Importing Data from a New Source

As part of our efforts to forecast revenue for travel services, the Pan-Geo marketing department would like to include data on average annual international air fares in the BI Semantic Model. The data comes to us as a Microsoft Excel file download.

Learn By Doing: Importing Data from an Excel File

Let's load the data from the Excel file:

Video 8-4 **Importing Data from an Excel File**

1. Click the Import from Data Source button on the toolbar. (You can also select Model | Import From Data Source from the main menu.) The Connect to a Data Source page of the Table Import Wizard appears.
2. Scroll through the list to become familiar with the types of data sources you can bring into a BI Semantic Model.
3. Scroll down to the Text Files group and click Excel File as shown in Figure 8-12.
4. Click Next.
5. Leave Excel as the friendly connection name, and click Browse to search for files. The Open dialog box appears.
6. Navigate to the folder where you saved the International Fare Information.xlsx file from the supporting files for this book.
7. Select the International Fare Information.xlsx file and click Open. The path to the file is now in the Excel File Path text box.
8. Select the Use first row as column headers check box.
9. Click Next. The Impersonation Information page of the Table Import Wizard appears.

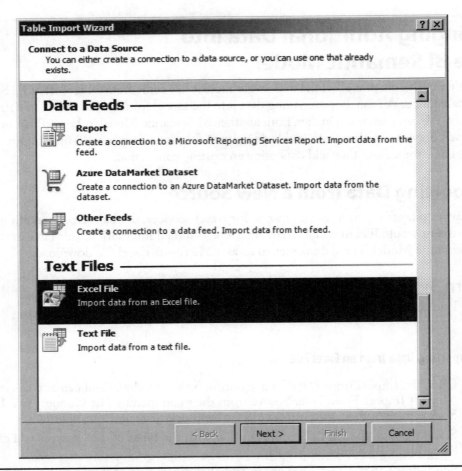

Figure 8-12   *The Connect to a Data Source page of the BISM Table Import Wizard*

10. The credentials you enter on this page will be used by Analysis Services to open this file when importing data. It is recommended you use a domain account name for a connection to a file on your network. Enter an appropriate username and password.

NOTE

When entering the username, include the domain name along with the username in the form DOMAIN\ UserName.

11. Click Next.
12. The data is in Sheet1 of the Excel workbook, so select the check box for Sheet1$.
13. Enter **International Fares** for the Friendly Name.
14. Make sure the Sheet1$ row is highlighted and click Preview & Filter. The Preview Selected Table dialog box appears as shown in Figure 8-13.

    We see an annual summary of fare information, including round-trip miles traveled, average reservation and bag fees, and several other measures. We should exclude blank rows. Also, there is a column labeled F10 that we don't need.

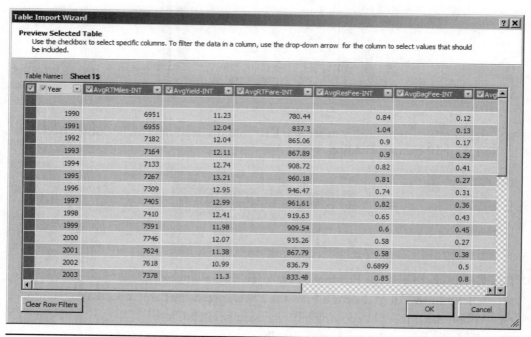

Figure 8-13   *The Preview Selected Table dialog box*

15. Click the drop-down arrow in the Year column heading. It may take a few moments for this drop-down box to populate. When it has populated, scroll down until you see the entry for (Blanks), uncheck the check box next to it, and click OK.

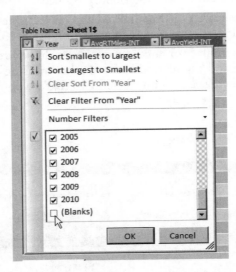

16. Scroll to the right until you see the F10 column heading. Uncheck the check box in the F10 column heading.

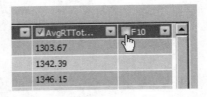

17. Click OK to exit the Preview Selected Table dialog box.
18. Click Finish. All of the rows from the Excel spreadsheet are imported to the model.
19. When the import has completed successfully, click Close.
20. Click the Save All button in the toolbar.

Adding Data Using an Existing Connection

There will be times when we need to import additional data from a data source we have already used in our model. In these situations, we need to be sure we don't create a duplicate connection to the same location. Instead, we use the existing connection to bring in the data.

Learn By Doing: Adding Data to a Model Using an Existing Connection

Let's import additional tables into our model from the PGHT_Tourism database. In order to reuse the connection to this SQL Server database, we access our existing connection from the Existing Connections dialog box.

Video 8-5 | **Adding Data to a Model Using an Existing Connection**

1. Choose Model | Existing Connections from the main menu or click the Existing Connections button on the toolbar. The Existing Connections dialog box appears. You see that our connection to SQL Server was imported along with the model from PowerPivot. There is also a connection to Microsoft Excel that we used to import the international air fare information.

NOTE

Even though you imported the SQL connection, it will be necessary to re-enter the impersonation credentials so the deployed model in Analysis Services can connect to the data source.

2. Select the connection created for the PGHT_Tourism database from the list, and click Edit. The Edit Connection dialog box appears.
3. Click Impersonation. The Impersonation Information dialog box appears.
4. Select the Specify Windows user name and password radio button and enter an appropriate Windows username (including the domain name) and password.
5. Click OK to exit the Impersonation Information dialog box.
6. Click Save to exit the Edit Connection dialog box.
7. With the connection to the PGHT_Tourism database selected, click Open. This opens the Choose How to Import the Data page of the Table Import Wizard. Now we can request additional tables from this data source.

   As we saw when we first created a BI Semantic Model using PowerPivot, we have two options when importing from a data source. We can import the entire content of tables or views. Alternatively, we can construct a SQL query to be more selective with the data we import. First, let's import data from a number of tables. There are several tables related to our hotel operations that we want to load into our model.

8. Keep the default "Select from a list of tables and views to choose the data to import" radio button selected and click Next.

Let's break the remaining steps down by table. For each table, we need to select that table, specify a friendly name, and preview and filter the data. The tables we're interested in at the moment are HotelFinancial and HotelRating. We have something special planned for the Hotel table a little later on.

HotelFinancial

1. Select the check box next to HotelFinancial.
2. Replace the name in the Friendly Name column with **Financial**.
3. With the HotelFinancial row selected, click Preview & Filter.
4. We want to import all of the fields from this table except HotelFinancialID. Uncheck the check box in the HotelFinancialID column heading.
5. Click OK.

HotelRating

1. Select the check box next to HotelRating. We're interested in all of the columns from this table, so it won't be necessary to do any filtering. When all is completed, the Table Import Wizard should appear as shown in Figure 8-14.
2. Click Finish to begin the import. For each table, data rows will be imported into our in-memory model. Depending on how many thousands, hundreds of thousands, or millions of rows are being imported, this can take a few minutes.
3. When the data has been imported successfully, click Close to return to the BI Semantic Model designer.
4. Click Save All in the toolbar to save your changes.

We now have a BI Semantic Model consisting of six tables. We still have one more table to import—the Hotel table. For this table we'll use a SQL query to import hotel data from the source.

Learn By Doing: Adding Data to a Model Using a Query

Using a SQL query to specify data to import into the BI Semantic Model gives us more flexibility and control over the characteristics of the data we are importing. We can join data from several tables or views, call a stored procedure that returns a result set, or exploit SQL system or user-defined functions. We can choose to include only the columns we need, or combine multiple columns into a single column.

When we import the Hotel table, we would like to include the name of the hotel chain from the HotelChain table.

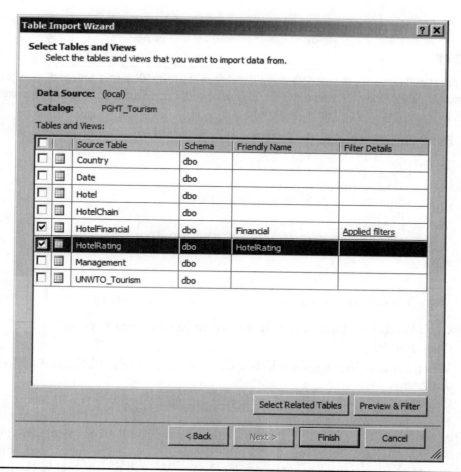

Figure 8-14   *The completed Select Tables and Views page of the BISM Table Import Wizard*

Video 8-6   **Adding Data to a Model Using a Query**

1. Once again, choose Model | Existing Connections from the main menu or click the Existing Connections button on the toolbar.

2. Select the connection to the PGHT_Tourism database from the list and click Open. This opens the Choose How to Import the Data page of the Table Import Wizard.

3. Select the "Write a query that will specify the data to import" radio button and click Next.

4. On the Specify a SQL Query page, enter **Hotel** for Friendly Query Name.

NOTE

You don't have to know SQL to write a SQL query. If you're new to writing SQL queries, you can click Design and an easy-to-use interactive query designer will help you craft a SQL query. Because our Hotel query is going to be brief, we'll enter it without the help of the query designer.

5. Enter the following for the SQL Statement:

```
SELECT
       h.HotelID
       ,"Chain Name" = chain.Name
       ,"Chain Logo" = chain.ChainLogo
       ,h.City
       ,h.CountryID
       ,"Number of Employees" = h.NumEmployees
       ,"Star Rating" = h.StarRating
FROM
       Hotel h
INNER JOIN
       HotelChain chain on chain.ChainID = h.ChainID
```

6. Click Validate to ensure the SQL statement has the correct syntax.
7. Click Finish.
8. When the data has transferred, click Close to return to the BI Semantic Model designer.
9. Click Save All in the toolbar to save your changes.

That completes our effort to bring data into our newly built BI Semantic Model. However, we still have some work to do. For example, as we design our models, it is a good idea to check the validity of the design choices. We will do just that in the next section by utilizing Microsoft Excel.

Making the Model Work

We have created a Tabular BI Semantic Model for Analysis Services that could be used by a Power View report author. But will the model, in its present form, do the job? Will users be able to analyze the data in meaningful ways? Is the model uncluttered and easy to use, or cryptic and unwieldy? To answer these questions, we need to spot-check the usability and validity of the model.

In its current form, our model consists of a group of tables, without any relationships or calculations. Thus, the model is not in its finished state. Even so, we want to make sure what we have in place thus far is clean and correct. After completing that verification, we will make additions and improvements to our model to enhance its effectiveness.

Testing the Model: Analyzing in Excel

To validate our model, we examine the model in the same way a business user might interact with it. We haven't yet deployed the model to a server (that comes in Chapter 11), which is a necessary step before the model can be utilized in Power View. So, rather than testing the model using Power View, we'll use the development workspace database (see the "Set the Default Workspace Server" section earlier in this chapter) and analyze our data model in Microsoft Excel.

It's quite simple to open our work-in-process model within a PivotTable in Excel. When we do this, we'll be asked how we want to connect to the model. This provides us with a chance to test security and perspectives, features we will cover later in this book. For now, we will connect using the current Windows user.

Learn By Doing: Analyzing Our In-Progress Model Using Microsoft Excel

So, let's see what our model looks like in Excel:

Video 8-7   ### Analyzing Our In-Progress Model Using Microsoft Excel

1. Select Model | Analyze in Excel from the main menu, or click the Analyze in Excel button on the toolbar. The Analyze in Excel dialog box opens as shown in Figure 8-15.

2. Leave the Current Windows User option selected and click OK.

   Microsoft Excel opens a new workbook with a worksheet containing a PivotTable as shown in Figure 8-16. We see the fields in our BI Semantic Model in the PivotTable Field List, as shown here. Go ahead and scroll through the field list to assess the model design. Here are a few things to note:

   ▶ The HotelID field occurs several times throughout the model. It clutters the tables and isn't useful for reporting.

   ▶ Many of the fields have cryptic names that came from the database and are not very meaningful to the business user.

   ▶ Numbers and categories are not in any particularly intuitive order or position in the model.

   You may also notice a number of other problems that won't be well received by a business user. Among them is the fact that each table exists in isolation from the others. At this point, you cannot, for example, view a financial measure by continent because no relationship is defined between the Financial and Country tables.

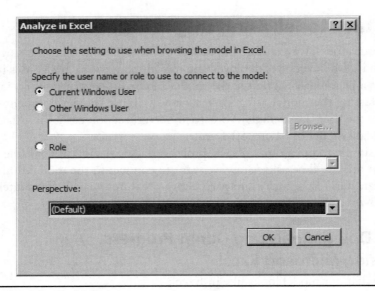

Figure 8-15 *The Analyze in Excel dialog box*

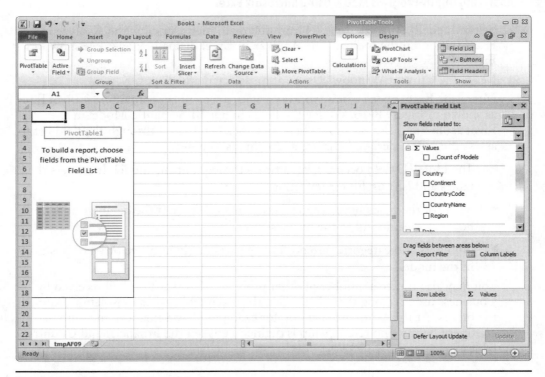

Figure 8-16 *A PivotTable in Microsoft Excel*

We can fix each of these problems so our BI Semantic Model is in tip-top shape. Let's return to the development environment.

3. Close Microsoft Excel without saving the workbook.

Enhancing the Model

By now you realize there is more to a BI Semantic Model than data alone. We add features—semantics—which describe the data in a manner that makes it readily useful to the business user. In order to rectify the problems we saw while browsing the model, we now add features to take the data model well beyond data alone.

In this section, we explore the following practices in turn and identify the significance of each:

▶ Renaming tables and columns

▶ Defining relationships between tables

▶ Creating calculated columns

▶ Creating measures

▶ Hiding unused columns and measures.

Renaming Tables and Columns

We need to ensure each item, table, field, and measure has a user-friendly name. When we loaded data, we paid attention to the names of the tables by assigning them friendly names. We now need to do the same thing for the fields and measures in our tables.

NOTE

It is possible to rename tables at this point, if you did not do so when the data was initially imported. The technique for renaming tables is very similar to the technique we use in the next Learn By Doing exercise for renaming columns.

Defining Relationships Between Tables

Table relationships determine how data elements can coexist on a report. For instance, we know our business users need to see financial data by country and by hotel. As our data was imported, the financial data was in a separate table from the hotel data, which was in a separate table from the country data. Unless relationships were already defined in the source database, each of these elements resides in its own silo until we define relationships between them.

This is very similar to the concept of relationships in a relational database (for those of you familiar with relational database design). We relate two tables using one or more fields common to both tables. For instance, the Financial table has a HotelID field that aligns with the HotelID field in the Hotel table. Thus, we can create a relationship between the Financial table and the Hotel table.

The Financial table does not have a field that will allow us to create a relationship with the Country table. Fortunately, the Hotel table does. Therefore, if we have a relationship between the Financial table and the Hotel table along with a relationship between the Hotel table and the Country table, we have sufficient means to report on financial data tied to countries.

We will create relationships between these tables in Chapter 9.

Creating Calculated Columns

Database designers cannot anticipate every piece of information required by business users. One possible solution to this situation would be to have the business users request a change to the model design each time a new piece of information is needed. That takes time and resources. Fortunately, our BI Semantic Model provides an alternative. We can calculate a new column from factors we do have, enabling us to solve the problem quickly and economically.

A BI Semantic Model affords us the option of extending data using expressions written in the Data Analysis Expressions (DAX) language. We'll see in the exercises a bit later in the chapter how easy it is to extend and supplement data in our existing tables using DAX.

Creating Measures

Similar to the way we add new calculated columns to our model using DAX, we can combine a calculation with a method of aggregation to create a measure. Where a calculation has a value for each row, a measure has a value when multiple rows are combined—say, all the rows for a given period of time or all the rows for a given hotel chain. Measures are created in the Measure Grid. In the coming exercises we'll create measures in some of our tables.

Hiding Unused Columns and Measures

Finally, we want to keep the BI Semantic Model neat and concise. We can enhance the value of our model significantly by hiding unnecessary data, which allows business users to take a straighter path to the answers they're looking for. We do this by hiding data that, although necessary for building the model, means nothing to the business user.

Putting It into Practice

Let's take one table at a time and get our model into shape. In this section, we're going to address four of the tables, paying closest attention to those tables we inherited from the PowerPivot model. For each table, we'll apply the enhancements discussed in the previous section.

Learn By Doing: Enhancing the Model

We'll start our model enhancement with the Country table, followed by the Date, Tourism, and International Fares tables in turn.

Video 8-8 **Enhancing the Model - Country, Date Tables**

Country   When we created our BI Semantic Model in SQL Server Data Tools, the Country table was loaded from the PowerPivot model. Now we are going to modify the Country table to better align it with the needs of the current model.

1. Click the Country tab at the bottom of the designer to select the Country table.
2. In the Properties window in the lower-right corner, click the Source Data property. The ellipsis (...) button will appear.
3. Click the ellipsis button. The Edit Table Properties dialog box appears. This dialog box looks like the Preview Selected Table dialog box we've seen before. Here, we can make changes to our initial filter settings.
4. Select the check box in the CountryID column heading.
5. Click the Filter icon to the right in the Continent column heading. The sort and filter options appear.
6. Click the Clear Filter From "Continent" item.

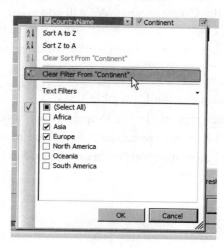

7. Click OK to exit the Edit Table Properties dialog box.

   Now, let's hide the CountryID and CountryCode columns. Although we need these columns to create relationships, we want to hide them from the business user.

8. Right-click the CountryID column heading and select Hide from Client Tools in the context menu.

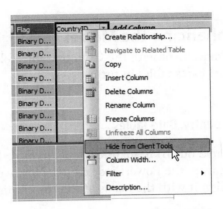

9. Right-click the CountryCode column heading and select Hide from Client Tools in the context menu.

10. Right-click the CountryName column heading and select Rename Column from the context menu. This puts the column heading in an edit state with the entire text of the heading selected.

11. Rename the column to **Country**.

12. Press ENTER to exit the column heading edit mode.

13. Click Save All in the toolbar.

That takes care of the Country table. We don't need to add any calculated columns or create any measures in the Country table. We will add relationships in Chapter 9.

Date   Let's move to the Date table, another of the tables we imported from the PowerPivot model:

1. Click the Date tab to select the Date table.

2. Click the Source Data property in the Properties window.

3. Click the ellipsis (...) button to open the Edit Table Properties dialog box.

4. Select the check box in the upper-left corner of the grid to uncheck all columns.

5. Select the check box for each of the following columns:
    ID
    Date
    MonthName
    ShortMonthName
    QuarterName
    ShortQuarterName
    Year
6. Click OK to exit the Edit Table Properties dialog box.
7. Right-click the ID column heading and select Hide from Client Tools from the context menu.

    Names consisting of two words merged together are great for computer programming, but they're not the most suitable for including in reports. We'll rename columns to put a space in between words where needed.
8. Insert spaces in the following column names (for each column, right-click the column heading, select Rename Column, insert the space(s), and then press ENTER to exit the column heading edit mode):

Current Column Name	New Column Name
MonthName	Month Name
ShortMonthName	Short Month Name
QuarterName	Quarter Name
ShortQuarterName	Short Quarter Name

As with the Country table, we don't need to add any columns or create any measures. Again, we will add relationships in Chapter 9.

Before we move to our next table, however, we need to take care of one more thing. A date table is a special type of table. As long as there is a column in the table with a data type of Date, the table can be designated a date table. This facilitates the time-based analytic capabilities of DAX formulas, which will be discussed in Chapter 10.

9. Choose Table | Date | Mark As Date Table from the main menu. The Mark as Date Table dialog box appears as shown in Figure 8-17.
10. In the Mark as Date Table dialog box, you're prompted to select which column is the unique date identifier. Leave the Date field selected in the drop-down list box.
11. Click OK to exit the Mark as Date Table dialog box.
12. Click Save All.

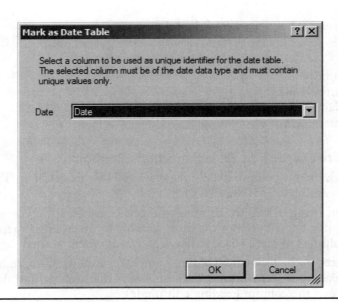

Figure 8-17   *The Mark as Date Table dialog box*

Video 8-9   **Enhancing the Model - Tourism Table**

Tourism   We're going to be a little bit busier making changes to the Tourism table. Several of the column names aren't user-friendly. In fact, they're quite long and cryptic. We're going to define several measures in this table as well. We will need to add a column from a related table. (Yes, we're going to need to define at least one relationship to make that happen.) As with our previous tables, we're going to hide some of the excess baggage (to use a little travel metaphor) we don't want the business user to see.

1. Click the Tourism tab to select the Tourism table.
2. Click the Source Data property in the Properties window.
3. Click the ellipsis (...) button to open the Edit Table Properties dialog box.
4. Check the check boxes in the following column headings:
   DeparturesInThousands
   OBTravelExpenditures
   TourismExpenditureAbroad
5. Click OK to exit the Edit Table Properties dialog box.
6. Select the NonResidentTouristArrivals column by clicking the column heading.
7. Select the Column Name property in the Properties window. You can rename columns here as well as by right-clicking the column heading. Change the column name to **Tourist Arrivals**, and press ENTER.

8. Repeat steps 6 and 7 to rename the following columns:

Current Column Name	New Column Name
NonResidentTouristHotelCheckins	Hotel Check-Ins
IBTravelExpenditures	Inbound Travel Spending
TourismExpenditureInCountry	Tourism Spending In-Country
DeparturesInThousands	Departures In Thousands
OBTravelExpenditures	Outbound Travel Spending
TourismExpenditureAbroad	Tourism Spending Abroad

In order to show tourism statistics by country, we need to create a relationship between the Tourism and Country tables. In this case, for each row in the Tourism table, we want the data model to look up the country associated with the statistics in that row. Therefore, Country is the lookup table. Actually, you don't have to worry about which way the relationship is supposed to go. No matter how you select it, SQL Server Data Tools will create the relationship in the correct manner.

9. Choose Table | Create Relationships from the main menu. The Create Relationship dialog box appears. The table selected when you opened this dialog box (in this case the Tourism table) is displayed in the Table drop-down list. The field selected when you opened the dialog box will be displayed in the Column drop-down list.

10. In the Column drop-down list, select CountryCode.

11. In the Related Lookup Table drop-down list, select Country.

12. In the Related Lookup Column drop-down list, select CountryCode. (This will probably already be selected by default.)

13. Click Create.

An icon appears in the CountryCode column heading indicating this column is being utilized in a relationship. We'll see the additional effects of creating this relationship the next time we review the model in Excel. Before we do, we have a few more steps to complete, starting with creating one more relationship.

14. Repeat steps 9 through 13 to create the following relationship:
Table: Tourism
Column: TravelYear
Related Lookup Table: Date
Related Lookup Column: ID

Next, we'll create some measures in the Tourism table. Before we do, you'll want to be able to see the Measure Grid below the table grid. By default, it should be showing, but in case it is not:

15. Click Table in the main menu and verify there is a check mark next to Show Measure Grid. If there isn't, select Show Measure Grid to check this item.

TIP

You can also right-click the tab for a given table and use the resulting context menu to toggle the Measure Grid.

You can enter DAX formulas in any cell in the Measure Grid to create measures. However, we're going to use the AutoSum shortcut to create measures from each of the numeric columns in the Tourism table. We're interested in showing the sum of each amount when we use tourism data on reports. A number of aggregation formulas are available, including Average, Min, Max, Count, and DistinctCount, in addition to Sum. AutoSum will enter the formula in the Measure Grid automatically.

16. Click the column heading for Tourist Arrivals.
17. In the main menu, select Column | AutoSum | Sum. A measure will appear beneath the column, in the Measure Grid.

NOTE

You can also create an AutoSum using the toolbar. The button with the Greek letter sigma (Σ) can create an AutoSum using various aggregate functions.

Video 8-10   **Enhancing the Model - Tourism Measures, International Fares Table**

18. Click the Measure Name property in the Properties window.
19. Change the Measure Name to **Total Tourist Arrivals**, and press ENTER.

    The formula for this measure is "Total Tourist Arrivals:=SUM([Tourist Arrivals])" where Total Tourist Arrivals is the display name of the measure. The rest of the formula might look familiar if you have used data functions in Microsoft Excel. It instructs the model to display the sum of all the values in the Tourist Arrivals column.

    You could type similar formulas anywhere in the grid for each of the other numeric columns. However, we use AutoSum to save time and effort.

20. Repeat steps 16 through 19 to create measures from the following columns:

Source Column for the Measure	Name for the New Measure
Hotel Check-Ins	Total Hotel Check-Ins
Inbound Travel Spending	Total Inbound Travel Spending
Tourism Spending In-Country	Total Tourism Spending In-Country
Departures In Thousands	Total Departures In Thousands
Outbound Travel Spending	Total Outbound Travel Spending
Tourism Spending Abroad	Total Tourism Spending Abroad

Finally, we're ready to hide the columns we don't want our business users to see.

21. Hide the TravelYear column (reminder: right-click its column heading and select Hide From Client Tools in the context menu).

22. Hide the CountryCode column.

23. Hide each of the numerical columns from which we created our measures. The measures will be used to display these values in reports. Having both the columns and the measures visible to the business user will only cause confusion.

TIP

To hide all of the columns in one operation, select the first column, press and hold down the SHIFT *key, and click the last column. This selects all the columns. Then, right-click anywhere within the selection and choose Hide from Client Tools. You'll notice there are no columns in the Tourism table visible to the users. In this particular table, the measures are all they need to see.*

International Fares   One more table to go. We're going to be brief and to the point about the changes that should be made to this table. Of course, you can refer to the steps presented earlier for the other tables if you need help accomplishing these tasks. International Fares does not lend itself readily to creating relationships with the other tables. In Chapter 9, we'll address this issue so the data can be integrated into the model. For right now, let's improve its usability by doing the following:

1. Create measures for the columns listed. Use Average rather than Sum for these measures. Rename the measures as shown:

Source Column for the Measure	Name for the New Measure
Average Of AvgRTMiles-INT	Average Round-Trip Miles
Average Of AvgRTFare-INT	Average Round-Trip Fare
Average Of AvgResFee-INT	Average Reservation Fee
Average Of AvgBagFee-INT	Average Baggage Fee
Average Of AvgRTTotal-INT	Average Round-Trip Total Cost

2. Hide all columns in the table.

3. Click Save All.

Checking Our Work   Now we're ready to check our work. We took several steps to convert the raw data model into a powerful and very usable BI Semantic Model. Let's analyze the result in Excel:

1. Select Model | Analyze In Excel from the main menu or click the Analyze in Excel button on the toolbar. The Analyze in Excel dialog box appears.

2. Click OK to exit the Analyze in Excel dialog box.

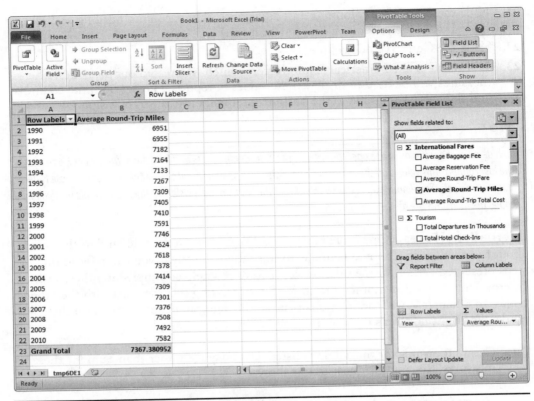

Figure 8-18 *Analyzing our model in an Excel PivotTable*

Now go ahead and browse the various features of the data model. You can see how our efforts have paid off as shown in Figure 8-18. Our column names are more concise and readable. We have measures appearing in the model. The business purpose of each field and the way the elements fit together are clear to the user.

Wrap-Up

In the next chapter, we go further into the best practices for creating and enhancing a BI Semantic Model. We look at how to create additional, more powerful measures and calculated columns. We examine the formatting and sorting of data. Also, we leverage Diagram View to make the model easier to understand and modify.

So, onward to give our model more power!

Chapter 9

BI Semantic Model: Additional Model Features

In This Chapter

- Diagram View
- Refining the Model
- Table and Column Options and Properties
- Table Storage and Security
- Wrap-Up

In Chapter 8, we built a basic BI Semantic Model that contains multiple tables, relationships between those tables, and measures that make the data more useful for analysis. We worked in the default view of the model, Grid View. This allowed us to see the data contained in the tables as we made our changes.

In this chapter, we look at the additional features available in the BI Semantic Model that enable the model to meet more of our users' needs. We explore a second view of the model, the Diagram View, and the changes we can make there. We revisit relationships within the model. We look at column properties such as measure formatting, sorting, and descriptions. We then add hierarchies, perspectives, and key performance indicators (KPIs) to our model. We close the chapter with a discussion of table enhancements such as partitioning and security.

Diagram View

One of the great improvements of the Tabular BI Semantic Model over previous data analysis models is the fact that changes to the model are immediately visible. When using the Tabular BI Semantic Model, gone are the days of adding a calculation, deploying the model to a server, processing the model, and then browsing the model to see if the calculation returned the desired values. This great feature is provided by Grid View in SQL Server Data Tools (SSDT). Grid View displays the data in the model in a manner similar to how users will work with the data once the model is deployed.

While Grid View is able to successfully show the contents of the model, it is not as good at illustrating the structure of the model. For example, you can view and create the relationships between the tables, but you can't get a good overall view of those relationships in Grid View.

Navigating the BI Semantic Model is similar to working with your family tree. There are often two views of the individuals in a family tree—the details view and the tree view. The details view shows you detailed information about an ancestor, such as name, gender, date of birth, date of death, occupation, spouse, and children. This view gives you a good idea of who the person was as an individual, but determining how this person is related to you is very difficult if not impossible—especially if they lived over 100 years ago.

When you look at the tree view of your family, similar to the example shown in Figure 9-1, the amount of detail per individual is decreased—you may only see the name, date of birth, and date of death for each person. The advantage of the tree view is that you can see all of the relationships between the individuals, so, for example, you can quickly find out that the person you were looking at in details view was your great-great grandfather on your mother's side.

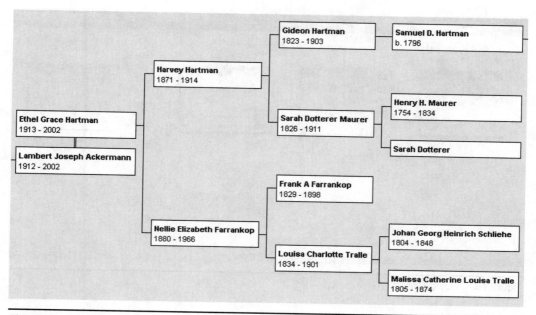

Figure 9-1   *Family tree diagram*

Diagram View provides the same capability for the BI Semantic Model as the tree view does for your family. Diagram View limits the amount of information that can be seen for each table, but it does a good job of illustrating the structure of the tables and the relationships between the tables.

You open Diagram View by clicking the Diagram button in the lower-right corner of the model design tab (as shown in Figure 9-2) or by selecting Model | Model View | Diagram View from the main menu. Diagram View is shown in Figure 9-3.

The tables within the model are displayed in Diagram View with arrows connecting the related tables. Very little detail is shown for each table. Diagram View displays the table name and column names for each table in addition to hierarchies and KPIs. The hidden columns in each table are grayed out.

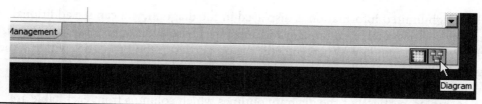

Figure 9-2   *Diagram button*

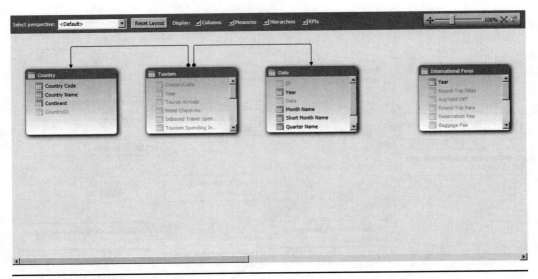

Figure 9-3   *Diagram View*

Navigating Diagram View

This section describes the navigation features available when you are working in Diagram View. Go ahead and experiment with these features in the Pan-Geo Tourism by Country model you created in Chapter 8.

Learn By Doing: Reopening a BI Semantic Model Project

To open the Pan-Geo Tourism by Country model in Diagram View:

1.   Open SQL Server Data Tools.
2.   Select the Pan-Geo Tourism by Country project in the Recent Projects area of the Start Page as shown in Figure 9-4.
3.   Click the Diagram button to switch to Diagram View.

Although limited information is displayed in the diagram, you can see additional details by clicking a table, column, or relationship. These additional details are found in the Properties window. When you edit the properties in the Properties window, the diagram will automatically reflect any changes you make.

When you select a relationship, not only does the Properties window display the relationship properties, but the diagram outlines which columns from each table are involved in the relationship. This visual cue makes it easy to see if the correct columns are being used in the relationship.

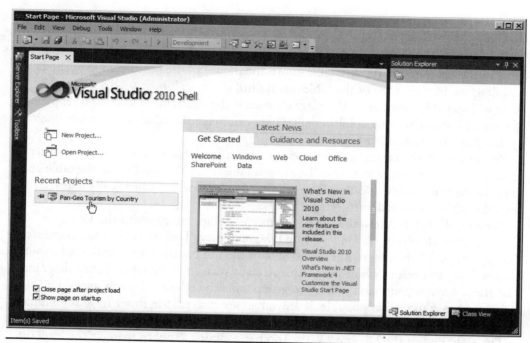

Figure 9-4   *The SQL Server Data Tools Start Page*

When you first open the diagram, the tables are all the same size in the diagram regardless of how many columns are in the table. As a result, some of the tables may not have all of the columns displayed in the diagram.

To get a quick view of all the columns in the table, you can maximize the table by placing the mouse in the table heading and clicking the Maximize button, as shown in Figure 9-5. The Maximize button appears when you hover the mouse over a table or when the table is selected. When you click the Maximize button, the table grows and centers itself on the screen. When a table is enlarged, a Restore button replaces the

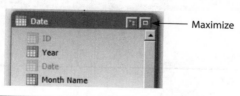

Figure 9-5   *Table Maximize button*

Maximize button in the table header. Clicking the Restore button causes the table to be restored to its normal size and position.

For a more permanent way to display all the columns in a table, you can resize the table in the diagram. To resize a table, move the mouse to the bottom edge of the table and drag the bottom edge of the table down until all the columns are displayed. The table will stay this new size in the diagram even if the diagram is closed and reopened. If your table contains long column names, you can make the table wider in the diagram by dragging its right or left edge.

You can move the tables in the diagram to arrange related tables near one another or make relationships easier to follow. To move a table, click the heading of the table and drag the table to its new location. The relationship lines will automatically adjust to keep the table connected to its related tables.

When in Diagram View, the top of the model design tab contains the Diagram View Toolbar, shown in Figure 9-6. The Diagram View Toolbar is used to customize the appearance of the diagram. The left side of the toolbar contains the Reset Layout button. You can click this button to automatically rearrange the tables in the diagram. The Reset Layout command will try to group tables by relationships to make the diagram as easy to read as possible. If any tables are resized, the Reset Layout command will not resize the tables but will leave the tables at their custom sizes.

The right end of the Diagram View Toolbar contains a tool to manage the level of zoom within the diagram. The zoom slider adjusts the view from 30% to 200% zoom. Clicking the Fit to Screen button causes the screen to zoom out so all of the tables in the diagram are shown on the screen. Clicking the Original Size button returns the zoom to 100%.

One challenge with diagrams is navigating the structure when the diagram is zoomed in so far that only a few tables are visible on the screen. To save you from having to scroll up and down and right and left through the diagram to find a specific table, the

Figure 9-6   *Diagram View Toolbar*

minimap offers a quick and easy way to get to the section of the diagram containing a desired table. Click the Open Minimap button to toggle the minimap on and off. The minimap shows a miniature view of the diagram and displays a rectangle to represent the part of the diagram that is visible on the screen. To get to a section of the diagram that is not currently displayed, drag the rectangle in the minimap to the desired section of the screen, and the diagram will show the tables within the rectangle.

The check boxes in the middle of the Diagram View Toolbar determine which details are displayed per table. For example, if the Measures check box is checked, the measures are displayed for each table. The Columns check box controls whether the table columns are displayed in the diagram. The Hierarchies and KPIs check boxes serve similar functions. The Select perspective drop-down list allows you to view the model items included in the selected perspective. (More about hierarchies, KPIs, and perspectives later in this chapter.)

Relationships in Diagram View

One of the advantages of Diagram View is that it visually displays the relationships between tables. You can easily create relationships in Diagram View by dragging the related column from one table to another.

Learn By Doing: Creating Relationships in Diagram View

Let's create the missing relationships in the model. We currently have the Tourism table connected to the Country table and the Date table, but the hotel tables are not related yet.

Video 9-1   **Creating Relationships in Diagram View**

1. If you modified the diagram using the zoom and layout tools described previously, reset the diagram by clicking the Reset Layout button on the Diagram View Toolbar. Click Reset Layout again in the Confirm dialog box.
2. Click the Original Size button in the zooming tool within the Diagram View Toolbar.
3. Move the Hotel and HotelRating tables near each other and adjust the screen so both tables are shown on the screen.
4. Drag the HotelID column from the HotelRating table and drop it on the HotelID column in the Hotel table. The relationship appears as an arrow from the HotelRating table to the Hotel table.

5. Perform steps 3 and 4 using the following tables and columns:

Source Table	Source Column	Destination Table	Destination Column
Financial	HotelID	Hotel	HotelID
Financial	PeriodEndDate	Date	ID
Hotel	CountryID	Country	CountryID
HotelRating	StayDate	Date	Date

6. Click the Reset Layout button to rearrange the tables.

Refining the Model

Our goal is to create a Tabular BI Semantic model for our business users that is easy to understand and easy to use. We continue to refine our model to move closer to that goal. In this section, we will add to the model while exploring features that improve the usability and the business insight that our model can provide.

Calculated Columns and Relationships

One table that is still not related to other tables is the International Fares table. In Chapter 8, we set up the model so users can analyze the International Fares data by year. This arrangement allows users to compare the total Average Baggage Fee and Average Round-Trip Fare between 2010 and 2011. Unfortunately, the Year column only works when it is selected from the International Fares table and not when used from the Date table (which would be a more logical place to retrieve the Year). To resolve this situation, we need to create a new relationship between the International Fares table and the Date table.

In their current states, we cannot relate the Year column from the International Fares table to the Year column in the Date table. The reason is the BI Semantic Model requires that the column in the lookup table in the relationship be a unique value. For example, the HotelID column is used to relate the Financial and Hotel tables. This relationship is successful because the values in the HotelID column are unique in the Hotel lookup table. Each row in the Hotel table has a different HotelID value.

In the relationship between the International Fares table and the Date table, the Year column is not unique in the Date table. Since the Date table holds a record per day, there are 365 or 366 records for each year in the Date table.

To remedy this situation, we could create a Year lookup table that just contains the distinct Year column values from the Date table. The problem with this approach is that there would be two tables—Year and Date—in the BI Semantic Model that would provide time information for the data.

The ID column in the Date table holds the date in YYYYMMDD format. In order to successfully relate the Date and International Fares tables, we will convert the Year column in the International Fares table to hold a date in the YYYYMMDD format to represent the first day of the year. For example, if the year is 2011, the International Fares table would hold the value 20110101 to represent the first date of that year.

Learn By Doing: Adding a Calculated Date Column

Since the first date value for the year is essentially the four-digit year with the characters "0101" added to the end of it, we can create a calculated column to represent this date.

Video 9-2   **Adding a Calculated Date Column**

1. Click the Grid button to switch to Grid View. You can create calculated columns, measures, and KPIs only in Grid View, and you can create hierarchies only in Diagram View.

2. Click the International Fares tab to view the data in the International Fares table.

3. Scroll to the right and click in the first cell under the Add Column heading.

4. Click within the formula box to enter a DAX expression for the calculated column. The formula box appears immediately above the grid, similar to the formula box in Excel.

5. Enter **=CONCATENATE([Year],"0101")** in the formula box. The CONCATENATE function joins together the values that are in the parameters of the function.

6. Press the ENTER key or click outside of the cell, and the table will be updated with the new value in the calculated column.

7. The new column is named CalculatedColumn1. Double-click the column header and change the column name to **Date**.

8. Click the Diagram View button to switch to Diagram View.

9. Drag the Date column from the International Fares table to the ID column in the Date table.

10. Hide the Date column in the International Fares table. To accomplish this, right-click the Date column and select Hide from Client Tools in the context menu.

11. Click the Reset Layout button to rearrange the tables based on the new relationship. The International Fares table and the Date table should look similar to Figure 9-7 (with the International Fares table resized to show all columns).

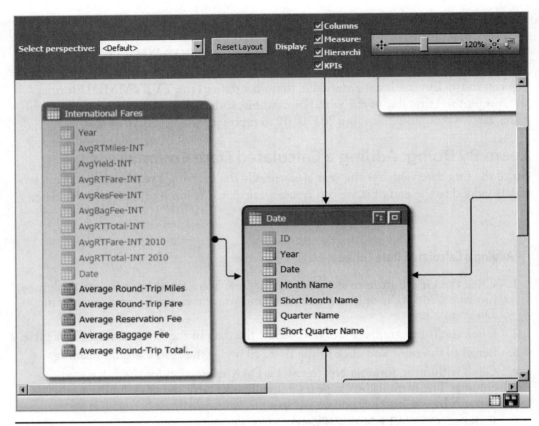

Figure 9-7   *Relationship between the International Fares and Date tables*

12. To validate the new relationship, click the Analyze in Excel button in the toolbar. The Analyze in Excel dialog box appears.

13. Click OK. Excel opens.

14. Place a check mark by the Average Round-Trip Fare column in the International Fares table.

15. Place a check mark by the Year column in the Date table. The pivot table shows the Average Round-Trip Fare grouped by Year.

16. Close Excel. You are prompted to save the workbook changes.

17. Click Don't Save.

Cleaning Up the Model

Through the work we did in this chapter and in Chapter 8, all of the tables are now related. However, there are a number of columns in the model that hold meaningless ID numbers that should be hidden to keep the model clean and understandable.

Learn By Doing: Hiding Columns Not Used for Business Analysis

Let's hide the following columns:

Video 9-3   **Hiding Columns Not Used for Business Analysis**

Table	Column
Financial	HotelID
	PeriodEndDate
Hotel	CountryID
	HotelID
HotelRating	HotelID
	StayDate

Using Diagram View, hide each of these columns. Right-click each column in turn and select Hide From Client Tools in the context menu.

Measures and Attributes

When browsing the model in Excel, you will notice two different types of items within the tables. *Attributes* are descriptive, such as Country or Year. *Measures* are quantities that can be aggregated for a particular attribute. Total Tourist Arrivals and Average Baggage Fee are examples of measures.

The users of the model combine these two types of items to do their analysis. For instance, they can view Total Tourist Arrivals grouped by Country or view Average Baggage Fee grouped by Year. In some client tools (such as Power View), columns with numeric values can automatically be used as measures even though they are not specifically defined as such in the model. Other client tools (such as the Excel Pivot Table Wizard that we use to analyze the model in Excel) read the structure of the model more literally. These client tools will aggregate only items specifically defined as measures in the model.

Learn By Doing: Creating Additional Measures

To make our model more useful in those clients that will aggregate only measures, let's create some additional measures in our model:

Video 9-4   **Creating Additional Measures**

1. Switch to Grid View by clicking the Grid button.
2. Click the Financial tab to select the Financial table.
3. Click any cell in the Revenue column.
4. Click the Sum button (represented by the Sigma symbol) in the toolbar to automatically create the Sum of Revenue measure.
5. Change the name of this new measure to **Total Revenue**.
6. Right-click the column header for the Revenue column and select Hide from Client Tools in the context menu.
7. Repeat steps 3 through 6 for the following two columns, using the indicated name for each newly created measure:

Column	Measure
CostOfSales	Total Cost of Sales
Expenses	Total Expenses

8. Click the HotelRating tab to select the HotelRating table.
9. Right-click the HotelRating tab and select Rename from the context menu. Change the name to **Hotel Rating**.
10. Creating a sum of hotel ratings does not make sense. So, instead of creating a measure using the sum aggregate, we will use the average aggregation. Click any cell in the Rating column.
11. Click the drop-down arrow next to the Sum button in the toolbar. The drop-down list displays the possible aggregations that can be used.
12. Select Average from the drop-down menu. The Average of Rating measure appears in the Calculation Area.
13. Change the name of this new measure to **Average Rating**.
14. Hide the Rating column.
15. Save the model and click the Analyze in Excel button to view the results.
16. Click OK. When Excel opens, explore the model.
17. Close Excel without saving the changes when you are done.

Hierarchies

We humans tend to use hierarchical classification of data as a way to group similar entities. Animal species are organized into a hierarchy of kingdom, phylum, class, order, family, genus, and species. The calendar is organized into a hierarchy of year, quarter, month, and day. Even department stores are hierarchically organized into department, product type, brand, and product.

Hierarchical organization enables us to determine some basic properties of an item just by knowing where it falls in the hierarchy. For example, if an animal is a member of the phylum Arthropoda, we know it has an external skeleton and jointed appendages. (Insects, spiders, centipedes, lobsters, and crabs are all arthropods.)

In addition, hierarchies allow us to navigate up and down the levels of the hierarchy and gather more or less detail as needed. Census data may indicate that 18 percent of U.S. households make over $100,000. A geographic hierarchy provides the ability to "drill down" from the country level to the state level to see what that percentage is for each state in the United States.

Although Microsoft Power View does not currently support hierarchies, it is being covered in this chapter because hierarchies are an important part of the BI Semantic Model and can be used in client tools such as Microsoft Excel. In addition, it may not be too long before hierarchies are supported in a future version of Power View.

Learn By Doing: Creating Hierarchies

At this point, our model contains no hierarchies. We do have tables that can contain hierarchical structures. Let's add hierarchies to the Date and Country tables so users can navigate through years, quarters, months, and dates and can navigate from continents to countries.

Video 9-5   **Creating Hierarchies**

1. Switch to Diagram View if you are in Grid View.
2. Navigate to the Date table and right-click the Date table header.
3. Select Create Hierarchy from the context menu, as shown in Figure 9-8. A new hierarchy named Hierarchy1 appears at the bottom of the table.

NOTE

You can also create a hierarchy by clicking the Create Hierarchy button in the table header or by right-clicking a column and selecting Create Hierarchy from the context menu.

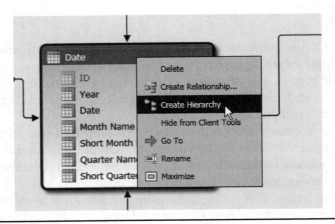

Figure 9-8   *Creating a hierarchy*

4. Rename the hierarchy to **Date Hierarchy**.

5. Enlarge the Date table to show all of the columns in addition to the Date Hierarchy with space below for four new columns.

6. Drag the Year column down on top of the hierarchy name until the hierarchy name turns gray. This creates the top level for the hierarchy.

NOTE

When adding columns to a hierarchy, drag the column to the hierarchy area and release when you see an insert line that goes most—but not all—of the way across the table's rectangle. If you see an insert line that extends all of the way across the table's rectangle, move your mouse up closer to the hierarchy entries.

7. Drag the Short Quarter Name column below the Year level in the hierarchy.

8. Double-click the Short Quarter Name level within the hierarchy and change the name to **Quarter**.

9. Drag the Month Name column below the Quarter level.

10. Rename the Month Name level to **Month**.

11. Drag the Date column below the Month level.

   Let's add another hierarchy to the model in the Country table:

12. Navigate to the Country table and right-click the Country table header.

13. Select Create Hierarchy from the context menu.

14. Rename Hierarchy1 to **Country Hierarchy**.

15. Enlarge the Country table to show all of the columns in addition to the Country Hierarchy with space below for two new columns.

16. Drag the Continent column on top of the hierarchy name to create the top level for the hierarchy.

17. Drag the Country column below the Continent level to create the next level in the hierarchy.

18. Save the model and click the Analyze in Excel button to view the results.

19. Click OK. Excel opens.

20. Scroll down to the Date table.

21. Expand the Date Hierarchy and the More Fields folder under Date. Note the Year, Month, and Quarter fields appear in both the hierarchy and the More Fields folder. These are actually the same field (with two slightly different names) showing up in two different places.

If all of the client tools using your model support hierarchies, it is a good idea to hide the columns in the table that are used in the hierarchy to simplify the model and avoid confusion. However, if your users are going to access the model with any client tool that does not recognize hierarchies, keep the items visible both in the hierarchy and in the table itself. Because we are targeting the Pan-Geo Marketing model for Power View, we will not hide the columns used in the hierarchy.

Learn By Doing: Setting Sort By Columns

Let's try using the Date Hierarchy:

Video 9-6 **Setting Sort By Columns**

1. While still in Excel, drag the Average Rating column in the Hotel Rating table into the Values area in the lower-right corner.

2. Drag the Date Hierarchy in the Date table to the Row Labels area. Because year is the top level of the Date Hierarchy, we see the Average Rating for each year.

3. Expand the 2011 entry to view the Average Rating for each quarter in 2011.

4. Expand the Q4, 2011 entry. You will notice the month names are in alphabetical order rather than in calendar order.

   The model does not recognize that the month column actually holds month values. We'll need to provide the proper sorting of months by adding a calculated column holding the month number of each date in the Date table.

5. Close Microsoft Excel and do not save changes.

6. Switch to Grid View by clicking the Grid button.

7. Click the Date tab to display the Date table and scroll to the end of the table.

8. Select any cell under the Add Column heading. Enter the following expression into the formula box **=FORMAT('Date'[Date],"yyyyMM")**. This expression provides the year and month number. For example, dates in the month of June 2012 have a value of 201206. This number format allows the months to sort in the proper calendar order.

9. Rename the column to **Month Number**.

10. Right-click the column and select Hide from Client Tools.

11. In the Properties window for the Month Number column, change the data type to Whole Number.

12. Now you can use the Month Number column to sort the Month Name column. Select any cell in the Month Name column.

13. Click the Sort by Column button near the right end of the Analysis Services toolbar. The Sort by Column dialog box appears.

14. Month Name should be selected in the left drop-down list box. Select the Month Number column in the right drop-down list, as shown in Figure 9-9.

15. Click the OK button.

16. Select any cell under the Add Column heading. Enter the following expression into the Formula Bar **=FORMAT('Date'[Date],"yyyyQ")**. This expression provides the year and quarter number. For example, dates in the month of June, 2012 will have a value of 20122. This number will allow the quarters to sort in the proper calendar order.

17. Rename the column to **Quarter Number**.

18. Right-click the column and select Hide from Client Tools.

19. In the Properties window for the Quarter Number column, change the data type to Whole Number.

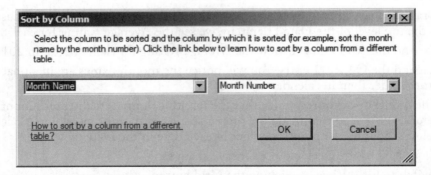

Figure 9-9 *Sort by Column dialog box*

20. Now you can use the Quarter Number column to sort the Quarter Name column. Select any cell in the Quarter Name column.

21. Click the Sort by Column button in the toolbar. The Sort by Column dialog box appears.

22. Quarter Name should be selected in the left drop-down list box. Select the Quarter Number column in the right drop-down list.

23. Click OK.

24. Save the model and click the Analyze in Excel button in the toolbar.

25. Click OK. Excel opens.

26. Repeat steps 1 through 4. The months are now in the proper order.

27. Exit Excel without saving changes when you are done exploring the model.

Formatting Columns and Measures

We worked with the Average Rating measure in the previous Learn By Doing exercise. You may have noticed that the Average Rating displays with nine decimal places—certainly more decimal places than necessary for this measure.

The columns are initially formatted in the model by interpreting the data type of the column in the data source. For example, the Financial table holds dollar amounts pulled from the HotelFinancial table in the database. These dollar amounts are stored using the money data type in SQL Server. By default, the model interprets the data type of the source data and formats the column appropriately. As Figure 9-10 shows, the Total Revenue column automatically formats the financial data using the currency format.

The Average Rating measure is calculated as an average of many integer values. The model assigns the General format to this measure. The General format determines the number of decimal places based on the significant digits available to the calculation. In this case, the General format determined that nine decimal places are appropriate for the Average Rating calculation. However, we can reduce that assigned number of decimal places, as described next.

Row Labels	Total Revenue
⊞ Africa	$1,614,056,339.99
⊞ Asia	$7,073,858,367.78
⊞ Europe	$1,998,038,899.17
⊞ North America	$2,158,587,859.80
⊞ Oceania	$315,258,624.38
⊞ South America	$1,790,958,600.53
Grand Total	$14,950,758,691.65

Figure 9-10 *Automatic currency format*

Learn By Doing: Formatting in the Model

Let's adjust the formatting of the column to display the Average Rating using two decimal places instead of nine:

Video 9-7 **Formatting in the Model**

1. Switch to Grid View.
2. Select the Hotel Rating table.
3. Select the Average Rating measure.
4. Find the Format property in the Properties window. The Format property should read General.
5. Select Decimal Number from the drop-down list. The Properties window automatically adjusts to display the Decimal places property.
6. The default Decimal Places property should be 2. If not, enter **2** for the Decimal Places property.
7. Click the Analyze in Excel button and analyze the model in Excel. The Average Rating should now display with two decimal places.
8. Exit Excel and don't save changes when you are done exploring the model.

In addition to adjusting the number of decimal places, another reason to modify the formatting of a measure is to include commas in the numbers. For example, the Total Tourist Arrivals in thousands within the model is 8612772.2. The addition of commas makes it easy to tell if the number 8 represents 8 million or 800 thousand. In this case, we can also remove the decimal because the decimal component is insignificant considering the size of the numbers.

To add commas to the measures and remove the decimal:

1. Select the Tourism table.
2. Select the Total Tourist Arrivals measure.
3. Switch the Format property to Whole Number.
4. Set the Show Thousands Separator property (located below the Measure Name property) to True.
5. Repeat steps 2 through 4 for the rest of the measures in the Tourism table and for the Average Round-Trip Miles measure in the International Fares table.
6. Click Save All and analyze the model in Excel. The Total Tourist Arrivals should now read 8,612,772.
7. Exit Excel and don't save changes when you are done exploring the model.

In addition to formatting measures, we can also adjust the formatting of columns. For example, the Data Format property of the Date column in the Date table can be used to present this date in a number of different formats. You can experiment with this on your own, if you like.

Perspectives

Perspectives provide the capability to present a limited view of a model to a set of users. For example, the accounting department may be interested only in the Financial table data and any tables related directly to the Financial table. We can create a perspective of the model that includes only those tables. We can then provide this perspective to the accounting department. Perspectives are not currently supported in Microsoft Power View, but they are supported by other client tools, so we will discuss them here.

Perspectives keep the model neat and efficient for different user groups. Each group sees only the data the group members are interested in. There is no need to provide to a group of users extra tables that do not apply to them. The extra tables only clutter up the model and make it more difficult to explore.

Learn By Doing: Creating a Perspective

Let's create an Accounting perspective within our model. The perspective will provide data from the Financial table. It will also include the Hotel table and the Date table, as these tables are directly related to the Financial table.

NOTE

Many of the commands performed here can be completed in both Grid View and Diagram View. In many cases, the view that is used is determined by personal preference. Since this chapter started with a discussion of Diagram View, many of the examples start in Diagram View for the sake of consistency.

Video 9-8

Creating a Perspective

1. Switch to Diagram View, if you are not already there.
2. Select Model | Perspectives from the main menu. The Perspectives dialog box opens (see Figure 9-11), displaying the fields in the model.
3. Click the New Perspective button. A column appears next to the field names, with a heading of New Perspective.

4. Change the column heading to **Accounting**.
5. The perspective can show either an entire table or selected columns and measures from a table. Place a check mark next to the Date, Financial, and Hotel tables. All of the columns and measures in each table are selected by checking the table itself. The completed Perspective dialog box is shown in Figure 9-11.
6. Click OK to exit the Perspectives dialog box.
7. To test out the new perspective, click Save All, and then click the Analyze in Excel button.
8. Instead of using the default values, select the Accounting perspective from the Perspective drop-down list, as illustrated in Figure 9-12.

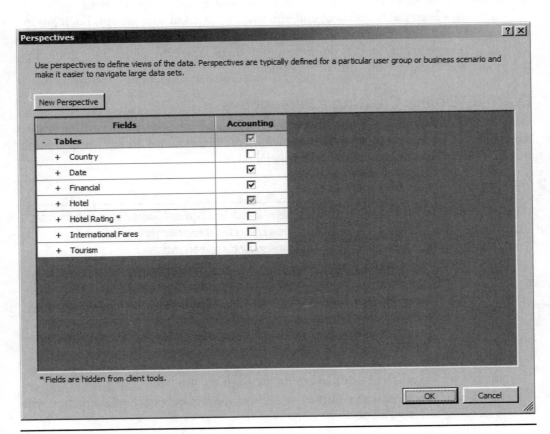

Figure 9-11 *Perspectives dialog box*

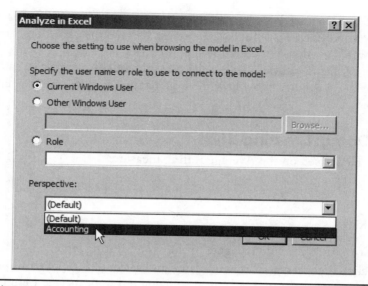

Figure 9-12   *Selecting the Accounting perspective*

9. Click the OK button.

    Excel opens and the PivotTable Field List contains only the three tables selected for the Accounting perspective along with any measures found in those tables. The user is presented with a much simpler view of the model, containing only the data that is important to the accounting user.

10. Close Excel and don't save changes when you are done exploring the Accounting perspective.

Key Performance Indicators

A key performance indicator (KPI) is used to provide quick feedback regarding the performance of an important measure against a targeted goal. For example, if the target gross margin is 50 percent, a KPI can be created to quickly show if the gross margin is currently above or below that goal. KPIs often have three distinct states, which can be indicated by a graphic such as a stoplight. A green light usually indicates the measure is at or beyond the goal (in our example, a gross margin of 50 percent or higher). A yellow light usually indicates the measure is somewhat short of the goal (a gross margin between 25 percent and 49 percent in our example). A red light usually indicates the measure is well off the mark (a gross margin at or below 24 percent in our example).

These KPIs can be placed in client software that supports them. SQL Server Reporting Services reports and Excel PivotTables can present KPIs to the user. Unfortunately, Microsoft Power View does not currently support KPIs.

KPIs make excellent additions to executive dashboards. An executive can view several KPIs each day and instantly know how the organization is performing against its most important goals.

Learn By Doing: Creating a KPI

Let's create a KPI based on the Average Rating measure:

Video 9-9

Creating a KPI

1. Switch to Grid View and navigate to the Hotel Rating table.
2. Right-click the Average Rating measure and select Create KPI from the context menu. The Key Performance Indicator dialog box appears (see Figure 9-13).

NOTE

The KPI can be a percentage of another measure in the model or it can be compared to a numeric value. The value that the KPI is compared against is called the target value.

3. In our case, the maximum rating is five. Select the Absolute Value radio button and enter **5** in the text box.
4. At the bottom of the screen, we choose a visual indicator to use for the KPI. Notice that quite a few are based on the red/yellow/green motif with three states. There are also a few that offer five states. Select the option that uses the red diamond, yellow triangle, and green circle.
5. The next step is to define the values that separate the red/yellow boundary and the yellow/green boundary. In the Define Status Thresholds area, leave the red/yellow boundary at 2 and change the yellow/green boundary to 3.5. You can change a value either by typing the value in the box or by dragging the marker below each box to the appropriate location. The completed KPI dialog box is shown in Figure 9-13.
6. Click OK to create the KPI.

The measure has now turned into a KPI, as indicated by the bar graph next to the name of the KPI in the Measure Grid. Let's see how the new KPI appears in Excel.

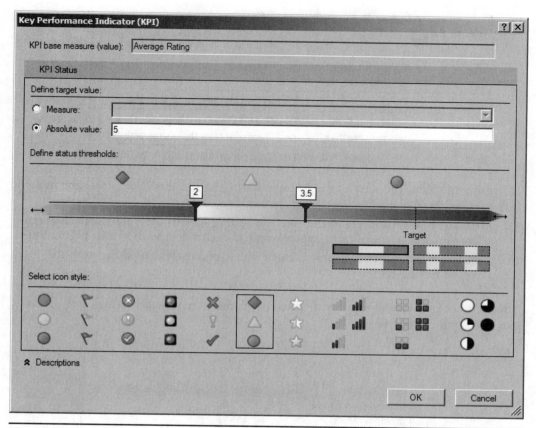

Figure 9-13   *Key Performance Indicator (KPI) dialog box*

7. Click Save All, and then click the Analyze in Excel button in the toolbar. The Analyze in Excel dialog box appears.

8. Leave the (Default) choice in the Perspective drop-down list box this time to browse the default perspective, and then click OK.

9. Drag the Chain Name column from the Hotel table into the Row Labels section.

10. The measure for Average Rating still appears under the Hotel Rating table, but now the PivotTable Field List contains a section called KPIs. Expand the KPIs section to view the Average Rating KPI.

11. Expand the Average Rating KPI. This KPI contains four properties that can be placed in the Pivot Table:

Value	The actual value of the KPI. The Value property correlates to the Average Rating measure in the Hotel Rating table.
Goal	The target value for the KPI that was entered when the KPI was created.
Status	The image indicating the value of the KPI. The image is determined by which indicator was selected when the KPI was created and what range the Value property falls into.
Trend	The Trend property does not currently have any functionality in the Tabular model.

12. Drag the Value property of the Average Rating KPI to the Values area. The numeric value of the Average Rating appears just as it did before.

13. Drag the Status property of the Average Rating KPI to the Values area. The red/yellow/green visual indicator appears next to each value, as shown in Figure 9-14.

14. Exit Excel and don't save your changes when you are done working with the Average Rating KPI.

It becomes immediately apparent which hotel chains have good ratings and which ones need improvement!

Row Labels	Average Rating	Average Rating Status
Grand Elegance Hotel	3.72	●
Great Stay Motel	0.98	●
Happy Tourist Inn	3.19	○
Hotel Sea Star	3.61	●
Hotel Truewater	3.42	○
Knockabout Motel	1.99	●
Luxury Lodge	3.76	●
Motel Greenstar	1.49	●
Posh Plaza	3.41	○
Saver Suite Motel	1.00	●
Skipping Stone Lodge	2.48	○
Swiftwater Suites	2.92	○
Tall Tower Hotel	3.73	●
Travel Quest Motel	3.21	○
Ultra-Suite Hotel	2.95	○
Verdant View Lodge	2.89	○
Grand Total	**2.77**	○

Figure 9-14 *Hotel Rating KPI*

Table and Column Options and Properties

As users browse the content of the Tabular model, questions might arise such as "Where did the data for the Hotel Ratings table come from?" and "How was the Average Baggage Fee calculated?" The current version of the model provides good information to help users make business decisions, but it lacks usability features. This section shows how to enhance the model to make it more user-friendly.

Images in the Model

In addition to data, images can be stored in the Tabular BI Semantic Model. In fact, we have already added an image within the Chain Logo column of the Hotel table. The logos can be displayed in Power View reports, Reporting Services reports, or other client tools that have image support.

Images can be stored in two ways in the model: stored directly in the table, or stored as a URL reference to an image file.

Images Stored in a Table

Images can be stored directly in the table as binary large objects (BLOBs). Just like text or numeric data, the entire content of the image is held within the model. The images can be imported directly from the data source along with the rest of the data. When an image is imported, it appears as a binary data type.

This can be a very convenient way to manage images because the images do not have to reside in a separate data store from the rest of the data. The consequence of using this approach is that images stored within the model may take up a large amount of memory. Part of the optimization of the Tabular model is that the data for the model is loaded into memory on the server. Image content tends to be larger than text or numeric data. As a result, the cells containing images are usually much bigger and therefore take up more memory in the model.

Images Referenced as URLs

The other way images can be used in a Tabular model is by storing the URL to the image file. Image URLs can be imported into the model along with the rest of the data. The URL will be created as a string column and will need to be converted to the Image URL data type so that client tools know the content points to an image file.

Since the pointer to the file is a URL, the image must be provided by a web server. This web server must be accessible from any client tool used to analyze the model. The Image URL does not work with a file path entered into the column.

The advantage of using the Image URL is that very little memory is required to reference the image from within the model. Since the content of the column is just URLs, the storage requirements are very low and only the URL itself is loaded into memory. The images themselves can also be updated very easily. To update an image with a new one, the image contents simply need to be overwritten on the web server hosting the images.

Descriptions

Each table has a Table Description property. Each column and measure within a table has a Description property. Many client tools display the content of these description properties as tooltips when the user hovers over a table, column, or measure.

We can use these description properties to supply additional information to the users of the model, such as an explanation of how a particular calculated value is derived. The description property could also be used to document the origin of the data in a particular table or column.

Determine if and how these description properties are presented to the user by each client tool being used. Then utilize these description properties appropriately to enhance your users' experience while exploring the model. (In Power View, these descriptions show up as tooltips when you hover over a table or field in the Field List.)

Identifiers and Defaults

A few of the column properties identify certain columns that play a special role within a table. They help a client tool determine how to construct a default visualization of the table in which they reside. These properties are

▶ **Row Identifier**   The Row Identifier property indicates the column that can be used to uniquely identify each row in the table. This column cannot have any duplicate values. At most, one column can be marked as the Row Identifier in each table.

▶ **Default Label**   The Default Label property indicates the column that provides a default name for each row in the table.

▶ **Default Image**   The Default Image property indicates the column that contains an image that should be used to identify each row in the table.

▶ **Default Field Set**   One or more columns can be identified as detail columns for the table. When the table as a whole is added to a visualization, any columns identified as detail columns are added to the visualization by default. The columns are added to the visualization in the order specified by the Table Detail Position property.

Learn By Doing: Setting Identifiers and Defaults

We'll go ahead and set these defaults where appropriate in our model:

Video 9-10

Setting Identifiers and Defaults

1. Click the Country tab to select the Country table.
2. Click any cell in the Country Code column.
3. In the Properties window, set the Row Identifier property to **True**.
4. Click any cell in the Country column.
5. In the Properties window, set the Default Label property to **True**.
6. Click any cell in the Flag column.
7. In the Properties window, set the Default Image property to **True**.
8. Again in the Properties window, select the Table Detail Position property. An ellipsis button (…) will appear.
9. Click the ellipsis button. The Default Field Set dialog box appears.
10. Select the Country field in the Fields in the table list.
11. Click Add to move the Country field to the Default fields, in order list.
12. Select the Continent field in the Fields in the table list.
13. Click Add to move the Continent field to the Default fields, in order list. The Default Field Set dialog box should now appear as shown in Figure 9-15.

> **NOTE**
>
> *You can use the Move Up and Move Down buttons to change the order of the fields in the Default fields, in order list.*

14. Click OK to exit the Default Field Set dialog box.
15. Click the Hotel tab to select the Hotel table.
16. Scroll right until you see the "Add Column" heading.
17. Click in the first cell under the "Add Column" heading.
18. Type the following in the formula box:

    ```
    =[Chain Name] & ", " & [City]
    ```

19. Press ENTER.
20. Change the name of the new calculated column to **Hotel Name**.
21. Click any cell in the HotelID column.

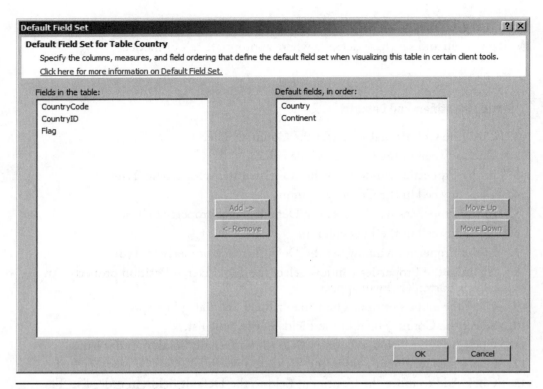

Figure 9-15   *Default Field Set dialog box*

22. In the Properties window, set the Row Identifier property to **True**.
23. Click any cell in the Hotel Name column.
24. In the Properties window, set the Default Label property to **True**.
25. Click any cell in the Chain Logo column.
26. In the Properties window, set the Default Image property to **True**.
27. Again in the Properties window, select the Table Detail Position property. An ellipsis button (…) will appear.
28. Click the ellipsis button. The Default Field Set dialog box appears.
29. Select the Chain Logo field in the Fields in the table list.
30. Click Add to move the Chain Logo field to the Default fields, in order list.
31. Repeat Steps 29-30 to add the following fields as Default fields:
    Hotel Name
    Number of Employees
32. Click OK to exit the Default Field Set dialog box.
33. Click Save All in the toolbar.

Table Storage and Security

As we have discussed, the Tabular BI Semantic Model is designed to take the PowerPivot data model and make it work at an enterprise level. Two important considerations when functioning at the enterprise level are scalability and security. In the Tabular BI Semantic Model, table partitioning is one method to facilitate scalability. Roles facilitate security.

We will conclude this chapter by looking at these two model features.

Table Partitioning

The goal of Tabular BI Semantic Models is to provide excellent performance when working with very large amounts of data. To achieve that lofty goal, the data needs to be processed by the model and loaded into memory. The model content does not change until the model is refreshed. The refresh loads and processes both the existing data and any new data. When the model is very large, refreshing the model can take a long time and stress the server's resources.

Refreshing the model would be faster if there were a way to leave the data already in the model untouched and to load only the new data. In this version of the Tabular BI Semantic Model, there is no feature that allows us to implicitly load only the new data. There is, however, a feature that allows us to explicitly create a scheme to do just that—or at least come close to it. That feature is table partitioning.

Table partitioning breaks the tables into pieces that can be refreshed individually. By placing older, static data in partitions separate from the partitions holding new, dynamic data, we can realize a significant reduction in the time required to get new data into the model. Only those partitions containing the new data need to be refreshed.

Learn By Doing: Partitioning a Table

Let's partition the Hotel Rating table so only the newest data is refreshed:

Video 9-11   **Partitioning a Table**

1. Click the Hotel Rating tab to select the Hotel Rating table.
2. In the main menu, select Table | Partitions. The Partition Manager dialog box appears.

    The Partition Manager shows the existing partitions for the table—which by default is one partition containing all of the data. It also enables us to create and modify additional partitions. We are going to create one partition for the data from the current year and one partition for the data from previous years.

The top of the screen displays the existing partition information. The middle of the screen shows the detail for the currently selected partition. The bottom of the screen displays the content of the partition by displaying either a table of data or the query that provides the data. Let's start by modifying the existing partition to hold the previous years' data.

3. Change the Partition Name field (near the center of the dialog box) to **HotelRatingHistorical**.

4. We need to add a filter to the query that provides the data to populate this partition. Click the Query Editor button, the small button with "SQL" on it. The query for the partition appears.

5. Enter the following text into the SQL Statement area. The screen should appear as illustrated in Figure 9-16.

```
SELECT * FROM HotelRating WHERE StayDate<'1/1/2011'
```

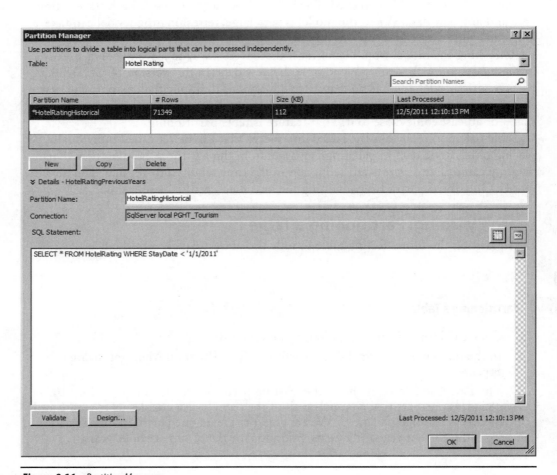

Figure 9-16 *Partition Manager*

6. Click the Copy button to create a new partition by copying the existing one. The new partition will contain the 2011 data. A new partition named HotelRatingHistorical - Copy appears below the HotelRatingHistorical partition.

7. Rename the new partition **HotelRatingCurrent**.

8. Modify the SQL Statement area to contain the following text:

```
SELECT * FROM HotelRating WHERE StayDate>='1/1/2011'
```

NOTE

Make sure the criteria for different partitions do not overlap. An overlap will cause data to be duplicated in two partitions. In our example, we used "StayDate<'1/1/2011'" for one partition and "StayDate>='1/1/2011'" for the other. This approach ensures the data for January 1, 2011 appears only in the HotelRatingCurrent partition.

9. Click OK to close the dialog box.

   Keep in mind that none of the data in the table has been changed. We currently have one partition with all of the data (the original partition that we renamed) and another partition with no data (the new partition we just created). Let's refresh the partitions so the rows are distributed appropriately.

10. Click the drop-down arrow next to the Process Table button in the toolbar and select Process Partitions, as shown in Figure 9-17.

11. The list of partitions for the table appears in the Process Partitions dialog box. Click the check box for each of the two partitions, as shown in Figure 9-18.

12. Click the OK button to begin the processing.

13. When the processing has completed, close the dialog box and click Save All.

NOTE

We are refreshing both partitions here to get the data initially distributed between the new partitions. In the future, the Hotel Ratings table can be updated by refreshing only the HotelRatingCurrent partition. We are not expecting any new hotel ratings for stays prior to 2011.

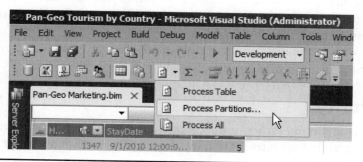

Figure 9-17   *Processing the partitions*

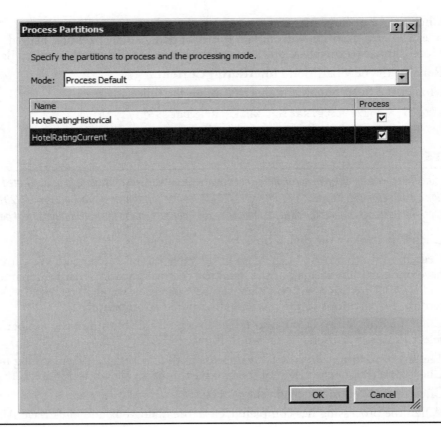

Figure 9-18 *Process Partitions dialog box*

The partitions refresh separately, so instead of having 100,000 rows in one partition, the rows are distributed across the two partitions, with less data in the HotelRatingCurrent partition and more data in the HotelRatingHistorical partition, as shown in Figure 9-19.

If the partitions are created using dates, as shown in this example, partition maintenance needs to take place on a periodic basis. For example, when a new year starts, the queries for the partitions need to be updated with a new date so the previous year's data appears in the historical partition and the current year's data appears in the current partition.

Role Security

Perspectives were covered earlier in the chapter. They are useful for showing only the parts of the model that are relevant to a set of users. Perspectives are not intended to

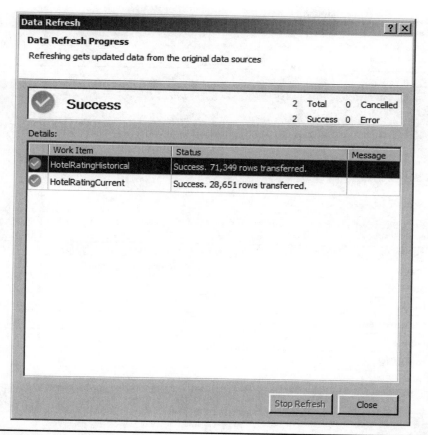

Figure 9-19 *Partition refresh results*

provide security for the model. Instead, the Tabular BI Semantic Model utilizes a role-based security approach. Users are authenticated to the model using their Windows credentials, and those credentials are assigned to roles within the model. Security is handled by restricting the rows in one or more tables that can be seen by the members of an individual role.

Open the Role Manager dialog box by clicking the Roles button in the toolbar. In Figure 9-20, the Role Manager dialog box contains a role called Brazil. As the description indicates, the members of this role are the employees from the Brazil office. The Row Filters tab shows for the Country table a DAX expression that limits the rows that can be seen by the members of the Brazil role. In fact, the filter limits these users so they can only see rows for the country of Brazil. The Members tab is used to assign Windows users or Windows groups to this role.

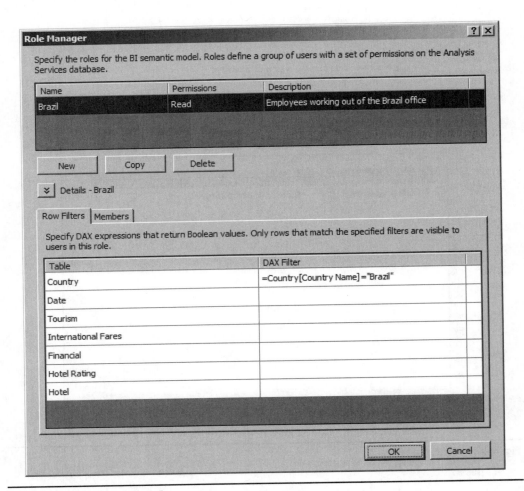

Figure 9-20 *Role Manager dialog box*

Wrap-Up

In this chapter, we took a basic model and added features to increase its usability. We have briefly touched on DAX expressions in both Chapter 8 and Chapter 9. The next chapter explores DAX expressions more thoroughly. We will see that DAX expressions enable us to make our model respond appropriately to any request thrown at it by our users.

Chapter 10

Using DAX Expressions

In This Chapter

► DAX Operators
► DAX Functions
► DAX Queries
► Wrap-Up

One of the reasons for creating a BI Semantic Model is to capture our organization's business logic in a single location. As we undertake the task of replicating the business logic—the various calculations and analytics utilized by our business users—we soon discover that some of those calculations and analytics are pretty complex. We need a capable yet easy-to-understand language to define the business logic within our models. Fortunately, we have just the tool for the job in the Data Analysis Expressions (DAX) language.

DAX is used with both Microsoft PowerPivot and Analysis Services Tabular BI Semantic Models. DAX is a set of functions and operators that can be leveraged to create expressions, calculations, and even query data from other tables in the model. DAX functions and syntax are based on the Excel scripting language and provide powerful analytical capabilities.

Thus far in Part II of this book, we have built a BI Semantic Model and enhanced that model. One of the ways we were able to customize and build out our model was by leveraging DAX. In Chapter 9, we used DAX to relate information between our tables and to create measures. We took one of those measures and used it to define a key performance indicator (KPI). We also saw how DAX is used to define filters when implementing security within a role.

This chapter explains how to use the different operators and functions available in the DAX language. Some of the more useful DAX commands are highlighted for you. Examples are provided to help you learn how to use these operators and functions. This is by no means a detailed explanation of every part of the DAX language. For that level of detail, pick up a book dedicated to the entire range of DAX features and functionality, such as *Practical PowerPivot & DAX Formulas for Excel 2010* by Art Tennick, available from McGraw-Hill Professional.

So let's take a look at the capabilities DAX provides and, at the same time, continue to enhance our model!

DAX Operators

DAX uses operators in expressions to do comparisons, perform arithmetic calculations, and to concatenate text. Let's take a quick look at each of these different types of operators and implement some examples in our existing BI Semantic Model.

Comparison Operators

Comparison operators are used to make a comparison between two values and return either True or False.

Comparison Operator	Meaning	Example
=	Equal to	[Continent] = "North America"
>	Greater than	[Revenue] > 10000
<	Less than	[CostOfSales] < 5000
>=	Greater than or equal to	[Rating] >= 1
<=	Less than or equal to	[Expenses] <= 2000
<>	Not equal to	[Country Name] <> "United States Of America"

Arithmetic Operators

Arithmetic operators are used to perform mathematical calculations such as addition, subtraction, and multiplication to provide a numeric result.

Arithmetic Operator	Meaning	Example
+	Addition	[CostOfSales] + [Expenses]
−	Subtraction or sign	[Revenue] − [CostOfSales]
*	Multiplication	−1 * [Expenses]
/	Division	[CostOfSales] / [Revenue]
^	Exponentiation	8 ^ 2

Learn By Doing: Using Arithmetic Operators to Create Calculated Columns

Let's take a look at using arithmetic operators within our existing Pan-Geo Tourism by Country model to create some additional calculated columns. These columns provide new values that can be used for analysis.

Video 10-1   **Using Arithmetic Operators to Create Calculated Columns**

1. Open SQL Server Data Tools and open the Pan-Geo Tourism by Country project (it has the extension .smproj). You can find the project under File | Recent Projects and Solutions in the main menu or in the Recent Projects area of the Start Page.
2. Click the Financial tab.

3. Scroll to the right and click in the first cell under the Add Column heading.
4. Type = **[Revenue] – [CostOfSales]** and press ENTER.
5. Change the name of the new calculated column to **Gross Profit**.
6. Select Column | Autosum | Sum from the main menu. A measure will be created below the Gross Profit column.
7. In the Properties window, change the name of the new measure to **Total Gross Profit**.
8. Select the Gross Profit column, right-click, and select Hide from Client Tools in the context menu.
9. Again, scroll to the right and click in the first cell under the Add Column heading.
10. Type = **[Gross Profit] – [Expenses]** and press ENTER.
11. Change the name of the new calculated column to **Net Income**.
12. Repeat steps 6–8 for this new column and change the name of the new measure to **Total Net Income**. The Financial tab should now look similar to Figure 10-1.
13. Click Save All.
14. Click the Analyze in Excel button in the toolbar.
15. Click OK in the Analyze in Excel dialog box to use the Current Windows User.
16. Place a check mark by the Total Gross Profit column in the Financial measures.
17. Place a check mark by the Total Net Income column in the Financial measures.
18. Place a check mark by the Country Hierarchy column in the Country table. The PivotTable shows the Total Gross Profit and Total Net Income grouped by Country, as shown in Figure 10-2.
19. Close Excel and click Don't Save.

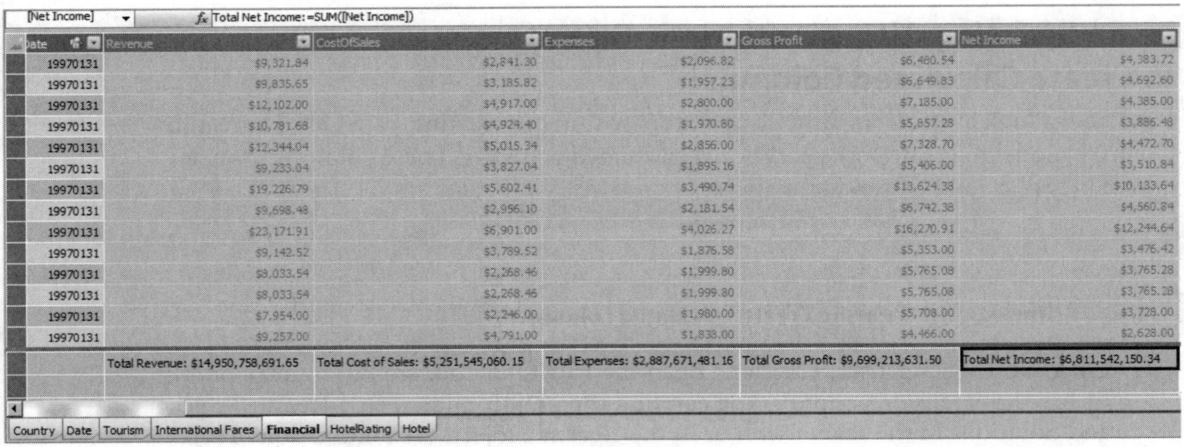
[Net Income] Total Net Income: =SUM([Net Income])

Date	Revenue	CostOfSales	Expenses	Gross Profit	Net Income
19970131	$9,321.84	$2,841.30	$2,096.82	$6,480.54	$4,383.72
19970131	$9,835.65	$3,185.82	$1,957.23	$6,649.83	$4,692.60
19970131	$12,102.00	$4,917.00	$2,800.00	$7,185.00	$4,385.00
19970131	$10,781.68	$4,924.40	$1,970.80	$5,857.28	$3,886.48
19970131	$12,344.04	$5,015.34	$2,856.00	$7,328.70	$4,472.70
19970131	$9,233.04	$3,827.04	$1,895.16	$5,406.00	$3,510.84
19970131	$19,226.79	$5,602.41	$3,490.74	$13,624.38	$10,133.64
19970131	$9,698.48	$2,956.10	$2,181.54	$6,742.38	$4,560.84
19970131	$23,171.91	$6,901.00	$4,026.27	$16,270.91	$12,244.64
19970131	$9,142.52	$3,789.52	$1,876.58	$5,353.00	$3,476.42
19970131	$8,033.54	$2,268.46	$1,999.80	$5,765.08	$3,765.28
19970131	$8,033.54	$2,268.46	$1,999.80	$5,765.08	$3,765.28
19970131	$7,954.00	$2,246.00	$1,980.00	$5,708.00	$3,728.00
19970131	$9,257.00	$4,791.00	$1,838.00	$4,466.00	$2,628.00
	Total Revenue: $14,950,758,691.65	Total Cost of Sales: $5,251,545,060.15	Total Expenses: $2,887,671,481.16	Total Gross Profit: $9,699,213,631.50	Total Net Income: $6,811,542,150.34

Country | Date | Tourism | International Fares | Financial | HotelRating | Hotel

Figure 10-1 *Gross Profit and Net Income columns in the Financial table*

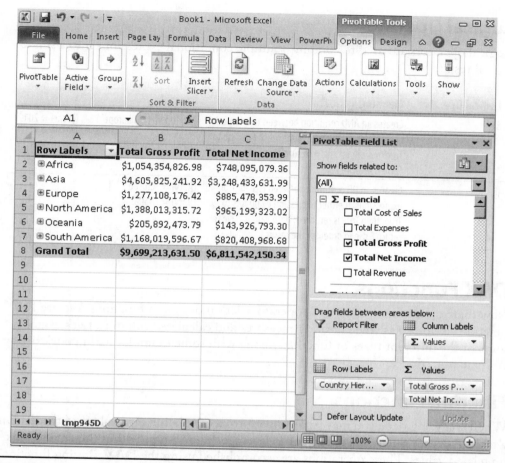

Figure 10-2 *Total Gross Profit and Total Net Income grouped by Country*

Text Operator

Use the ampersand (&) to concatenate two text values, creating a single string.

Text Operator	Meaning	Example
&	Concatenate	[Month Name] & " " & [Year]

Logical Operators

Logical operators are used to combine multiple conditional expressions into a single logical result.

Logical Operator	Meaning	Example
&&	Creates an AND condition between two logical expressions. Both expressions must evaluate to True in order for this to return True; otherwise, False is returned.	([Continent] = "Europe") && ([Year] = 2012)
||	Creates an OR condition between two logical expressions. If either expression evaluates to True, then True is returned; both values have to return False in order for the result to be False.	([City] = "Chicago") || ([City] = "Dallas")

DAX Functions

Now that you are familiar with the operators, let's move on to functions. We use DAX functions in formulas when creating measures and calculated columns. Let's examine some of the different types of functions, along with some examples within our existing BI Semantic Model.

Filtering Functions

When analyzing data, you may want to perform a calculation on a subset of the data in a table. At other times, you may want to leverage relationships within the data to look up related values. These operations are accomplished using the DAX filtering functions. The filtering functions are some of the most powerful functions provided by DAX.

RELATED(<column>)

The RELATED() function provides us with a way to look up a value in one table and pull it into another table. We do this by using the relationships between tables defined in the model (thus, the name of the function). The RELATED() function takes a single parameter. That parameter is a fully qualified reference to a field in another table. "Fully qualified" means we need to specify both the name of the table and the name of the field. A relationship must exist in the model between the table that contains the calculated column using the RELATED() function and the table referred to by the fully qualified parameter.

For example, in our model we have a relationship between the Hotel table and the Country table. The relationship in the model specifies that the CountryID field in the Hotel table is a foreign key reference to the CountryID field in the Country table. Because of this relationship, we can create the following calculated column in the Hotel table:

```
=RELATED(Country[Country])
```

This returns the content of the Country field in the Country table that is related to the given row in the Hotel table.

RELATEDTABLE(<table>)

The RELATEDTABLE() function is similar to the RELATED() function. It makes use of a one-to-many relationship between the table where the function is used and the table specified by the <table> parameter. Whereas the RELATED() function works from the "many" side of the relationship to find the "one," the RELATEDTABLE() function works from the "one" side of the relationship to find the "many." The RELATED() function takes a foreign key and uses the relationship to find the single record containing the matching primary key. The RELATEDTABLE() function takes a primary key and uses the relationship to find all the rows containing a matching foreign key.

The following example can be used in the Hotel table to create a table of all the rows in the Financial table related to each hotel:

```
RELATEDTABLE(Financial)
```

As we will see later in this chapter, we can then use the table that results from the RELATEDTABLE() function as a parameter to an aggregate function. This enables us to sum a field or count rows in a related table.

FILTER(<table>, <filter>)

The FILTER() function allows us to create a subset of a given table. We do so by applying a filter condition to the rows of the table. Only those rows where the filter condition evaluates to True are included in the result.

The following example returns all of the rows in the Financial table where the HotelID is equal to 20:

```
FILTER(Financial, Financial[HotelID] = 20)
```

CALCULATE(<expression>, <filter1>, <filter2>...)

The CALCULATE() function is almost identical to the RELATED() function. Even though the word RELATED is not present in the name of the function, the CALCULATE() function utilizes any relationship that exists between the table where the function is used and the table specified by the <expression> parameter. The only difference is the CALCULATE() function allows us to add filters by specifying additional filter parameters.

The following example can be used in the Hotel table to return a total from a table of all the rows in the Financial table related to each hotel where the Year is 2011:

```
CALCULATE(SUM(Financial[Revenue]), 'Date'[Year] = 2011)
```

ALL(<table> | <column>)

The ALL() function is used to return all of the values in a table or in a field, while overriding any filters that might be applied. This is useful when calculating things like percent of total. When making these types of calculations, we want to compare a number to all of the values in the table, not just those that happen to meet the current filter criteria.

This example will return all of the values of the Year field in the Date table no matter what filters might be in place:

```
ALL('Date'[Year])
```

DISTINCT(<column>)

The DISTINCT() function returns a one-column table that includes the distinct values of a column. The following example will return all of the distinct chain names in the Hotel table:

```
DISTINCT(Hotel[Chain Name])
```

HASONEVALUE(<columnname>)

The HASONEVALUE() function returns True when the context of the column name returns only one distinct value. If the column has more than one distinct value in the given context, the function returns False. For example, the following function will return True, if the Year field in all of the rows in the current context for the Date table have the same value:

```
HASONEVALUE('Date'[Year])
```

USERELATIONSHIP(<columnname1>, <columnname2>)

The USERELATIONSHIP() function specifies the relationship to be used in a calculation. A relationship between the specified tables using the specified columns must already exist in the model. If this is not the case, the function will result in an error.

This function is used when there is more than one relationship defined between the same two tables in the model. For example, if we had a table containing information on hotel stays, we could have one relationship defined between this HotelStay table and the Date table based on check-in date. A second relationship could exist between these two tables based on check-out date. The USERELATIONSHIP() function would then be used to identify which relationship should be used for a given calculation. For example, to use the relationship based on check-out date, we would specify:

```
USERELATIONSHIP(HotelStay[CheckOutDate], 'Date'[ID])
```

Learn By Doing: Using Filter Functions

Let's take a look at using a couple of the filter functions with our existing model. In the process, we will utilize some of the relationships that have been defined in our model.

Video 10-2   **Using Filter Functions**

1. Click the Hotel tab.
2. Scroll to the right and click in the first cell under the Add Column heading.
3. Type **=RELATED(Country[Country])** and press ENTER.
4. Change the name of the new calculated column to **Country**.
5. Click the Financial tab.
6. Click in an empty cell in the Measure Grid below the rows of data. If this area is not displayed, simply right-click the Financial tab and select Show Measure Grid.
7. Type the following formula:

```
Revenue for 2009:=CALCULATE(SUM(Financial[Revenue]), 'Date'[Year]=2009)
```

8. Press ENTER.
9. In the Properties window, change the Format property for the new measure from General to Currency. The Financial tab should now look similar to Figure 10-3.
10. Click Save All.

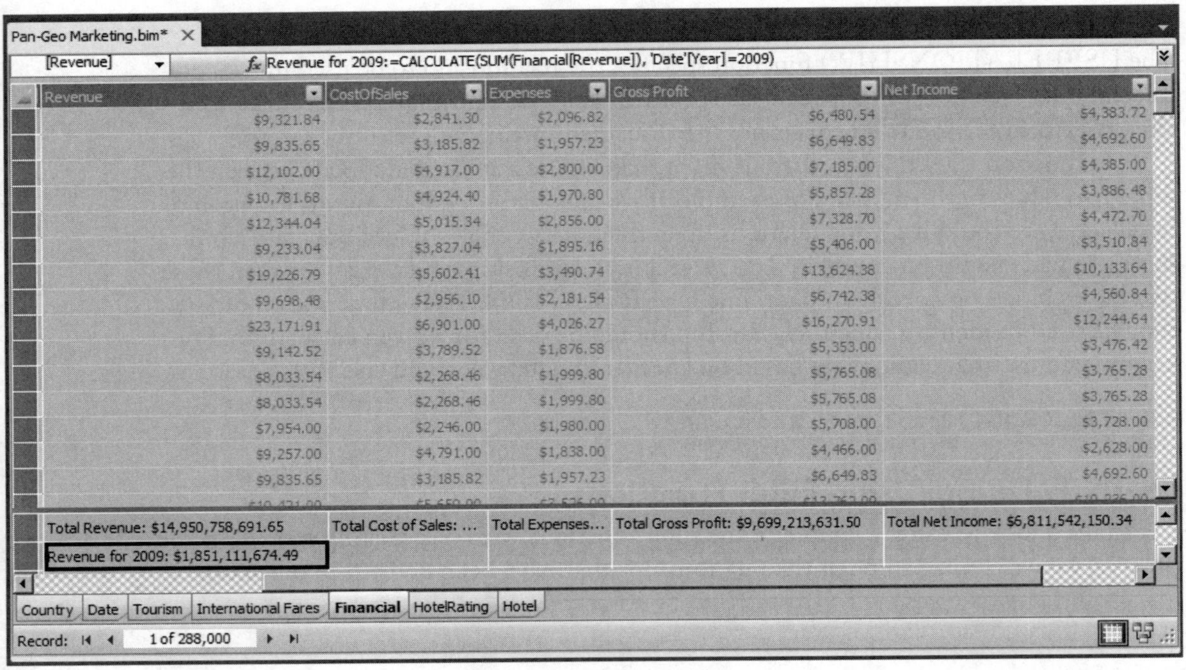

Figure 10-3 *Revenue for 2009 measure in the Financial table*

11. Click the Analyze In Excel button in the toolbar, and then click OK to use the Current Windows User.

12. Place a check mark by the Revenue for 2009 column in the Financial measures.

13. Place a check mark by the Chain Name and Country columns in the Hotel table. The PivotTable shows the Revenue for 2009 grouped by the Chain Name broken out by Country, as shown in Figure 10-4.

14. Close Excel and click Don't Save.

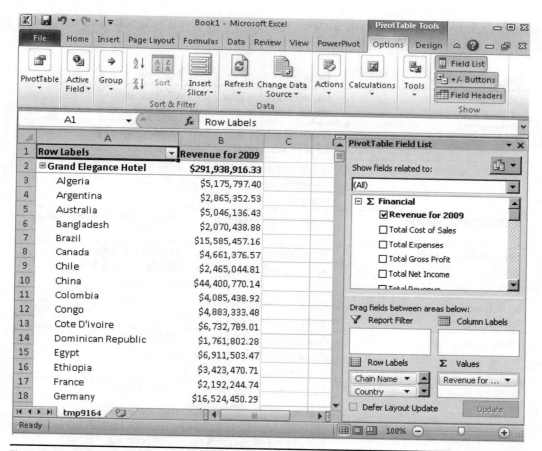

Figure 10-4   *Revenue for 2009 grouped by Chain Name by Country*

Math and Statistical Functions

The math and statistical functions in DAX are all very similar, if not identical, to the Excel mathematical, trigonometric, and aggregation functions. Some of the functions differ slightly in the way they work with tables in DAX versus ranges in Excel and in the way they work with Boolean and text values.

Syntax	Meaning	Example
ABS(<value>)	Returns the absolute value of a number	ABS([Expenses])
AVERAGE(<column>)	Returns the average (mean) of all the values in a column	AVERAGE([Rating])
CURRENCY(<value>)	Evaluates the argument and converts the value to a currency data type	CURRENCY([CostOfSales])
DISTINCTCOUNT(<column>)	Returns the distinct count of values in a column	DISTINCTCOUNT(Hotel[Chain Name])
RANKX(<table>, <expression>)	Returns a ranking based on a number for each row in the table	RANKX(ALL(Hotel), SUMX(RELATEDTABLE(Financial), [Total Revenue]))
ROUND(<number>, <number digits>)	Rounds a number based on the specified number of digits	ROUND([Revenue], 2)
STDEV.P(<column>)	Calculates the standard deviation of a column of numbers based on the entire population	STDEV.P([Rating])
STDEV.S(<column>)	Estimates the standard deviation of a column of numbers based on a sample	STDEV.S([Revenue])
SUM(<column>)	Adds all of the values in a column	SUM([Revenue])
SUMMARIZE(<table>, <groupby_column>[, <name>, <expression>])	Returns a summary table grouped on the expression	SUMMARIZE(Hotel, [Chain Name], [City], "Total Revenue", [Total Revenue])
SUMX(<table>, <expression>)	Returns the sum of values based on the evaluation of the expression	SUMX(All(Hotel[Chain Name]), [Total Revenue])
TOPN(<n_value>, <table>, <orderby_expression>, <order>)	Returns the top N records from the table based on the expression and ordered as specified (0 = descending, 1 = ascending)	TOPN(10, Hotel, [Total Revenue], 0)

Learn By Doing: Using Mathematical and Statistical Functions

Let's take a look at using some of these functions with our existing model so we can see how they can be used to create rankings and other business calculations within measures.

Video 10-3 **Using Mathematical and Statistical Functions**

1. Click the Hotel tab.
2. Scroll to the right and click in the first cell under the Add Column heading.
3. Type the following formula:

   ```
   =SUMX(RELATEDTABLE(Financial),Financial[Total Revenue])
   ```

4. Press ENTER.
5. Change the name of the new calculated column to **Life to Date Revenue**.
6. Click in an empty cell in the Measure Grid in the Hotel tab below the rows of data.
7. Type the following formula:

   ```
   Hotel Chain Rank:=RANKX(ALL(Hotel[Chain Name]), [Total Revenue])
   ```

   This calculation allows us to return the ranking of a hotel chain based on total revenue compared to all of the hotel chains. Initially we will see the result of one hotel chain. When we analyze the hotel chains against each other, we will see that this result will change to show the individual rank of each hotel chain relative to the others.

8. Press ENTER.
9. Click in another empty cell in the Measure Grid in the Hotel tab.
10. Type the following formula:

    ```
    Hotel Chain Count:=DISTINCTCOUNT(Hotel[Chain Name])
    ```

11. Press ENTER.
12. Click the Financial tab.
13. Click in an empty cell in the Measure Grid below the rows of data.
14. Type the following formula:

    ```
    % of Total Revenue:=SUM([Revenue])/SUMX(ALL(Financial), [Revenue])
    ```

15. Press ENTER.

16. In the Properties window, change the Format property for the new measure from General to Percentage.

17. Click in another empty cell in the Measure Grid in the Financial tab.

18. Type the following formula:

    ```
    Gross Profit Margin:=[Total Gross Profit]/[Total Revenue]
    ```

19. Press ENTER.

20. In the Properties window, change the Format property for the new measure from General to Percentage. The Financial tab should now look similar to Figure 10-5.

21. Click Save All.

22. Click the Analyze in Excel button in the toolbar, and then click OK to use the Current Windows User.

23. Place a check mark by the Hotel Chain Rank and Hotel Chain Count columns in the Hotel measures.

24. Place a check mark by the % of Total Revenue and Gross Profit Margin columns in the Financial measures.

25. Place a check mark by the Chain Name column in the Hotel table. The PivotTable should show all of the values grouped by the Chain Name, as shown in Figure 10-6.

26. Close Excel and click Don't Save.

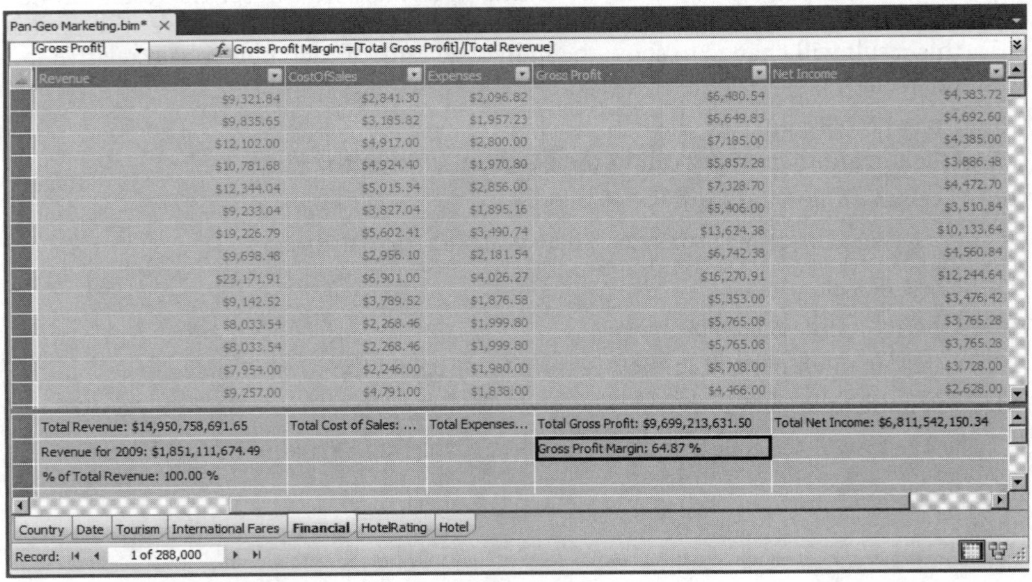

Figure 10-5   *% of Total Revenue and Gross Profit Margin measures in the Financial table*

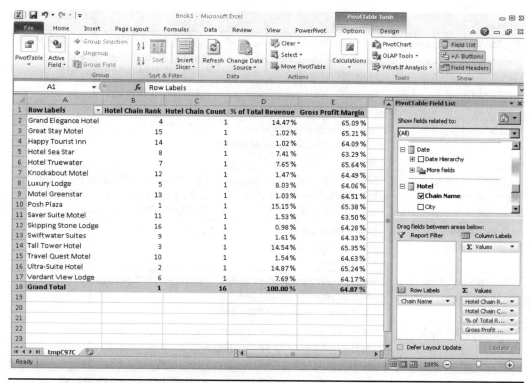

Figure 10-6 *Multiple measure values grouped by Hotel Chain Name*

Date and Time Intelligence Functions

The DAX library provides many of the same date and time functions that are found in Excel. In addition to the typical date and time functions such as MONTH() and YEAR(), DAX also provides a set of time intelligence functions that can be used to compare dates across time periods.

Syntax	Meaning	Example
DATE(<year>, <month>, <day>)	Returns the specified date in datetime format	DATE(2012, 4, 21)
DATEADD(<dates>, <number_of_intervals>, <interval>)	Returns a table that contains a column of dates back or forward in time based on the number of intervals and interval specified	DATEADD('Date' [Date], −1, YEAR)

(Continued)

Syntax	Meaning	Example
FIRSTNONBLANK(<column>, <expression>)	Returns the first value in the column based on the filter context where the expression is not blank	FIRSTNONBLANK(DATESBETWEEN('Date' [Date], BLANK(), LASTDATE('Date' [Date])), CALCULATE(COUNTROWS(Financial)))
HOUR(<datetime>)	Returns the hour number from 0 (12:00 A.M.) to 23 (11:00 P.M.)	HOUR('Date' [Date])
LASTDATE(<dates>)	Returns a table with a single row and column that contains the latest date in the column of dates specified	LASTDATE('Date'[Date])
LASTNONBLANK(<column>, <expression>)	Returns the last value in the column based on the filter context where the expression is not blank	LASTNONBLANK(DATESBETWEEN('Date' [Date], BLANK(), LASTDATE('Date' [Date])), CALCULATE(COUNTROWS(Financial)))
MONTH(<datetime>)	Returns the month specified as a number from 1 (January) to 12 (December)	MONTH('Date' [Date])
PREVIOUSYEAR(<dates> [, <year_end_date>])	Returns a table that contains a column of all dates from the previous year based on the year end date if specified	PREVIOUSYEAR('Date' [Date])
SAMEPERIODLASTYEAR(<dates>)	Returns a table that contains a column of all dates one year prior based on the specified column and context	SAMEPERIODLASTYEAR('Date' [Date])
TOTALMTD(<expression>, <dates> [, <filter>])	Calculates the value based on the expression for the month to date based on the current context	TOTALMTD(SUM(Financial[Revenue]), 'Date' [Date])
WEEKDAY(<date>, <return_type>)	Returns the day of the week specified as a number. If return_type is not specified or is 1, then Sunday is 1 and Saturday is 7. If return_type is 2, then Monday is 1 and Sunday is 7. If return_type is 3, then Monday is 0 and Sunday is 6.	WEEKDAY('Date' [Date])

Learn By Doing: Using Date and Time Intelligence Functions

Again, we'll use some of these functions with our existing model. Here, we see how these functions provide a new column to be used for evaluation purposes. We also see how time intelligence is used to provide some new insights and discover trends.

Video 10-4 **Using Date and Time Intelligence Functions**

1. Click the Date tab.
2. Scroll to the right and click in the first cell under the Add Column heading.
3. Type the formula **=WEEKDAY([Date])** and press ENTER.
4. Change the name of the new calculated column to **DayNumberOfWeek**. This column will be used later in another calculated column as a reference point in the "Logical Functions" section.
5. Click the Hotel tab.
6. Scroll to the right and click in the first cell under the Add Column heading.
7. Type the following formula:

```
=LASTNONBLANK(DATESBETWEEN('Date'[Date], BLANK(), LASTDATE('Date'[Date])),
                          CALCULATE(COUNTROWS(Financial)))
```

This will return the last date that a hotel had revenue.

NOTE

The COUNTROWS() function returns the number of rows in the specified table.

8. Press ENTER.
9. Change the name of the new calculated column to **Last Revenue Date**.
10. In the Properties window, change the Data Format from General to Short Date.
11. Once again, click in the first cell under the Add Column heading.
12. Type the formula **=TODAY() – [Last Revenue Date]** and press ENTER.
13. Change the name of the new calculated column to **Days Since Last Revenue**.
14. In the Properties window, change the Data Type from Auto (Date) to Decimal Number. We can now determine the number of days since a hotel generated revenue.
15. Click the Financial tab.
16. Click in an empty cell in the Measure Grid below the rows of data.
17. Type the following formula:

```
LY Total Revenue:=IF(ISBLANK(SUM([Revenue])), BLANK(),
                CALCULATE(SUM([Revenue]), SAMEPERIODLASTYEAR('Date'[Date])))
```

LY is being used here as an abbreviation for Last Year.

18. Press ENTER.
19. In the Properties window, change the Format from General to Currency.
20. Click another empty cell in the Measure Grid in the Financial tab.

21. Type the following formula:

```
YoY Growth Total Revenue:=[Total Revenue] - [LY Total Revenue]
```

YoY is being used here as an abbreviation for Year over Year.

22. Press ENTER.
23. In the Properties window, change the Format from General to Currency.
24. Click another empty cell in the Measure Grid in the Financial tab.
25. Type the following formula:

```
YoY % Growth Total Revenue:=IF(ISBLANK([LY Total Revenue]), BLANK(),
                              [YoY Growth Total Revenue]/[LY Total Revenue])
```

26. Press ENTER.
27. In the Properties window, change the Format from General to Percentage. The Financial tab should now look similar to Figure 10-7.
28. Click Save All.
29. Click the Analyze in Excel button in the toolbar, and then click OK to use the Current Windows User.
30. Place a check mark by the Total Revenue, LY Total Revenue, YoY Growth Total Revenue, and YoY % Growth Total Revenue columns in the Financial measures.

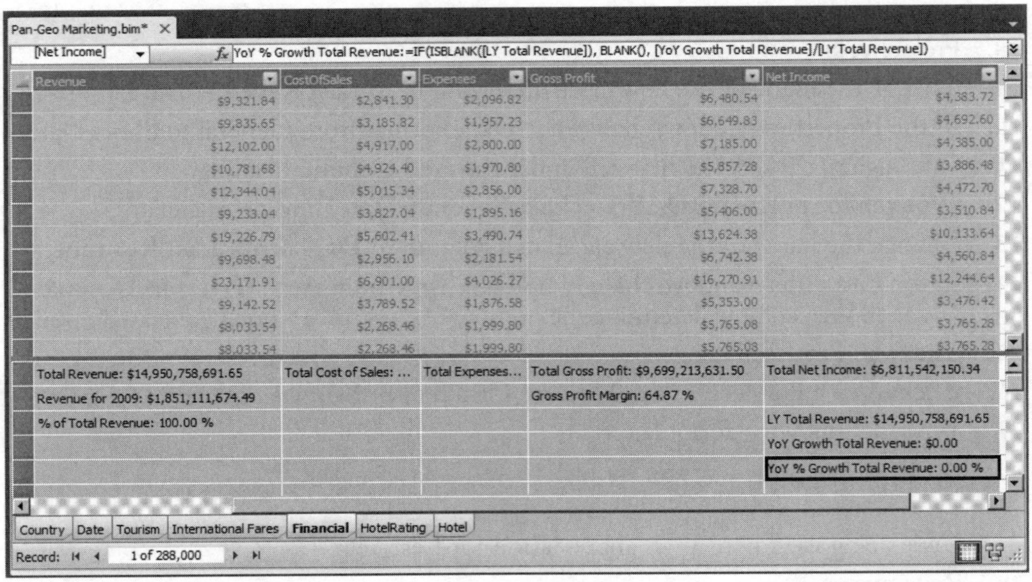

Figure 10-7   *Time-related measures in the Financial table*

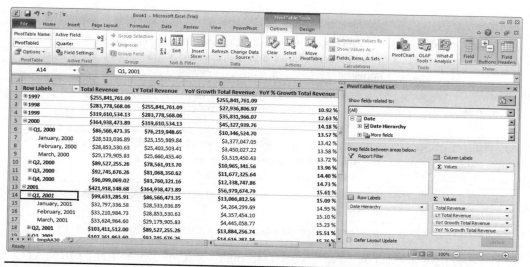

Figure 10-8   *Multiple measure values grouped by Date Hierarchy*

31. Drag the Date Hierarchy from the Date table to the row labels area in the PivotTable Field List. The PivotTable should show all of the values grouped by the Date Hierarchy, as shown in Figure 10-8.

32. Close Excel and click Don't Save.

Text Functions

The DAX library also contains a set of text functions that can be utilized to work with data in the tables and columns. These functions are very similar to those provided in Excel.

Syntax	Meaning	Example
BLANK()	Returns a blank	BLANK()
CONCATENATE(<text1>, <text2>)	Combines two text strings into a single text string and accepts only two arguments	CONCATENATE([Year], "0101")
FIND(<find_text>, <value> [, <start_num>])	Returns the starting position number of one text string within another. This is a case-sensitive operation, and if the start number position is omitted, the value will be 1, which indicates where to start the search.	FIND(Chain[Name], "Hotel")
FORMAT(<value>, <format_string>)	Converts a value to the text string format specified	FORMAT('Date'[Date], "yyyyMM")

(Continued)

Syntax	Meaning	Example
LEFT(<text>, <num_chars>)	Returns a text string based on the number of characters specified from the start of the text string	LEFT('Date'[ID], 6)
MID(<text>, <start_num>, <num_chars>)	Returns a text string based on the number of characters specified from the start number provided	MID('Date' [ID], 5, 2)
SUBSTITUTE(<text>, <old_text>, <new_text> [, <instance_num>])	Returns a text string replacing existing text with the new text specified based on the occurrence specified (or all if omitted)	SUBSTITUTE('Date' [Date], "/", "-")
TRIM(<text>)	Removes all spaces from the start and end of a text string	TRIM(Hotel[Chain Name])
UPPER(<text>)	Converts a text string to all uppercase letters	UPPER(Country[Country Name])

You may have noticed we have already used the CONCATENATE(), FORMAT(), and BLANK() functions in our examples in this chapter and in Chapter 9. For this reason, we will not do any additional exercises with the text functions. That does not mean it is not important to know they are available and understand how you can use them. Along with the ampersand (&) operator, the text functions can be particularly useful when creating additional calculated columns in your tables. The TRIM() function is also particularly valuable for removing any unneeded spaces at the beginning or end of data that was imported.

Logical Functions

Logical functions are used in expressions to perform evaluations and return information about the values being referenced in the model. Once again, these functions are based on similar functions available in Excel.

Syntax	Meaning	Example
AND(<logical1>, <logical2>)	Performs a check to see if both expressions are True; returns True if they are, else returns False	AND([Total Revenue] > [Total Expenses], [Total Revenue] > [LY Total Revenue])
IF(<logical_test>, <value_if_true> [, <value_if_false>])	Checks a logical expression and returns a True or False value based on the evaluation; if False value is omitted, then an empty string is returned	IF(ISBLANK([LY Total Revenue]), BLANK(), [YoY Growth Total Revenue]/ [LY Total Revenue])

Syntax	Meaning	Example
IFERROR(<expression>, <value_if_error>)	Evaluates an expression and returns a value specified if an error occurs or returns the value based on the expression if no error occurs	IFERROR(([YoY Growth Total Revenue]/ [LY Total Revenue]), 0)
OR(<logical1>, <logical2>)	Performs a check to see if one of the expressions is True; if so, returns True, else returns False	OR([Gross Profit Margin] > .7, [YoY % Growth Total Revenue] > .20)
SWITCH(<expression>, <value1>, <result1> [, <value2>, <result2>, ..., <else>])	Evaluates an expression against a list of values and returns a result based on the comparison	SWITCH([DayNumberOfWeek], 1, "Sunday", 2, "Monday", 3, "Tuesday", 4, "Wednesday", 5, "Thursday", 6, "Friday", 7, "Saturday", "Unknown weekday")

Learn By Doing: Using Logical Functions

We have already used the IF() logical function when setting up some of our time-based calculations, but let's take a look at using a few more logical functions with our existing model.

Video 10-5 **Using Logical Functions**

1. Click the Date tab.
2. Scroll to the right and click in the first cell under the Add Column heading.
3. Type the following formula:

   ```
   =SWITCH([DayNumberOfWeek], 1, "Sunday", 2, "Monday", 3, "Tuesday",
    4, "Wednesday", 5, "Thursday", 6, "Friday", 7, "Saturday", "Unknown weekday")
   ```

4. Press ENTER.
5. Change the name of the new calculated column to **Day of Week**.
6. Set the Sort By Column property to DayNumberOfWeek for the new calculated column.
7. Right-click the DayNumberOfWeek column and select Hide from Client Tools. The Date tab should now look similar to Figure 10-9.
8. Click the Hotel tab.
9. Click in an empty cell in the Measure Grid below the rows of data.
10. Type the following formula:

    ```
    Top Performers:=IF(OR([Gross Profit Margin] > .7,
                         [YoY % Growth Total Revenue] > .20), "Top Performer")
    ```

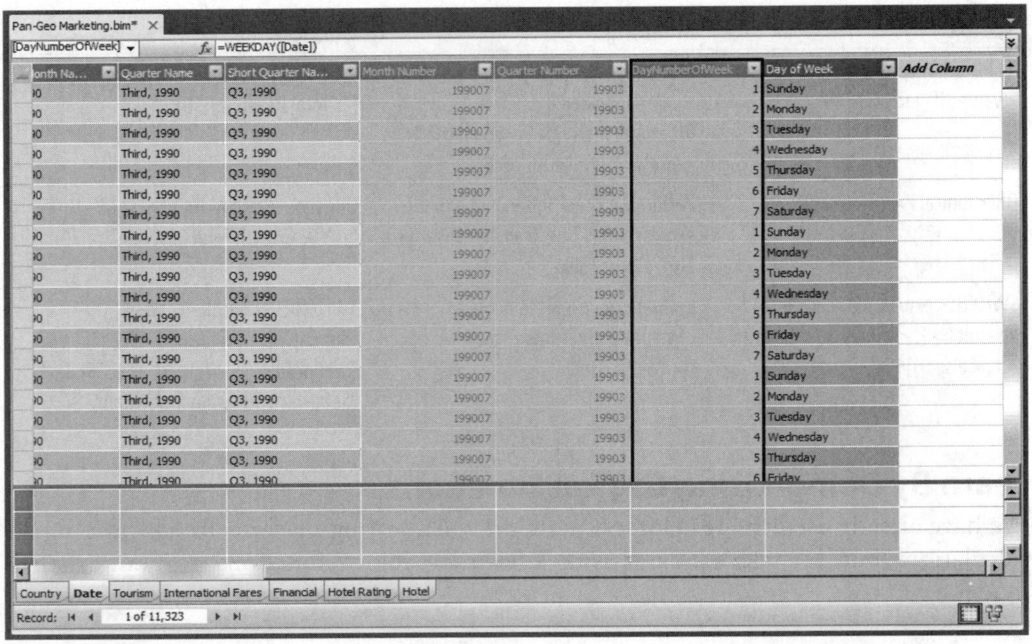

Figure 10-9 *Current View of the Date table*

This calculation will not provide any results in its current state. We will see results only after we start to analyze our hotels.

11. Press ENTER.

12. Click Save All

13. Click the Analyze in Excel button in the toolbar, and then click OK to use the Current Windows User.

14. Place a check mark by the Gross Profit Margin and YoY % Growth Total Revenue columns in the Financial measures.

15. Place a check mark by Top Performers in the Hotel measures.

16. Place a check mark next to Chain Name column in the Hotel table.

17. Drag the Date Hierarchy from the Date table to the Row Labels below Chain Name in the PivotTable Field List. The PivotTable should show all of the values grouped by the Chain Name and Date Hierarchy, as shown in Figure 10-10.

18. Close Excel and click Don't Save.

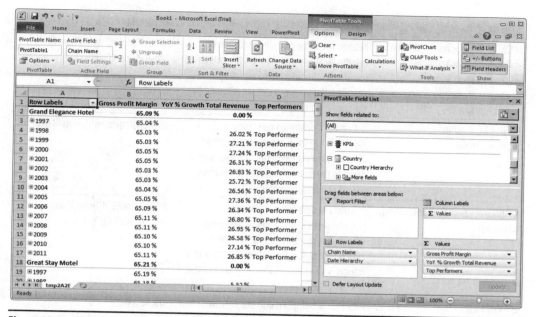

Figure 10-10 *Multiple measure values grouped by Chain Name and Date Hierarchy*

Information Functions

The information functions come in several different flavors. One set of information functions performs evaluations on values and returns True or False accordingly. We have already used one such function, ISBLANK(), to determine if a value is returned by a given expression.

There are also information functions that can be used in parent/child hierarchy evaluations to perform lookups and to retrieve information. This is explained in more detail in the following section. Finally, to determine the credentials being used for the current connection to the model, you can use the USERNAME() function.

Syntax	Meaning	Example
CONTAINS(<table>, <column1>, <value1> [, <column2>, <value2>, …])	Evaluates whether or not a specific value exists in a table column; returns True or False, respectively	CONTAINS(Financial, [HotelID], 20)
ISBLANK(<value>)	Checks whether or not the value is blank; returns True or False, respectively	ISBLANK([LY Total Revenue])

(Continued)

Syntax	Meaning	Example
LOOKUPVALUE(<result_column>, <search_column1>, <search_value1> [, <search_column2>, <search_value2>, …])	Returns the value provided in the result column for the row that meets the criteria specified in the search columns and values specified. If multiple values are returned by the search, an error is returned.	LOOKUP(Hotel[City], [Chain Name], "Posh Plaza", [Country], "Argentina")
PATH(<ID_column>, <parent_column>)	Returns a "|" delimited text string with the identifiers of all the parents of the current identifier, starting with the top-level parent down to the current identifier (useful for parent/child relationships)	PATH(Hotel[HotelID], Hotel[ChainID])
PATHITEM(<path>, <position> [, <type>])	Returns the item value at the specified position number in the delimited string provided by the PATH() function. The data type is returned as text by default (0) or as an integer if specified (1). Positions are evaluated left to right.	PATHITEM(PATH(Hotel[HotelID], Hotel[ChainID]), 2, 1)
USERNAME()	Returns the domain name and username from the credentials provided by the connection (<domain_name>\<user_name>)	USERNAME()

Parent/Child Hierarchies

Many organizations have parent/child hierarchies that must be represented in the BI Semantic Model. The best example of this is an organizational chart showing who reports to whom, such as shown in Figure 10-11. If the employee records shown in Figure 10-11 were imported into a Tabular BI Semantic Model, we could use three DAX functions to turn the parent/child relationship into a hierarchy.

Employees

EmpNum	Name	Position	Supervisor
129	Sandra	Team Leader	239
235	Eva	Developer	129
239	Peter	Development Manager	303
293	Maya	CEO	
303	Frank	IT Director	470
470	Tia	CFO	293
487	Juan	System Administrator	303

Figure 10-11 *An employee table with a parent/child relationship*

The PATH() function uses the primary key field and the parent foreign key field to traverse up the parent/child relationship. As it does, it builds a list of each of the primary key values it encounters along the way. The primary key values are delimited by the "|" character. In the structure shown in Figure 10-11, we could use the following PATH() function:

```
=PATH([EmpNum], [Supervisor])
```

In the record for Eva, this function returns the following path:

```
293|470|303|239|129|235
```

This path results because Eva, who is employee number 235, has a supervisor whose employee number is 129—Sandra. Sandra's supervisor is employee number 239—Peter. Peter's supervisor is employee number 303—Frank. Frank's supervisor is employee number 470—Tia. Tia's supervisor is employee number 293—Maya. Maya is the CEO, so her Supervisor field is empty.

The PATHITEM() function extracts one of the primary key values from the delimited list created by the PATH() function. To use the PATHITEM() function, a calculated field must first be created using the PATH() function. The "path field" can then be referenced as the first parameter (<path>) of the PATHITEM() function.

The value extracted from the list is determined by the second parameter (<position>) of the PATHITEM() function. A position value of 1 extracts the leftmost primary key value in the path, a position value of 2 extracts the primary key value that is second from the left, and so on.

If we use the PATH() function to create a calculated field called SupervisorPath for our structure in Figure 10-11, we can then use the following PATHITEM() function:

```
=PATHITEM([SupervisorPath], 3)
```

In the record for Eva, this function returns the following foreign key value:

```
303
```

This is the third item from the left in the list created by the PATH() function.

Finally, we can use the LOOKUP() function to find the name associated with a key value. The following expression would get the name of the person at the third level in the relationship:

```
=LOOKUPVALUE([Name], [EmpNum], PATHITEM ([SupervisorPath], 3))
```

In the record for Eva, this function returns

```
Frank
```

because Frank is the name corresponding to the employee number found at the third level of the path.

Learn By Doing: Using Information Functions

Even though the data we have does not have a typical parent/child relationship, we will work with something similar in our model:

Video 10-6 **Using Information Functions**

1. Click the Hotel tab.
2. Scroll to the right and click in a cell within the Add Column column.
3. Type the following formula:
   ```
   =IF(IFERROR(FIND("Hotel", Hotel[Chain Name]),0)>0, "Hotel",
       IF(IFERROR(FIND("Motel", Hotel[Chain Name]),0)>0, "Motel",
           IF(IFERROR(FIND("Lodge", Hotel[Chain Name]),0)>0, "Lodge", "Other")))
   ```
4. Press ENTER.
5. Change the name of the new calculated column to **Chain Type**.
6. Once again, click in the first cell under the Add Column heading.
7. Type the following formula:
   ```
   =SWITCH(Hotel[Chain Type], "Hotel", 4, "Motel", 1, "Lodge", 12, 11)
   ```
8. Press ENTER.
9. Change the name of the new calculated column to **ChainParentID**.
10. Click in the first cell under the Add Column heading.
11. Type the following formula:
    ```
    =PATH(Hotel[HotelID], Hotel[ChainParentID])
    ```
12. Press ENTER.
13. Change the name of the new calculated column to **ChainPath**.
14. Click in the first cell under the Add Column heading.

15. Type the following formula:

```
=LOOKUPVALUE(Hotel[Chain Name],Hotel[HotelID],
PATHITEM(Hotel[ChainPath], 1,1))
```

16. Press ENTER.
17. Change the name of the new calculated column to **Level1**.
18. Click in a cell in the Add Column column.
19. Type the following formula:

```
=IF(ISBLANK( PATHITEM(Hotel[ChainPath], 2,1)),Hotel[Chain Name],
   LOOKUPVALUE(Hotel[Chain Name],Hotel[HotelID], PATHITEM(Hotel[ChainPath], 2,1)))
```

20. Press ENTER.
21. Change the name of the new calculated column to **Level2**. The Hotel tab should now look similar to Figure 10-12. Switch over to Diagram View of the model.
22. Right-click the Level1 column in the Hotel table and select Create Hierarchy from the context menu.
23. Change the name of the hierarchy to **Chain Hierarchy**.

	Life to Date...	Last Revenue Date	Days Since Last Revenue	Chain Type	ChainParentID	ChainPath	Level1	Level2	Add
	$11,485,789.16	12/31/2011	71	Hotel	4	4|38	Tall Tower Hotel	Tall Tower Hotel	
	$15,890,720.08	12/31/2011	71	Hotel	4	4|61	Tall Tower Hotel	Tall Tower Hotel	
	$16,500,354.96	12/31/2011	71	Hotel	4	4|362	Tall Tower Hotel	Tall Tower Hotel	
	$19,288,755.75	12/31/2011	71	Hotel	4	4|407	Tall Tower Hotel	Tall Tower Hotel	
	$20,064,801.62	12/31/2011	71	Hotel	4	4|501	Tall Tower Hotel	Tall Tower Hotel	
	$38,448,448.22	12/31/2011	71	Hotel	4	4|578	Tall Tower Hotel	Tall Tower Hotel	
	$14,571,770.01	12/31/2011	71	Hotel	4	4|581	Tall Tower Hotel	Tall Tower Hotel	
	$16,246,243.56	12/31/2011	71	Hotel	4	4|582	Tall Tower Hotel	Tall Tower Hotel	
	$16,452,725.91	12/31/2011	71	Hotel	4	4|608	Tall Tower Hotel	Tall Tower Hotel	
	$36,629,080.17	12/31/2011	71	Hotel	4	4|837	Tall Tower Hotel	Tall Tower Hotel	
	$33,746,397.37	12/31/2011	71	Hotel	4	4|878	Tall Tower Hotel	Tall Tower Hotel	
	$22,295,217.19	12/31/2011	71	Hotel	4	4|1049	Tall Tower Hotel	Tall Tower Hotel	
	$14,115,050.96	12/31/2011	71	Hotel	4	4|1110	Tall Tower Hotel	Tall Tower Hotel	
	$36,256,135.69	12/31/2011	71	Hotel	4	4|1119	Tall Tower Hotel	Tall Tower Hotel	
	$17,319,842.30	12/31/2011	71	Hotel	4	4|1360	Tall Tower Hotel	Tall Tower Hotel	
	$39,828,880.25	12/31/2011	71	Hotel	4	4|1413	Tall Tower Hotel	Tall Tower Hotel	

an-Geo Marketing.bim* ×

[Level2] fx =IF(ISBLANK(PATHITEM(Hotel[ChainPath], 2,1)),Hotel[Chain Name], LOOKUPVALUE(Hotel[Chain Name],Hotel[HotelID], PATHITEM(Hotel[ChainPath], 2,1)))

Country | Date | Tourism | International Fares | Financial | Hotel Rating | **Hotel**

Record: 1 of 1,600

Figure 10-12 *Hotel table in Grid View*

24. Drag the Level2 column below the Level1 column in the Chain Hierarchy to complete the new hierarchy.

25. Click the ChainParentID column in the Hotel table, hold the SHIFT key, and click the Level2 column (the one right above the Hotel Chain Rank). Now right-click the selected columns and select Hide from Client Tools in the context menu.

26. Click the Reset Layout button in Diagram View and click Reset Layout in the confirm dialog box. Your model diagram should look somewhat similar to Figure 10-13.

27. Click Save All.

28. Click the Analyze in Excel button in the toolbar, and then click OK to use the Current Windows User.

29. Place a check mark by the Total Net Income column in the Financial measures.

30. Place a check mark next to Chain Hierarchy from the Hotel table. (Remember, the hierarchies are listed at the bottom of the Pivot Table Field List.)

31. Place a check mark next to Date Hierarchy from the Date table. The PivotTable should show the Net Income grouped by the Chain Hierarchy and Date Hierarchy, as shown in Figure 10-14.

32. Close Excel and click Don't Save.

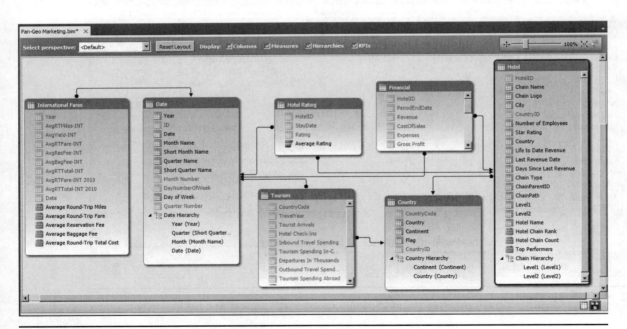

Figure 10-13 *Pan-Geo Marketing model in Diagram View*

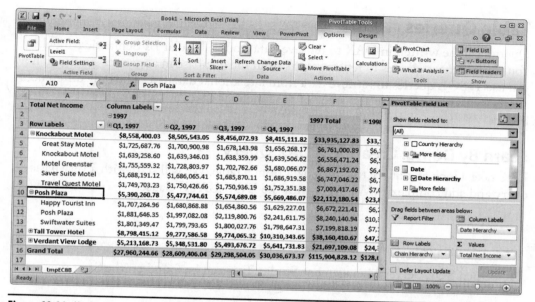

Figure 10-14 *Net Income measure grouped by Chain Hierarchy and Date Hierarchy*

DAX Queries

Up to this point in the chapter, we have focused on using DAX functions to enhance our model. Although DAX queries do not enhance our model, we want to touch on them briefly. We can use DAX queries to perform validation on a tabular model once it has been deployed to a server as an alternative to analysis in Excel.

DAX queries are executed behind the scenes when a tool like Power View is used to explore a Tabular BI Semantic Model. You will see this if you run a trace against the Analysis Services database hosting the tabular model using SQL Server Profiler. Some tools, such as Reporting Services, will require you to have a more intimate knowledge of DAX queries in order to retrieve data from the model.

Table Queries

Queries can be written in DAX to retrieve data from a Tabular BI Semantic Model. You can use these queries to return results from the database in a manner similar to how you use T-SQL queries to retrieve data from a relational database. The only differences are the syntax that you use and some of the functions that you can leverage in the DAX library.

Learn By Doing: Creating a DAX Query

Let's take a look at a query to return data from a table. We will start with a very basic query and add complexity. We begin with the EVALUATE clause.

Video 10-7

Creating a DAX Query

1. Open SQL Server Management Studio. This can be found on the Start menu at Start | All Programs | Microsoft SQL Server 2012.

2. Connect to your Tabular instance of Analysis Services.

3. Expand the Databases folder.

4. Right-click the database named Pan-Geo Tourism By Country_ Administrator_<guid>. (Your Pan-Geo Tourism By Country project must be open in SQL Server Data Tools for this database to exist on the server.) This is the working database for our Tabular BI Semantic Model project. In Chapter 11 we'll deploy our project to establish the released version of the model for our users.

5. Select New Query | MDX from the context menu. MDX is the query language for Multidimensional BI Semantic Models. Because this was the first type of model available for Analysis Services, this is the menu choice used to launch the query window for both Multidimensional and Tabular instances of Analysis Services.

6. In the query window, type the following:

```
EVALUATE Hotel
```

7. Press F5 or click the Execute button in the toolbar to execute the query. Your query window should look like Figure 10-15. Here you can see that you have returned all of the rows and columns of data from the Hotel table in the database including the calculated columns.

8. Modify the query to add the bold text shown here:

```
EVALUATE Hotel
ORDER BY Hotel[Chain Name], Hotel[Number of Employees] DESC
```

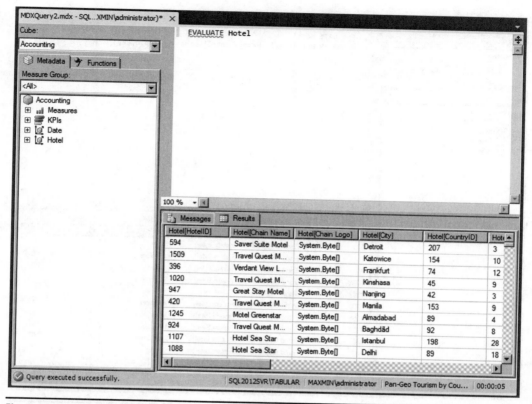

Figure 10-15 *EVALUATE Hotel query window*

9. Execute the query. Your query window should now look like Figure 10-16. You will see that the results are ordered by the Hotel Chain Name in ascending order and then by Number of Employees in descending order.

10. Modify the query to add the bold text shown here:

```
EVALUATE Hotel
ORDER BY Hotel[Chain Name], Hotel[Number of Employees] DESC
START AT "Posh Plaza"
```

11. Execute the query. Your query window now shows the table rows starting at the Posh Plaza hotel chain with all of the previous rows removed from the results.

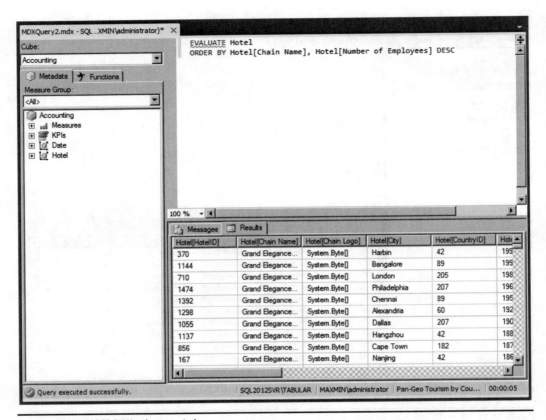

Figure 10-16 *ORDER BY Hotel query window*

12. Insert two blank lines below your existing query and enter the following:

```
EVALUATE ADDCOLUMNS( Hotel, "Total Net Income", Financial[Total Net Income],
    "Total Gross Profit", Financial[Total Gross Profit], "Parent Chain",
    Hotel[Level1])
ORDER BY [Parent Chain], [Chain Name], [Total Gross Profit] DESC
```

13. Select the text of this new query and press F5. If you scroll to the right, you will see the additional columns that we have added into the Hotel table results shown in Figure 10-17.

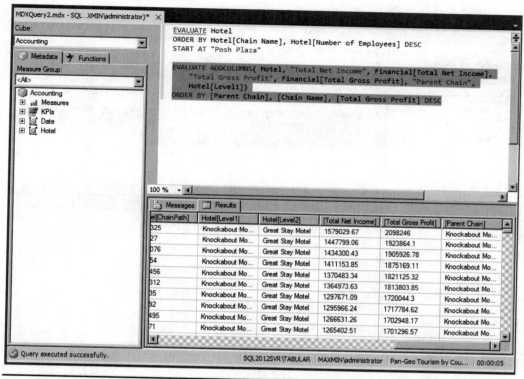

Figure 10-17 *ADDCOLUMNS Hotel query window*

14. Insert two blank lines below the second query and enter the following:

```
EVALUATE SUMMARIZE(Financial, 'Date'[Year], Hotel[Chain Name], "Total Revenue",
    FORMAT(Financial[Total Revenue], "Currency"), "Gross Profit Margin",
    FORMAT(Financial[Gross Profit Margin], "Percent"))
ORDER BY [Year] DESC, [Gross Profit Margin] DESC
```

15. Select the text of this third query and press F5. Your query window should now look like Figure 10-18. In this example you can see that we created a grouping with the SUMMARIZE() function. We have also included the select columns we wanted, ordered the results, and even included some additional formatting on the values returned.

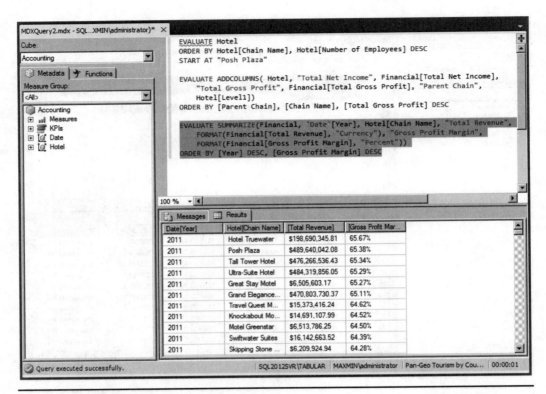

Figure 10-18 *SUMMARIZE Financial query window*

As you can see, the syntax for the DAX query is quite different from the syntax of the T-SQL and MDX query languages you may have used in the past. However, the results that can be returned are similar. With DAX we get some new features such as the START AT clause, which allows you to jump right to a row of data in our table. One way to learn more about DAX queries is to explore your Tabular BI Semantic Model with a client tool and then use SQL Server Profiler to determine the actual DAX queries that are being created behind the scenes. This technique is shown in Figure 10-19.

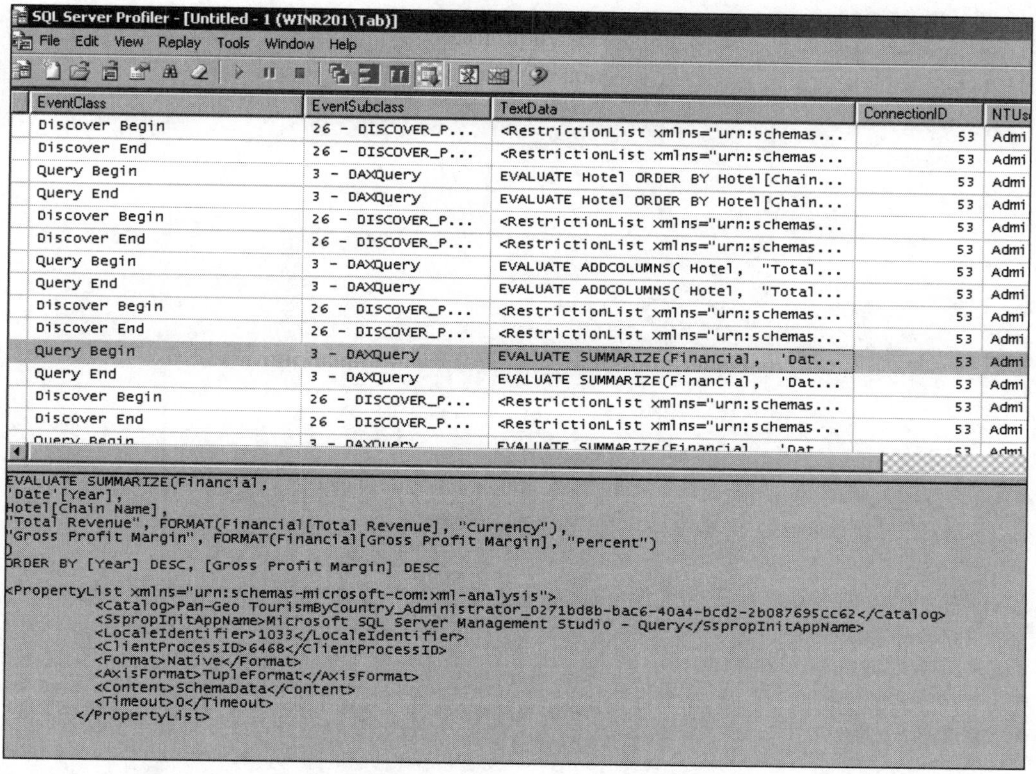

Figure 10-19 *SQL Server Profiler trace results*

Wrap-Up

You now have more exposure to the DAX language—particularly some of the different operators, functions, and query usage. This chapter by no means provides complete coverage of what is available in DAX, but it gives you sufficient familiarity to provide a good starting point. We were also able to add a number of enhancements to our model.

Now that we have built out the model, we are ready to deploy it to an environment where it can start to benefit our business users. By deploying the database, we make it available to the users so they can begin to analyze our model and gain business insight. In Chapter 11 we complete our journey and ship our model off to the users.

Chapter 11

Deploying Tabular BI Semantic Models

In This Chapter

- ▶ When to Deploy
- ▶ Deploying and Processing
- ▶ How to Deploy and Process a Tabular BI Semantic Model
- ▶ What You Have Learned in This Book

Now that you have seen the power of the Tabular BI Semantic Model, you likely are imagining how the Tabular BI Semantic Model will work for your business and how much value it will add. As you know, the Tabular BI Semantic Model can empower the people in your organization who are looking to gain insight from your data. Free of the technical roadblocks and jargon associated with the raw data sources, they can focus their efforts on truly understanding the data and quickly zeroing in on the facts they need.

Users will be able to spend less time on data and report design and more time on information delivery and decision making. In fact, in virtually no time at all, users will be presenting business intelligence for ad hoc requirements. Depending on the audience, the ultimate value of your Tabular BI Semantic Model could be huge. Perhaps you're already starting to add up the personal rewards of recognition for a job well done!

But let's stop a moment to consider this reality: Thus far, we haven't had an audience. We have been testing our model by analyzing the data in Excel against the workspace database. It looks like a good design, and that in-memory cache really performs well, but no one else can benefit from the model unless we share it. All the work we have done in Chapters 8 through 10 has been with sharing in mind. Now, it's time to learn how that sharing is accomplished.

Deploying is the term we use to refer to the act of sharing a Tabular BI Semantic Model by making it accessible to consumers. We can also use the term *publishing* to refer to the same act. Throughout this chapter, generally we refer to sharing models built using PowerPivot as *publishing* to SharePoint, and sharing models built with SQL Server Data Tools as *deploying* to an Analysis Services server.

In this chapter, we first discuss when to deploy your Tabular BI Semantic Model. Next, we look at what comprises deployment and the considerations affecting where and how you deploy the model. Then, we cover the mechanics of deploying a Tabular BI Semantic Model.

When to Deploy

As discussed in the introduction to this book, deployment is not necessarily an end to the entire model development process. You don't wait until the Tabular BI Semantic Model is flawless before you deploy it for the first time. In fact, you can't really know how well your model will function until you share it with your users and obtain their feedback. It is generally good practice to build and deploy a Tabular BI Semantic Model as part of a feedback cycle (refer to Figure I-2 in the introduction to this book). This is particularly true in cases where the consumer base is large or high profile. The risks are too high to wait until the very end of a project's funding or timeline to unveil your masterpiece.

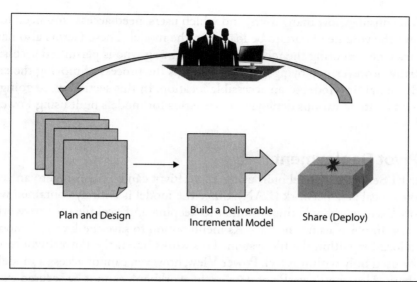

Figure 11-1   *A Tabular BI Semantic Model development sprint*

So, we advise that you develop in short phases (we'll call them "sprints"), a period of days during which you conduct daily status reviews. At the end of the sprint, deploy the model and solicit feedback. Feedback can be applied when planning the next development phase. Repeat this process, shown in Figure 11-1, until potential users give your model their stamp of approval.

At the culmination of the project, the model is deployed one final time; or it may already be deployed, with full user acceptance, as part of this cyclical process.

Deploying and Processing

Deployment almost always involves both deploying and processing the Tabular BI Semantic Model. Using any of the methods we'll cover in this chapter, you first deploy the Tabular BI Semantic Model to the location from which users will access it. Then, you may refresh the data in the model, which traditionally is called *processing* the model. Let's look first at what is involved in deploying a model.

What Is Deployment?

The deployment of a Tabular BI Semantic Model can take several forms depending on where the model originated—PowerPivot or SQL Server Data Tools—and how users will access the model. In all cases, you have choices as to where the model will reside.

You need to consider how many users, and which users, need access. You need to take into account the volume of data to be loaded in the model. These factors also have implications when securing the model and determining who is permitted access.

Essentially, however, deploying (or publishing) is the process of moving the entire Tabular BI Semantic Model to an accessible location. In this section we're going to compare and contrast various deployment scenarios for models built using PowerPivot and Analysis Services.

PowerPivot Deployment

A Tabular BI Semantic Model built using PowerPivot can be published to an accessible location on a local area network (LAN). Since the model is entirely contained within a Microsoft Excel workbook, this is similar to keeping an Excel file on a network file share. It is as simple as using the Save As menu option to save the Excel workbook to a specified location within the file system. This works fine if the PowerPivot model is going to be used only within Excel. Power View, however, cannot access a model stored on a file share. Also, the PowerPivot data in the workbook cannot be secured except by denying access to the file itself.

A PowerPivot file stored in a file share may be analyzed using PivotTables or PivotCharts in Microsoft Excel. In addition, data from this file in the file system may be imported into other Tabular BI Semantic Models.

Alternatively, a PowerPivot model may be published to a SharePoint document library, as shown in Figure 11-2. In SharePoint, the PowerPivot model is accessible to Power View users. The model still resides in an Excel workbook and can still be

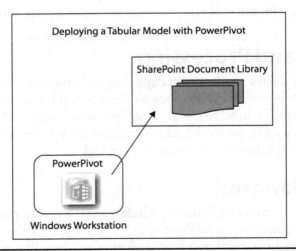

Figure 11-2   *Deploying a PowerPivot model to SharePoint*

explored using the tools within Excel. Now, however, users have the added bonus of server resources, such as memory and processors, along with more sophisticated data loading and unloading, sharing of caches, collaboration, document management, and SharePoint authentication and authorization.

Another benefit of publishing to SharePoint is the PowerPivot Gallery, a particular type of document library that has powerful features for supporting models. This will be described in more detail later in this chapter.

Analysis Services Deployment

An Analysis Services server running in tabular mode will be the host for any Tabular BI Semantic Model built using SQL Server Data Tools. The Tabular BI Semantic Model in Analysis Services, similar to one that uses PowerPivot for SharePoint, has the benefit of exploiting the resources of the server for query processing horsepower and for providing lots of RAM for in-memory data caching. In addition, Analysis Services provides capabilities for securing specific data within the model using role-based security. Finally, tables can be partitioned, resulting in improved processing and query performance over a larger volume of data. Analysis Services truly is the high-performance, scalable platform that is suitable for the needs of a larger enterprise.

You will recall that our Tabular BI Semantic Model uses an Analysis Services server to host the workspace database. This transient database allows us to see the data in the model as the model is being built. The workspace database is hosted by either an instance of Analysis Services running locally on the development workstation or an instance of Analysis Services running on a development server. When we actually deploy the model, we create a copy of it on a production Analysis Services server, as shown in Figure 11-3.

We'll discuss additional characteristics and options for an Analysis Services deployment in the upcoming "How to Deploy and Process a Tabular BI Semantic Model" section of this chapter.

What Is Processing?

As mentioned at the start of this section, *processing* is a term that describes refreshing the data in the Tabular BI Semantic Model. You can think of this data as a cache, or a copy of the data that is set aside specifically for analysis and reporting. The Tabular BI Semantic Model stores data. Potentially a lot of data. This is what makes it a wonderfully powerful tool for browsing and analyzing information.

When we build the Tabular BI Semantic Model and request data from a source, the data is loaded into each table in the model. That's an initial refresh of the cache. Every moment thereafter, the model can be considered increasingly out of date—what we consider its *latency*. Therefore, unless the model is set up to use *DirectQuery*, where data

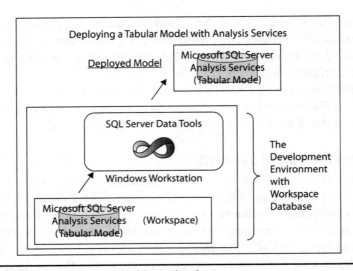

Figure 11-3 *Deploying a Tabular BI Semantic Model to Analysis Services*

isn't actually cached in the model but is retrieved directly from the data source for each request, the model must periodically refresh its cache of data from the data source.

NOTE

DirectQuery is a query and storage mode that is supported only in models built for Analysis Services using SQL Server Data Tools; it is not supported by PowerPivot. DirectQuery mode is covered in greater detail in Table 11-2, later in this chapter.

As was true in our discussion of deployment, there are a number of ways to refresh the cache depending on whether we're using a model from PowerPivot in SharePoint or a model hosted by an Analysis Services server. In the next section, we'll walk step by step through the process of both deploying and processing both types of Tabular BI Semantic Models.

How to Deploy and Process a Tabular BI Semantic Model

Let's first examine the deployment process as it relates to a Tabular BI Semantic Model that originates within PowerPivot. Then we'll turn our attention to a model built for Analysis Services. In each case we'll examine both deployment and processing; then we'll discuss the various means which are available for each type of model to be secured against unauthorized access. Finally, we'll create connections to the deployed Analysis Services Tabular Model for use with Power Pivot (and Reporting Services, if desired).

Publishing a PowerPivot Model

As previously mentioned, a PowerPivot BI Semantic Model is entirely contained within a Microsoft Excel workbook document. If you have had any experience uploading or adding a document to a SharePoint document library, you already know how to publish a PowerPivot BI Semantic Model. For those of you who haven't had any experience with this procedure, we'll step through it in the next exercise.

Learn By Doing: Publishing a PowerPivot Workbook to SharePoint

We're going to upload an Excel workbook to a document library on a SharePoint server. We could utilize any library included among the Trusted File Locations for Excel Services. Of course, Excel is recognized by SharePoint as a standard content type (of type "Document"), so the workbook will appear in SharePoint like any other Excel document.

Video 11-1

Publishing a PowerPivot Workbook to SharePoint

1. Open the SharePoint site and locate the document library where your Power View reports are saved.
2. Click the Add Document link (shown here) or select Upload Document from the Documents tab of the ribbon. (You must be on a document library page in SharePoint for the Documents tab to be present.) The Upload Document form for the library appears. ⊕ Add document
3. Click the Browse button. The Choose File to Upload dialog box appears.
4. Browse to find the file you wish to publish. We're going to deploy the model in an Excel file called PGHT Tourism PowerPivot Model.xlsx. (This was downloaded with the supporting materials for the book.)
5. Select the document and click Open to exit the Choose File to Upload dialog box.
6. Click OK to publish this document. If the document uploads successfully, you'll be presented with the upload form for the document, as shown in Figure 11-4.
7. You can place a description of the document in the Title field, if desired.
8. Click Save to finish publishing the document. Figure 11-5 shows the entry for the model in the SharePoint document library.

NOTE

Certain permissions and SharePoint site settings (such as document size restrictions) might prevent a successful document upload. If this occurs, contact your site administrator to request the necessary permissions or site settings.

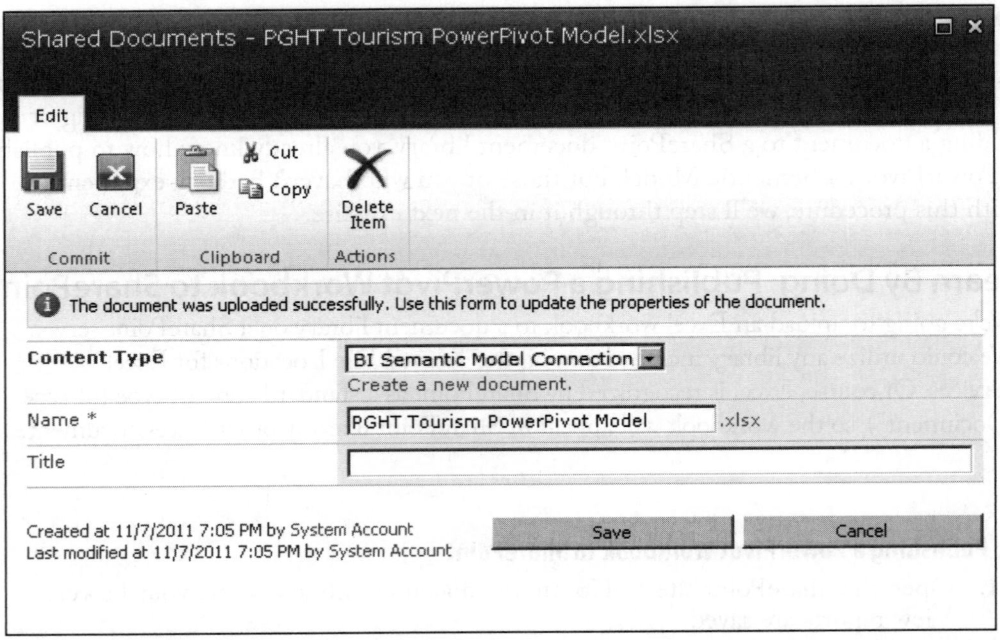

Figure 11-4 *Upload properties for PGHT Tourism PowerPivot Model.xlsx*

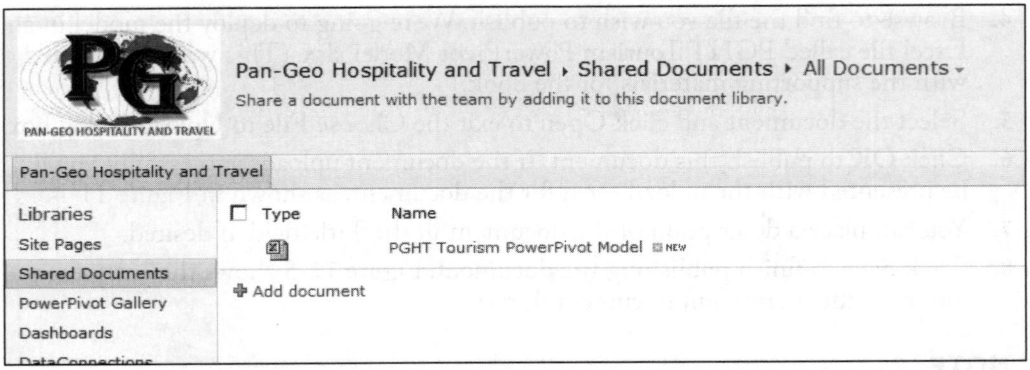

Figure 11-5 *A PowerPivot BI Semantic Model in SharePoint*

The PowerPivot BI Semantic Model published in SharePoint will not automatically provide the option of creating a Power View report using the model. Hover your mouse pointer over the entry for the document you just uploaded and click the drop-down arrow that appears. In the menu that appears, you'll see you *are* able to browse the document using Excel Services. You are also able to manage the PowerPivot data refresh (as shown here; more details are provided later in the chapter).

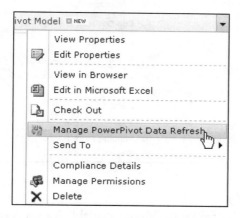

However, if you wish to analyze this model using Power View, you need to create a BI Semantic Model connection to the model using the BI Semantic Model connection file introduced in Chapter 1. Let's give this a try.

1. On the Documents tab of the ribbon, click the drop-down arrow on the New Document button.
2. Select BI Semantic Model Connection from the menu that appears.
3. In the File Name field, enter **PGHT Tourism PowerPivot Model**.
4. Enter a description in the Description field, if desired.
5. For Workbook URL or Server Name, enter the URL of the Excel document in the SharePoint document library. This will be the URL of the SharePoint server along with the name of the document library and the name of the document. It will be similar to the following:

   ```
   http://{servername}/ {documentlibraryname}/PGHT Tourism PowerPivot
   Model.xlsx
   ```

   where *{servername}* is the name of the SharePoint server and *{documentlibraryname}* is the name of the SharePoint document library.
6. Click OK to create the BI Semantic Model connection file.

If you look at the context menu for the BI Semantic Model connection file, as shown next, you will see that we now have the option to create a Power View report from the PowerPivot model.

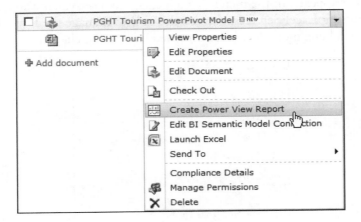

PowerPivot Gallery

Having the PowerPivot BI Semantic Model available for users to access in a SharePoint document library provides numerous advantages, as we have mentioned. This approach is most beneficial in those cases where users wish to leverage the Excel workbook in addition to the PowerPivot model contained within, and wish to work primarily within Microsoft Excel.

An alternative approach is to publish the PowerPivot model to the PowerPivot Gallery. This is the recommended approach if the goal is to make the PowerPivot model available for Power View reporting. The PowerPivot Gallery is a SharePoint document library created from a special template optimized for use with PowerPivot models.

Learn By Doing: Publishing a PowerPivot Workbook to the PowerPivot Gallery

Let's publish our PowerPivot model again, this time to the PowerPivot Gallery:

1. On the SharePoint site, click the PowerPivot Gallery link on the left.
2. Select the Documents tab of the ribbon.
3. Click Upload Document (the upper portion of this item, not the lower, drop-down arrow portion).
4. In the PowerPivot Gallery – Upload Document form that appears, click the Browse button.
5. In the Choose File to Upload dialog box that appears, browse to the location of the Excel document called PGHT Tourism PowerPivot Model.xlsx.

6. Select the document and click Open to exit the Choose File to Upload dialog box.
7. Click OK to publish this document to the PowerPivot Gallery. The PGHT Tourism PowerPivot Model document is shown in the PowerPivot Gallery in Figure 11-6.

NOTE

Initially, the PowerPivot Gallery entry for the Excel document will show a generic placeholder for each spreadsheet. Eventually, these generic placeholders will be replaced by thumbnail views of each spreadsheet in the Excel document as shown in Figure 11-6.

Features of the PowerPivot Gallery

The PowerPivot Gallery provides the following features that are not available in a standard document library:

▶ Capability to preview the content of the PivotTables or PivotCharts in document worksheets. For each workbook, the user can preview thumbnails of each worksheet within the workbook.

▶ Multiple views. A user can easily search among published models using Gallery View (the default), Theater View, or Carousel View.

▶ Convenient one-click capability to utilize the model within Microsoft Excel or Power View.

▶ Convenient access to manage the data refresh schedule.

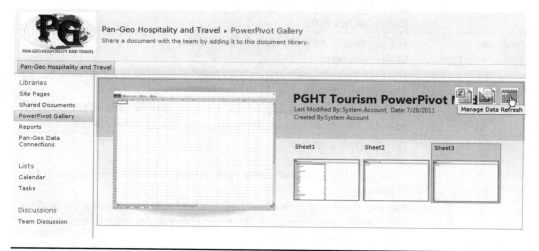

Figure 11-6   *The PowerPivot Gallery*

It still is possible to create a BI Semantic Model connection file and access the model by a document's URL in its PowerPivot Gallery location, as you would with a standard document library. Therefore, the PowerPivot Gallery provides an easy-to-browse single source for your BI Semantic Models created using PowerPivot. We recommend publishing your PowerPivot models to the PowerPivot Gallery whenever possible so you can take advantage of its enhanced features.

Securing a PowerPivot Model

Standard SharePoint authentication and authorization are utilized to govern access to the PowerPivot BI Semantic Model within an Excel workbook. The workbook is stored as standard SharePoint content and is processed by SharePoint shared services in a SharePoint server farm. Whether a user has access to the workbook and the PowerPivot data in that workbook depends on whether the user has the right to view a workbook. Once a user has rights to view the workbook, that user can see all of the data in the PowerPivot model.

Users can perform other actions against the document (configure refresh, use the PowerPivot data as a data source, create workbooks based on the model, etc.) depending on their permission level, as outlined in Table 11-1.

Permission Level	Allows These Tasks
Farm or Service Administrator	Install, enable, and configure services and applications. Use PowerPivot Management Dashboard and view administrative reports.
Full Control	Activate PowerPivot feature integration at the site collection level. Create a PowerPivot Gallery library. Create a data feed library.
Contribute	Add, edit, delete, and download PowerPivot workbooks. Configure data refresh. Create new workbooks and reports based on PowerPivot workbooks on a SharePoint site. Create data service documents in a data feed library.
Read	Access PowerPivot workbooks as an external data source, where the workbook URL is explicitly entered in a connection dialog box (for example, in Excel's Data Connection Wizard).
View Only	View PowerPivot workbooks. View data refresh history. Connect a local workbook to a PowerPivot workbook on a SharePoint site, to repurpose its data in other ways. Download a snapshot of the workbook. The snapshot is a static copy of the data, without slicers, filters, formulas, or data connections. The contents of the snapshot are similar to cell values copied from the browser window.

Table 11-1   *SharePoint Permissions for Managing a PowerPivot BI Semantic Model*

Processing the PowerPivot BI Semantic Model

Once we deploy the PowerPivot model to the SharePoint server, we must set up a process that will update the data in the model cache. Our users will not find the model very useful if the data is never refreshed. Processing a PowerPivot model to update the cache can be done either manually, or scheduled to happen automatically.

First, just as when we created the model, a user can manually open the Excel workbook, navigate to the PowerPivot ribbon and open the PowerPivot window. Select Get External Data, if it is visible. Select Refresh | Refresh All (or Refresh, for the current table only), as shown here.

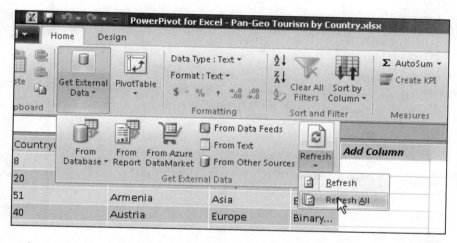

The refresh of a PowerPivot model may also be configured to happen automatically from within SharePoint. In a SharePoint document library, clicking the drop-down arrow for an Excel workbook provides a menu option for configuring the PowerPivot model's data refresh settings, as shown here.

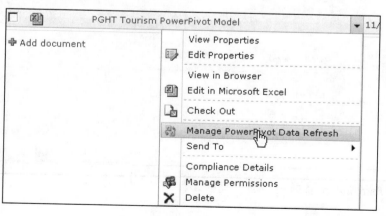

In a PowerPivot Gallery, click the Manage Data Refresh icon, which can be seen in Figure 11-6. Either method will take you to the page used to configure a PowerPivot model's data refresh (or processing) settings as shown in Figure 11-7. This includes the scheduled frequency of the data refresh, the credentials to use when accessing the source data, and the data sources that should participate in this scheduled refresh.

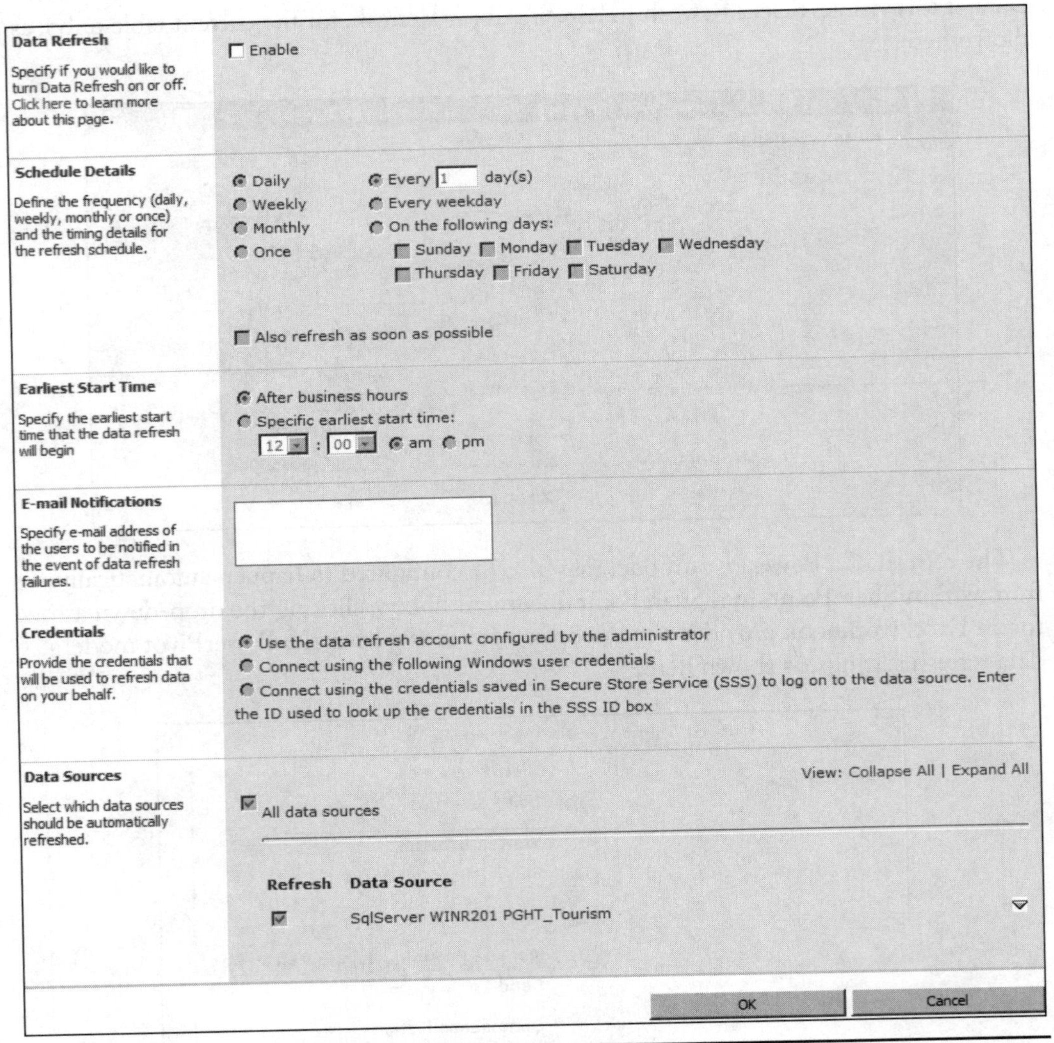

Figure 11-7 *PowerPivot Refresh Settings form*

A Windows user account is used for refreshing the model within SharePoint. The Data Refresh settings form allows SharePoint users with Contribute permissions to configure whether the refresh uses the credentials stored with the data source (defined when we first bring data into the model), a Secure Store Service ID, or another Windows account.

Deploying the Analysis Services Tabular Model

Deploying, processing, and providing access to a Tabular BI Semantic Model created in SQL Server Data Tools require a set of tasks that differ from those we looked at for the PowerPivot models. The first thing to be aware of is that a deployed Tabular BI Semantic Model does not reside in SharePoint. A BI Semantic Model connection file or a Reporting Services Data Source is configured in SharePoint to point to the Tabular BI Semantic Model. The model itself, however, resides as a database on an Analysis Services server.

Interactive Deployment from SQL Server Data Tools

Initial deployment of an Analysis Services Tabular BI Semantic Model is usually accomplished during the development cycle using SQL Server Data Tools. Let's look at the properties of the Pan-Geo Tourism by Country model project. The Property Pages dialog box for this project will appear similar to Figure 11-8.

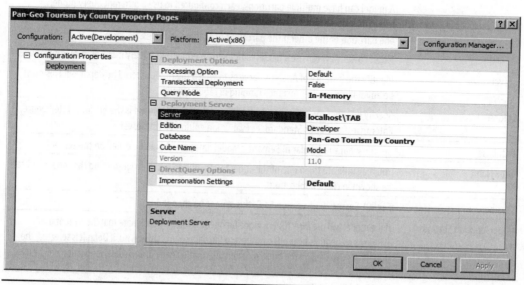

Figure 11-8   *Tabular BI Semantic Model Property Pages dialog box*

In the Property Pages dialog box, we specify where and how the model will be deployed and processed. Table 11-2 lists and describes each of the properties available in this dialog box.

Deployment Property	Description
Processing Option	Specify whether you wish to process the model upon deployment. If the Default option is selected, the Analysis Services server will determine which items need to be processed after deployment.
Transactional Deployment	Deployment consists of several commands (using the XMLA language) that must be executed on the Analysis Services server. These commands can be executed in a single transaction by setting this property to True. When executing as a single transaction, if a task fails, all tasks are rolled back. The default setting is False.
Query Mode	In-Memory mode designates that queries against the model should be satisfied from the in-memory cache. This requires processing the model to create the in-memory cache. DirectQuery mode indicates that queries should be satisfied using real-time data from the data source. Using DirectQuery does not utilize the cache, so processing is not required. The hybrid modes, DirectQuery with In-Memory and In-Memory with DirectQuery, allow client applications to use either mode while indicating what the default mode should be. For example, the default mode is DirectQuery when DirectQuery with In-Memory is chosen. If there will be client applications using MDX queries, the cache must be used, so either In-Memory or In-Memory with DirectQuery must be selected. A model can have multiple partitions, each configured to use a different query mode; however, a single query cannot use data from both the cache and the data source. It must use one partition or the other if the partitions use different modes. **Note:** Power View can use a model configured for either DirectQuery mode or In-Memory mode.
Server	Identify the instance of Analysis Services to which the model should be deployed. This must be an Analysis Services instance running in tabular mode.
Edition	Specify whether the server to which the model will be deployed is the Business Intelligence, Enterprise, Developer, Standard, or Evaluation edition of SQL Server.
Database	Specify what the Tabular BI Semantic Model database should be called on the server.
Cube Name	You may indicate the name of the Cube; this is utilized when programming the model and can be shown in client applications.
Version	For SQL Server 2012, version 11.0, this cannot be changed.
Impersonation Settings	If the model will use DirectQuery mode for queries, you may designate that the current user's Windows credentials be used to connect to the data source. Otherwise, if Default is selected, the credentials specified on the Impersonation Information page of each data connection will be used.

Table 11-2   *Tabular BI Semantic Model Project Properties*

Learn By Doing: Deploying from SQL Server Data Tools

Let's deploy our model using SQL Server Data Tools:

Video 11-2 **Deploying from SQL Server Data Tools**

1. Start SQL Server Data Tools.
2. Open the Pan-Geo Tourism by Country project.
3. Select Project | Pan-Geo Tourism By Country Properties from the main menu. The Pan-Geo Tourism by Country Property Pages dialog box appears.
4. In the Server field, enter the name of the tabular instance of Analysis Services that will host the deployed model.

NOTE

Do not use a production Analysis Services server to complete these training exercises.

5. Enter **Pan-Geo Tourism by Country** in the Database field.
6. Click OK to exit the Pan-Geo Tourism by Country Property Pages dialog box.
7. Right-click the project name in the Solution Explorer window and select Deploy from the context menu.
8. Provide the appropriate credentials, if prompted.
9. The definition (or metadata) that defines the model structure is deployed to the Analysis Services server and each of the tables is processed. The progress is shown in the Deploy dialog box. When the processing is complete, as shown in Figure 11-9, click Close.

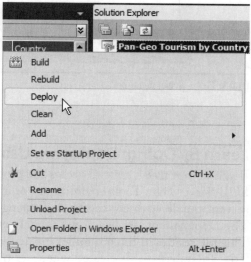

If the Processing Option project property is set to Do Not Process, only the Deploy Metadata line will appear in the Deploy dialog box.

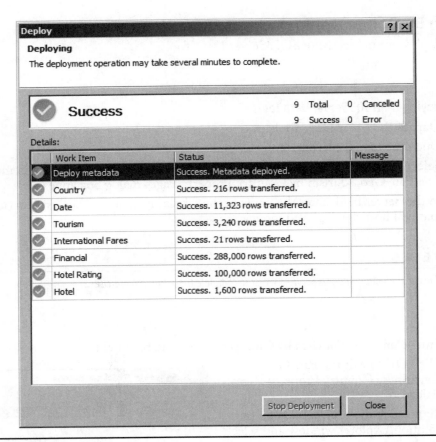

Figure 11-9   *Deploy dialog box*

Learn By Doing: Deploying Using the Deployment Wizard

If you do not have rights to access the production Analysis Services server from your SQL Server Data Tools environment or if the model is to be deployed to multiple servers, the deployment can be done using the Analysis Services Deployment Wizard. The Deployment Wizard uses a model definition file with the extension .asdatabase. This file resides in the bin folder inside the folder containing the project definition files. The .asdatabase file is created whenever the model is built or deployed.

Let's deploy our model again through the Deployment Wizard:

Video 11-3 **Deployment Using the Deployment Wizard**

1. Open the Pan-Geo Tourism by Country project in SQL Server Data Tools and select Build | Build *{projectname}* from the main menu. This will ensure you have an up-to-date .asdatabase file to be deployed.
2. Select Start | All Programs | Microsoft SQL Server 2012 | Analysis Services | Deployment Wizard.
3. Click Next on the welcome page.
4. On the Specify Source Analysis Services Database page, click the browse button (ellipsis) to display the Open dialog.
5. Navigate to the .asdatabase file in the bin folder for the project. (This is located in the folder containing the source files for the project.)
6. Double-click the .asdatabase file to select it. This will return you to the Specify Source Analysis Services Database page of the wizard, as shown in Figure 11-10.

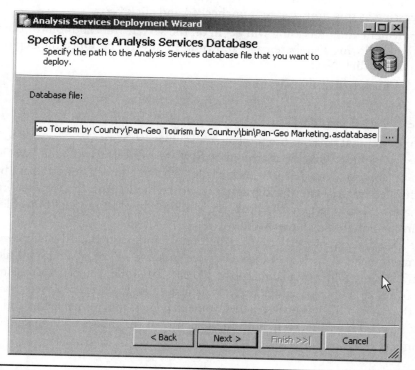

Figure 11-10   *The Specify Source Analysis Services Database page of the Wizard*

7. Click Next.
8. On the Installation Target page of the wizard, the server and database names will default to the values specified in the project properties. You may change them if desired, and then click Next.
9. On the Specify Options for Partitions and Roles page of the wizard, you can choose whether to update partitions and security roles on the server. By default, new partition and role information is deployed; however, if a role already exists in your project, its membership won't be changed. Click Next.
10. The Specify Configuration Properties page of the wizard enables you to override connection and other configuration settings, if desired. Click Next.
11. On the Select Processing Options page of the wizard, choose a processing method, and whether to process in a single transaction. Again, these settings default from project properties. Click Next.
12. Finally, on the Confirm Deployment page of the wizard, indicate whether to create a deployment script from your Deployment Wizard choices, for later use. This script, using XMLA commands, can be executed from within SQL Server Management Studio, Integration Services, and other XMLA clients. A script can be generated on a development computer and executed on a production server. If you select Create Deployment Script, the wizard will not begin deployment and processing at this time. Leave it unchecked and click Next.
13. Deployment and processing will begin on the server. You can monitor the progress on the Deploying Database page, shown in Figure 11-11. Once the deployment completes, click Next.
14. Click Finish to exit the wizard.

Restore from a Backup

Another method that you can use to deploy a Tabular BI Semantic Model is to restore a database backup file. This file is created by SQL Server Data Tools and has an extension of .abf (Analysis Services backup file). The creation of this database backup file is controlled by the Data Backup property of the model. You can view and modify the setting for this property in the Property window when the model (.bim) file is selected in the Solution Explorer window.

Set the Data Backup property to "Back up to disk" and select Build | Build {projectname} from the main menu. A backup of the workspace database will be created. This file is created in the same folder that contains the project's BIM file. You can also create an ABF file by backing up an Analysis Services database that has been deployed to a server.

Once the backup file has been created, you can copy it to another server and restore it on that server. This will restore both the structure of the model and the data cached for that model.

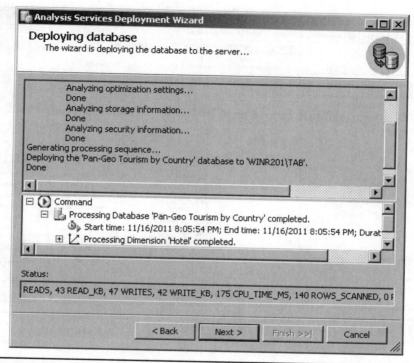

Figure 11-11 *The Deploying Database page of the wizard*

Processing the Model

When a model is deployed from SQL Server Data Tools, it is automatically processed as a part of that operation, unless the Processing Option property for the project is set to Do Not Process. Of course, to keep the data in the model current, we need to process the model more often than just when it is deployed. We need to create a scheduled task that will process the model. The best way to do this is to first create a SQL Server Integration Services (SSIS) package to process the model, and then create a SQL Agent job to execute that SSIS package on a regular basis.

SSIS provides a control flow task called Analysis Services Processing Task. This task is configured to connect to a database on a tabular instance of Analysis Services. It is then set to process some or all of the tables in that database. This task is shown in Figure 11-12.

For each table you'll be processing in the model, you may choose from several processing options, several of which are shown in the following illustration. The options listed in Table 11-3 are relevant to Tabular BI Semantic Models in Analysis Services.

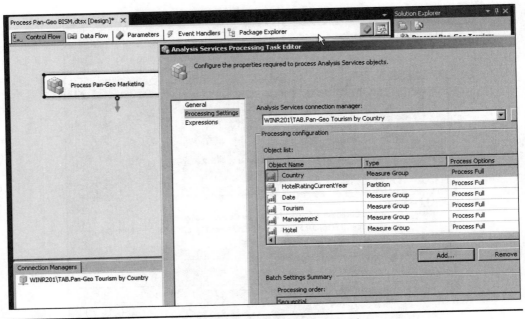

Figure 11-12 *Using SQL Server Integration Services to process the BI Semantic Model*

Before you review the specific options, though, you should be aware of which options are suitable for the various types of objects in the model (note that Process Clear, Process Default, and Process Full are suitable for all four types):

- ▶ **For a database**   Process Clear, Process Default, Process Recalc, and Process Full
- ▶ **For a Model (Cube)**   Process Clear, Process Default, Process Full, Process Data, Process Add, and Process Structure.
- ▶ **For a table**   Process Clear, Process Default, Process Defrag Process Full, Process Data, and Process Add
- ▶ **For a partition**   Process Clear, Process Default, Process Full, and Process Data

Option	Description
Process Full	If any data already exists in the table, it is dropped and the table is processed. Process Full is needed whenever a structure change (such as the addition of columns, or a change to a hierarchy) occurs in the model.
Process Data	Processes only the data in a table without rebuilding indexes. Like Process Full, it also drops existing data.
Process Clear	Removes data from the table.
Process Add	Adds new data to the table based on criteria specified for the table or its partitions.
Process Default	Based on the existing processing state of the table, does whatever process is required to bring the table to a fully processed state.
Process Structure	Updates the model structure.
Process Defrag	Updates the model's internal data about each partition.
Process Recalc	Updates the calculated columns, rebuilds hierarchies and relationships.

Table 11-3   *Analysis Services Processing Modes*

NOTE

The Process Index option may be displayed in the user interface, but is not appropriate for a Tabular BI Semantic Model.

Once you have deployed your model and have a schedule in place to process it periodically, your users can enjoy up-to-date, fast access to their data. As you have seen throughout this book, the Tabular BI Semantic Model will likely prove crucial to making timely decisions that impact business.

Creating Connections to the Model

Once our model is in place on the Analysis Services server, we need to create a connection to the model in order for it to be used to create Power View reports. We have two options for this connection: the BI Semantic Model connection and the Reporting Services data source.

Learn By Doing: Creating a BI Semantic Model Connection

First, we'll create a BI Semantic Model Connection:

Video 11-4

Creating a BI Semantic Model Connection

1. Open Internet Explorer and navigate to the home page of the SharePoint site.
2. Navigate to the document library where your Power View reports will be saved.

3. Select the Documents tab of the ribbon.

4. In the ribbon, click the New Document drop-down arrow. The New Document drop-down menu appears.

5. Select BI Semantic Model Connection. The New BI Semantic Model Connection page appears.

6. Enter **PGHT Tourism** for File Name.

7. For Workbook URL or Server Name, enter the name of the tabular instance of Analysis Services where the Pan-Geo Tourism by Country model has been deployed.

8. Enter **Pan-Geo Tourism by Country** for Database.

9. Click OK.

Learn By Doing: Creating a Report Data Source

Next, we'll create a Report Data Source:

Video 11-5

Creating a Report Data Source

1. In the document library where your Power View reports will be saved, select the Documents tab of the ribbon.

2. Click the New Document drop-down arrow. The New Document drop-down menu appears.

3. Select Report Data Source. The Data Source Properties page appears.

4. Enter **PGHT Tourism RS** for Name.

5. Select Microsoft BI Semantic Model for Power View from the Data Source Type drop-down list.

6. Enter the following for Connection string:

```
Data Source={servername};Initial Catalog="Pan-Geo Tourism by
Country"
```

where {*servername*} is the name of the tabular instance of Analysis Services on which the Pan-Geo Tourism by Country model has been deployed.

7. Specify credentials appropriate for making this connection.

8. Click Test Connection to ensure the Report Data Source has been created correctly.

9. Click OK.

What You Have Learned in This Book

This book has given you a full set of tools for taking the greatest possible advantage of a revolutionary new report authoring tool introduced with Microsoft SQL Server 2012—Power View. Beyond Power View, the Tabular BI Semantic Model provides a means to capture your organization's data and metadata in a format easily explored by business users. The Tabular BI Semantic Model becomes an empowering view of your organization's data, facilitating rapid and high-impact report authoring using Power View.

Part I: Using Power View

In Part I of the book, you became familiar with Power View and discovered what a powerful tool it is for leveraging a Tabular BI Semantic Model and quickly discovering business intelligence.

In Chapter 1, you launched Power View, got acquainted with the screen, and became familiar with the world through the eyes of a Power View report author.

Chapter 2 gave you your first taste of report development within Power View, creating your first visualizations, customizing the look of your report, adding totals, and understanding relationships between columns in a Tabular BI Semantic Model.

Chapter 3 built upon your experience in Chapter 2, giving you a mastery of more powerful features for communicating the truths that are found in the model.

Adding sophisticated charting to your repertoire, Chapter 4 introduced the graphical visualizations in Power View that make important business intelligence easier to interpret at a glance.

In Chapter 5, you increased your knowledge of chart types and other visualization techniques. You dug down to the deeper layers of feature integration within Power View, including synchronized Slicers, Banding, the Play Axis, and other powerful tools.

Finally, in Chapter 6 you discovered the process of sharing reports in order to put business intelligence to work within an organization.

Part II: Creating a BI Semantic Model (BISM)

Part II offered a comprehensive set of topics, examples, and exercises that enabled you to take complete advantage of the underlying data structure required by Power View—the Tabular BI Semantic Model. This model offers numerous features foreshadowed by PowerPivot that are now available within Analysis Services. It provides an enterprise-ready means for working with large, in-memory sets of data.

Chapter 7 introduced you to elements of the computing environment that are needed to support construction of the Tabular BI Semantic Model.

Chapter 8 provided Tabular BI Semantic Model development basics, giving you the information needed to begin molding your organization's data into the tabular shape required by the Power View report authoring tool.

Chapter 9 added layers of improved usability to the BI Semantic Model, extending well beyond what was provided by the source data so that the model supports critical decision making.

Chapter 10 expanded the skill set of the model developer with Data Analysis Expressions (DAX), which enables you to extend the model beyond simple data elements to provide sophisticated calculations, enhanced infrastructure, and powerful composite data elements.

This chapter, Chapter 11, provided techniques and practices for sharing the Tabular BI Semantic Model with small, medium, and large groups throughout an organization. By deploying and processing the Tabular BI Semantic Model, you provide the raw material for those who are building reports using Power View.

Now that report authors in your organization have Power View for extremely fast, powerful, and easy ad hoc report construction, and the smart, well-designed data model you have built to support their efforts, they have more business intelligence leverage than ever before!

We wish you a great journey as you continue to explore the newfound capabilities of both Power View and the Tabular BI Semantic Model. In the words posted above the door of the Pan-Geo Hospitality and Travel IT department, "Bon voyage!"

Part III

Appendixes

Appendixes

Appendix A

Installing and Configuring the Sample Data

In This Chapter

▶ **Restoring the Databases**
▶ **Additional Data Setup**
▶ **Ready to Begin**

ppendix A and Appendix B guide you through the process of setting up an
environment for completing the Learn By Doing exercises in this book. If
you have a development or test installation with the necessary components
installed and configured, you can use the steps in Appendix A to complete this process.
The necessary components are

- ▶ SQL Server 2012 relational database engine
- ▶ Tabular instance of SQL Server 2012 Analysis Services
- ▶ SharePoint 2010 Enterprise Edition hosting the following:
  - ▶ An instance of SQL Server Reporting Services in SharePoint Integrated mode
  - ▶ SQL Server PowerPivot for SharePoint
- ▶ Microsoft Excel 2010 with the Microsoft SQL Server 2012 PowerPivot for Microsoft Excel 2010 Add-In
- ▶ SQL Server Management Studio
- ▶ SQL Server Data Tools
- ▶ Microsoft Silverlight 5

If you do not have this type of environment available, you can use the steps in
Appendix B to create a virtual environment with limited-time, evaluation versions of
the software.

CAUTION

Do not use a production server to host the materials for the Learn By Doing exercises in this book.

If you have an environment that fits the preceding list of requirements, you simply
need to restore the sample data and sample Tabular BI Semantic Model, and create the
necessary connections. This appendix walks you through this process.

Restoring the Databases

We have provided two database backups with this book. The first is a backup of
the SQL Server relational database containing all of the sample data for Pan-Geo
Hospitality and Travel (PGHT). The second is a backup of a SQL Server Analysis
Services Tabular database that contains the Tabular BI Semantic Model. This second
backup is identical to the Tabular database and Tabular BI Semantic Model that is
created through the Learn By Doing exercises in Part II of this book.

If you are interested in learning how to create models in addition to learning how to use Power View, you can build your own version of the model by first completing the exercises in Part II of the book. Then, you can use the model you created to complete the exercises in Part I. If you are not planning on completing all of the Learn By Doing exercises in Part II of the book, you can simply restore the databases and get started with Part I. In either case, you need to restore the relational database.

| Video A-1 | **Restoring the Database Backups** |

Step 1: Restoring the SQL Relational Database Backup

This section covers the steps required to create and restore the PGHT database in your environment. If you do not have an environment set up, refer to Appendix B, which discusses the software that is required and leads you through the steps to create your very own virtual learning environment.

NOTE

The database backups are located on the DVD accompanying this book. You cannot restore the backups directly from the DVD; instead, you must first copy the backup files to the hard drive. The following instructions assume that the database backups and their accompanying SQL and XMLA script files have been placed in a new folder called PGHTSetup created at the root of the C: drive (C:\PGHTSetup).

Learn By Doing: Creating and Restoring the Relational Database

Complete the following:

1. Click Start | Microsoft SQL Server 2012 | SQL Server Management Studio.
2. From the Server type drop-down list, select Database Engine.
3. Enter the name of the SQL Server 2012 relational server instance that will host this database, and click Connect.
4. Click the Open File button (the folder icon) in the toolbar or select File | Open | File from the menu.
5. Browse to the C:\PGHTSetup folder.
6. Select the "Create and Restore PGHT Database" file and click Open.
7. Click the Execute button in the toolbar (or press the F5 key). If the Execute button is not available in the toolbar, select View | Toolbars | SQL Editor.
8. When the execution is complete, close SQL Server Management Studio.

Step 2: Restoring the Tabular SSAS Database Backup

In order to work on the Learn By Doing exercises in Part I of the book, you need to have the Tabular Analysis Services database in place. This Analysis Services database contains the Tabular BI Semantic Model. This section covers the steps required to create and restore the Pan-Geo Tourism by Country database in your environment. It is not necessary to restore the Tabular SSAS Database if you plan to create and deploy the model using Part II of this book prior to completing the Learn By Doing exercises in Part I. If you do not have an environment set up, refer to Appendix B, which discusses the software that is required and leads you through the steps to create your very own virtual learning environment.

Learn By Doing: Creating and Restoring the Tabular Database

Complete the following:

1. Click Start | Microsoft SQL Server 2012 | SQL Server Management Studio.
2. From the Server type drop-down list, select Analysis Services.
3. Enter the name of the Tabular instance of SQL Server 2012 Analysis Services that will host this database, and click Connect.
4. Click the Open File button (the folder icon) in the toolbar or select File | Open | File from the menu.
5. Browse to the C:\PGHTSetup folder.
6. Select the "Restore Pan-Geo Tourism by Country Tabular Database" file and click Open.
7. Click the Execute button in the toolbar (or press the F5 key). If the Execute button is not available in the toolbar, select View | Toolbars | SQL Editor.
8. When the execution is complete, close SQL Server Management Studio.

Additional Data Setup

There are a few more items that you need to set up if you are going to get started with Part I. The necessary steps for these items are covered as part of Learn By Doing exercises in Part II of this book.

PowerPivot File

Chapter 1 refers to an Excel file called "PGHT Tourism PowerPivot Model.xlsx" that contains a PowerPivot model. To upload this file to the SharePoint site, complete the Learn By Doing exercise in Chapter 11 entitled:

▶ Learn By Doing: Publishing a PowerPivot Workbook to the PowerPivot Gallery

You can also refer to the final third of the accompanying video, Video 11-1: Publishing a PowerPivot Workbook to SharePoint.

Connections

In addition, you need to create two connection files in a SharePoint document library. One is a BI Semantic Model connection file and the other is a Reporting Services data source file. To create these two files, complete the final two Learn By Doing exercises in Chapter 11:

- ▶ Learn By Doing: Creating a BI Semantic Model Connection
- ▶ Learn By Doing: Creating a Report Data Source

You can also refer to the accompanying videos for the exercises: Video 11-4: Creating a BI Semantic Model Connection, and Video 11-5: Creating a Report Data Source.

Ready to Begin

Your learning environment is now complete and you are ready to work through the Learn By Doing exercises in this book.

Appendix B

Creating a Virtual Learning Environment

In This Chapter

- ► **Required Software**
- ► **Configuring the Environment**
- ► **Additional References**
- ► **Installing the Sample Data and Connections**

I n this appendix, we cover the process of creating a virtual learning environment. We go over the steps to install and configure the software that is needed to complete the Learn By Doing exercises in this book. To complete this process, you will:

▶ Create a virtual machine

▶ Install a trial or licensed version of Windows Server 2008 R2

▶ Configure Windows Server 2008 R2 as a domain controller

▶ Install and configure trial versions of:

  ▶ SQL Server 2012

  ▶ SharePoint 2010

  ▶ Office 2010

  ▶ various add-ins

You have several options when choosing the virtual machine software to host this learning environment. Any of the following products can be used:

▶ Microsoft Hyper-V

▶ Oracle VM VirtualBox

▶ VMware Workstation

Whichever virtual machine software you choose, be aware it must support a 64-bit operating system. Microsoft SharePoint Server 2010 requires that you use a 64-bit version of Windows. The virtual machine software must also support the mounting of an ISO image. (If your virtual machine software does not provide this feature, you may be able to use a software product such as Virtual CloneDrive, www.slysoft.com/en/virtual-clonedrive.html.)

Use the virtual environment with which you are comfortable to create a virtual machine. Then, install a version of Windows Server 2008 R2—either the limited-time trial version or a licensed version, if you have one available. (You can use a different 64-bit version of the Windows operating system to host the learning environment software; however, the operating system configuration steps in this appendix are specific to Windows Server 2008 R2.) The steps in this appendix begin with the configuration of the operating system. They assume you have already built the virtual machine and installed the operating system. If you have chosen Hyper-V and need help building the virtual machine, refer to Table B-2 in the "Additional References" section at the end of this appendix for an article on how to build it. Table B-2 also has links to other resources that you may find helpful during the following process.

Software	Download Link
Windows Server 2008 R2 Evaluation	www.microsoft.com/download/en/details.aspx?id=19994
Microsoft SharePoint Server 2010 Evaluation (Enterprise Client Access License features version)	http://technet.microsoft.com/en-us/evalcenter/ee388573
SP1 for Microsoft SharePoint Server 2010	Foundation: www.microsoft.com/download/en/details.aspx?id=26640 Server: www.microsoft.com/download/en/details.aspx?id=26623
Microsoft SQL Server 2012 Evaluation	www.microsoft.com/download/en/details.aspx?id=29066
Microsoft Office Professional Plus 2010 Evaluation (64-bit)	http://technet.microsoft.com/en-us/evalcenter/ee390818
Visual Studio 2010 Tools for Office Runtime (64-bit)	www.microsoft.com/download/en/details.aspx?id=20479
Microsoft SQL Server 2012 PowerPivot for Microsoft Excel 2010 (64-bit)	www.microsoft.com/download/en/details.aspx?id=29074
Silverlight 5 End-User Runtime for Windows	32-bit: http://go.microsoft.com/fwlink/?LinkId=229320 64-bit: http://go.microsoft.com/fwlink/?LinkId=229321

Table B-1   *Required Software*

Required Software

Table B-1 lists the software used to create the virtual learning environment and provides links to download evaluation versions of each product. The following steps utilize evaluation versions of the software.

The space required for all of the downloads will be approximately 9GB and the virtual hard drive space needed will be approximately 30GB. (We suggest you use an 80GB dynamic virtual hard drive.)

Download (or otherwise obtain) all the required software. The following instructions assume the downloaded software has been placed in a new folder called PGHTSetup at the root of the C: drive (C:\PGHTSetup). This folder will be referenced in the video as well as in the Learn By Doing exercises.

Configuring the Environment

Now that you have the software downloaded and available, we will go over the steps for setting up the server.

Step 1: Setting Up the Server

The steps in this appendix assume you have already set up the virtual hard drive and have installed the base operating system. The steps provided here and in the accompanying video use the Windows Server 2008 R2 Standard Edition 180-day evaluation download. This download includes Service Pack 1 (SP1).

Learn By Doing: Creating a Domain Controller

To configure the server, start up your virtual server and complete the following steps:

Video B-1

Creating a Virtual Learning Environment: Windows Server, SharePoint

1. Log on to your virtual server with an account that has local administration rights.
2. Select Start | Administrative Tools | Server Manager to open Server Manager.
3. Select Roles in the left pane.
4. In the Roles pane on the right, click Add Roles. This launches the Add Roles Wizard and displays the Before You Begin page of the wizard.
5. On the Before You Begin page of the wizard, click Next.
6. On the Select Server Roles page, select Active Directory Domain Services.
7. Click Add Required Features when prompted.
8. Click Next.
9. On the Active Directory Domain Services page, click Next.
10. On the Confirm Installation Selections page, click Install.
11. When the install is complete, click the hyperlink that says "Close this wizard and launch the Active Directory Domain Services Installation Wizard (dcpromo.exe)."
12. Click Next in the Active Directory Domain Services Installation Wizard.
13. On the Operating System Compatibility page, click Next.
14. On the Choose a Deployment Configuration page, select the Create a new domain in a new forest radio button and click Next.
15. On the Name the Forest Root Domain page, enter **corp.com** for the fully qualified domain name and click Next.
16. On the Set Forest Functional Level page, select Windows Server 2008 R2 from the drop-down list and click Next. This may take a few minutes to complete.
17. On the Additional Domain Controller Options page, uncheck the box for DNS Server and click Next. Again, this may take a few minutes to complete.

18. When prompted, click Yes to continue.
19. On the Location for Database, Log Files, and SYSVOL page, leave the default locations and click Next.
20. Enter a password for Directory Services restore mode, using strong name requirements—for example, **Pass@word1**.
21. Confirm the password and click Next.
22. Click Next on the Summary page.
23. Check the Reboot on completion check box, and then wait for the domain controller setup to complete.
24. After the reboot, log in, and then choose Start | Administrative Tools | Active Directory Users and Computers.
25. Expand corp.com in the left pane and click the Users folder.
26. Double-click Administrator in the right pane.
27. In the Properties dialog box, click the Account tab.
28. In the Account Options section, check the Password Never Expires check box.
29. Click Apply.
30. Click OK.
31. Open Server Manager as we did in step 2.
32. Select Server Manager in the left pane.
33. In the right pane, under Security Information, click the hyperlink for Configure IE ESC.
34. In the dialog box that opens, select both the Off radio buttons and click OK.
35. Select Features in the left pane of Server Manager and click Add Features in the right pane.
36. In the Add Features Wizard that opens, check the Desktop Experience check box.
37. Click the Add Required Features button when prompted.
38. Click Next.
39. Click Install.
40. Click Close.
41. Click Yes to restart the server.
42. After the reboot, log in and click Close on the Install Results page after the configuration completes.
43. Close Server Manager.

Step 2: Installing SharePoint 2010

Now we move on to actually installing software we will be using on the new Windows server. We will begin with Microsoft SharePoint Server 2010 Evaluation, which has a 180-day evaluation period. The version that we downloaded is the Enterprise Client Access License features version.

Learn By Doing: Installing SharePoint 2010 and SP1

1. Open Windows Explorer and navigate to the PGHTSetup folder where you placed the install software.
2. Double-click the SharePointServer executable. The installation software will take a minute or so to open.
3. Click the Install software prerequisites link to open the Microsoft SharePoint 2010 Products Preparation Tool. (An Internet connection is required.)

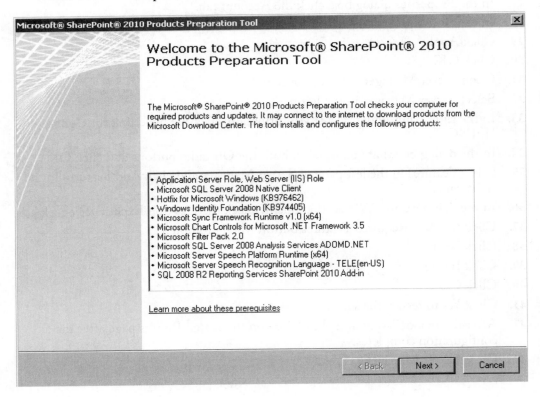

4. Click Next.
5. Check the box to accept the software license terms, and click Next.

6. The installation of the software prerequisites will take several minutes. Click Finish when the Installation Complete page appears.

7. Click the Install SharePoint Server link.

8. Enter the SharePoint Server evaluation product key and click Continue. You should receive a SharePoint Server evaluation product key as part of requesting and downloading the evaluation software.

9. Check the box to accept the software license terms, and click Continue.

10. Click Install Now. The installation process will take several minutes.

11. Uncheck the Run the SharePoint Products Configuration Wizard now check box and click Close.

12. Click the Exit link to close the SharePoint Server 2010 install home page.

13. Return to the PGHTSetup folder.

14. Double-click the sharepointfoundation2010sp1-kb2460058-x64-fullfile-en-us executable (your version name may vary based on the region code—"en-us").

15. Check the box to accept the software license terms, and click Continue.

16. When the installation is complete, click OK.

17. Return to the PGHTSetup folder.

18. Double-click the officeserver2010sp1-kb2460045-x64-fullfile-en-us executable (your version name may vary based on the region code—"en-us").

19. Check the box to accept the software license terms and click Continue.

20. When the installation is complete, click OK.

Step 3: Installing SQL Server 2012, Round 1

Now that we have SharePoint installed, we move on to the database. We will be installing the Evaluation edition of the product, which has a 180-day evaluation period. It is not possible to include all of the required components of SQL Server 2012 in all of their required configurations in a single installation. Instead, we must do this in three rounds.

Learn By Doing: Installing SQL Server—Database, SSAS Tabular, SSMS, SSDT

Video B-2

Creating a Virtual Learning Environment: SQL Server Database, PowerPivot

1. Mount the ISO image you downloaded for SQL Server.

2. Run the setup executable from the mounted image.

3. Click the Installation link on the left side of the SQL Server Installation Center page.

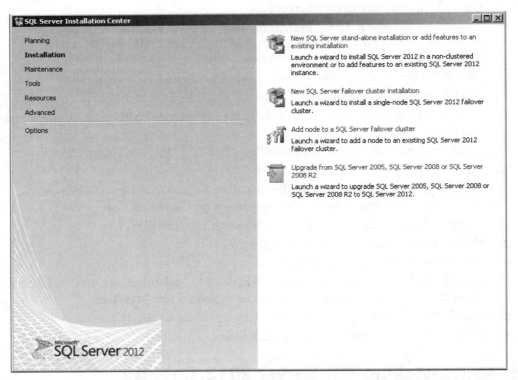

4. Click the "New SQL Server stand-alone installation or add features to an existing installation" link.

5. On the Setup Support Rules page, click Show Details to confirm all items passed. Review the information for any items that did not pass. After reviewing, click OK.

6. On the Product Key page, click Next. (A product key is not necessary for the Evaluation edition.)

7. Check the box to accept the software license terms, and click Next.

8. A second version of the Setup Support Rules page is displayed. Again review the information for any items that did not pass. It is not a problem to have a yellow triangle with an exclamation point next to the Computer domain controller and Windows Firewall items. After reviewing, click Next.

9. On the Setup Role page, make sure SQL Server Feature Installation is selected and click Next.

10. On the Feature Selection page, check the boxes for the following features (as shown below the list):

    ▶ Database Engine Services

    ▶ Analysis Services

    ▶ SQL Server Data Tools

    ▶ Client Tools Connectivity

    ▶ Client Tools Backwards Compatibility

    ▶ Client Tools SDK

    ▶ Management Tools – Basic (also make sure Management Tools – Complete is checked)

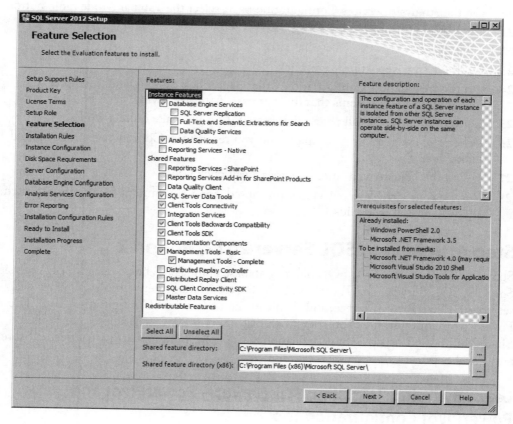

11. Click Next.

12. On the Installation Rules page, click Show Details. Review the information for any items that did not pass. After reviewing, click Next.

13. On the Instance Configuration page, make sure the Default instance radio button is selected and click Next.

14. On the Disk Space Requirements page, click Next.

15. We will run the SQL Server Analysis Services service with the Administrator login. This is the reason earlier in this process we set the password for this account to never expire. On the Server Configuration page, enter **corp\Administrator** for the Account Name next to SQL Server Analysis Services.

16. Enter the password for the Administrator login in the Password column.

17. Click Next.

18. On the Database Engine Configuration page, leave the Authentication Mode set to Windows authentication mode and click Add Current User.

19. Click Next.

20. On the Analysis Services Configuration page, select the Tabular Mode radio button.

21. Click Add Current User.

22. Click Next.

23. On the Error Reporting page, click Next.

24. On the Installation Configuration Rules page, click Show Details. Review the information for any items that did not pass. After reviewing, click Next.

25. On the Ready to Install page, click Install. This will take quite a while.

26. When the installation is complete and you receive the Computer restart required dialog box, click OK.

27. When the "Please wait" message goes away, click Close.

28. Restart your virtual server. When prompted, enter a comment for the restart, such as "SQL install" and click OK.

Step 4: Installing SQL Server 2012, Round 2

So far, we have installed the SQL Server database engine, a Tabular instance of Analysis Services, SQL Server Data Tools, and SQL Server Management Studio. Now we will set up the PowerPivot instance, and then run the PowerPivot Configuration Tool. The PowerPivot Configuration Tool, new with SQL Server 2012, will help us configure SharePoint by setting up a web application, a site collection, PowerPivot, a Secure Store, and Excel Services.

Learn By Doing: Installing SQL Server—PowerPivot and PowerPivot Configuration Tool

1. Open Windows Explorer and navigate to CD/DVD drive containing the mounted ISO image.

2. Double-click the setup application.

3. Click the Installation link on the left side of the SQL Server Installation Center page.

4. Click the "New SQL Server stand-alone installation or add features to an existing installation" link.

5. On the Setup Support Rules page, click OK.

6. On the Product Updates page, click Next.

7. A second version of the Setup Support Rules page is displayed. Again review the information for any items that did not pass. It is not a problem to have a yellow triangle with an exclamation point next to the Computer domain controller and Windows Firewall items. After reviewing, click Next.

8. On the Installation Type page, select the option to Perform a new installation of SQL Server 2012 and click Next.

9. On the Product Key page, click Next.

10. On the License Terms page, check the box to accept the software license terms, and click Next.

11. On the Setup Role page, select the SQL Server PowerPivot for SharePoint radio button.

12. Uncheck the box for "Add SQL Server Database Relational Engine Services to this installation."

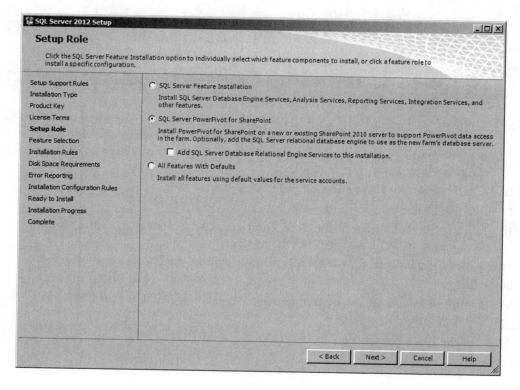

13. Click Next.

14. On the Feature Selection page, click Next.

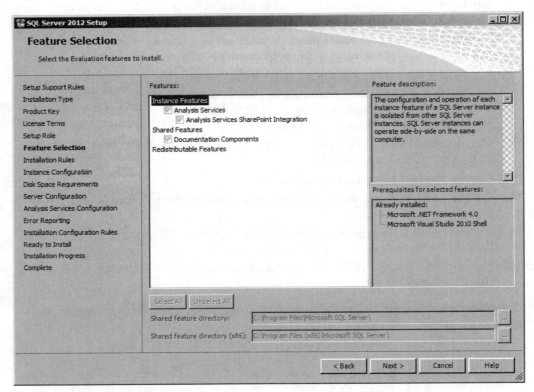

15. On the Installation Rules page, click Show Details. Review the information for any items that did not pass. It is not a problem to have a yellow triangle with an exclamation point next to the Recommendation for installing the Database Engine. After reviewing, click Next.

16. On the Instance Configuration page, click Next.

17. On the Disk Space Requirements page, click Next.

18. On the Server Configuration page, enter **corp\Administrator** for the Account Name next to SQL Server Analysis Services.

19. Enter the password for the Administrator login in the Password column.

20. Click Next.

21. On the Analysis Services Configuration page, Click Add Current User.

22. Click Next.

23. On the Error Reporting page, click Next.

24. On the Installation Configuration Rules page, click Show details. Review the information for any items that did not pass. After reviewing, click Next.
25. On the Ready to Install page, click Install.
26. When the Complete page appears, click Close.
27. Click the Tools link on the left side of the SQL Server Installation Center page.
28. Click the PowerPivot Configuration Tool link. (You may need to close the SQL installation and open it again in order for this to recognize your new PowerPivot instance and become active.)

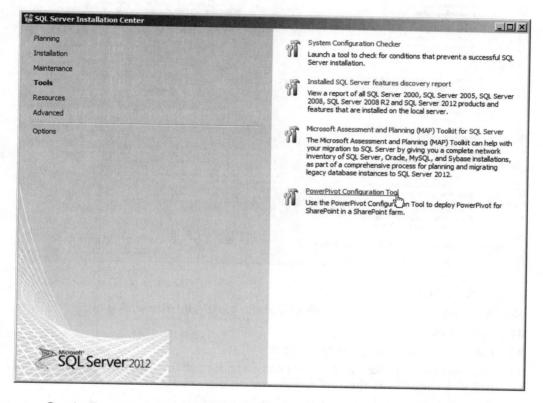

29. On the PowerPivot Configuration Tool page, click OK.
30. After a minute or two, a larger PowerPivot Configuration Tool window will appear with multiple tabs on the right side. On the Parameters tab, complete the following fields that are not filled in with default values:

   ▶ Default Account Password (the password for the login shown next to Default Account Username)

   ▶ Database Server (this is the name of your virtual computer)

> ▶ Passphrase (such as **Pass@word1**)
>
> ▶ Confirm Passphrase (again **Pass@word1**)

31. Change the SharePoint Central Administration Port number to 11111.

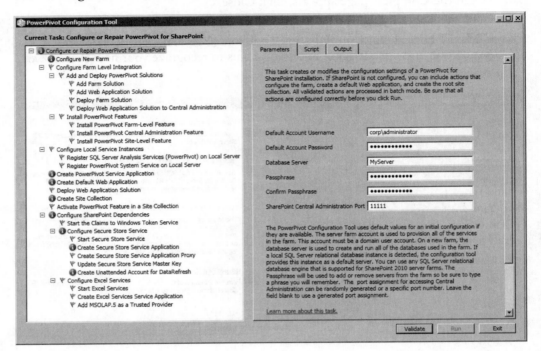

32. Click Validate.

33. After validation completes, click OK in the Task Validation dialog box.

34. Click Run.

35. Click Yes in the dialog box to confirm.

36. This process will take some time to complete. Be patient! After the process is finished, click OK in the Task Configuration dialog box.

37. Click Exit to close the PowerPivot Configuration Tool.

38. Verify that SharePoint Central Administration is running properly. Click Start | All Programs | Microsoft SharePoint 2010 Products | SharePoint 2010 Central Administration. This will launch the Central Administration page. The Central Administration page will take some time to load the first time.

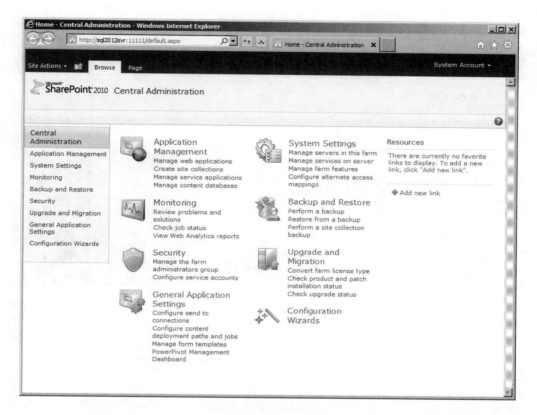

39. If you receive a Set up Internet Explorer 9 dialog box, select the Use recommended Security and Compatibility settings radio button and click OK. Close the resulting browser window tab.

40. If you receive a Windows Security prompt, enter the Administrator user name and password.

41. If you receive any Internet Explorer content blocked dialog boxes, click Add. Then in each resulting Trusted sites dialog box, uncheck the "Require server verification (https:) for all sites in this zone" check box, click Add, and then click Close.

42. Next, navigate to your SharePoint site collection. To do this, in the URL area of your browser, delete the ":11111" and everything after it.

43. Press ENTER. Again, it will take some time to load the first time.

44. If you receive a Windows Security prompt, enter the Administrator user name and password.

45. When the SharePoint site collection page appears, as shown in the next illustration, you may want to bookmark this URL in the browser favorites so you can easily return to it later.

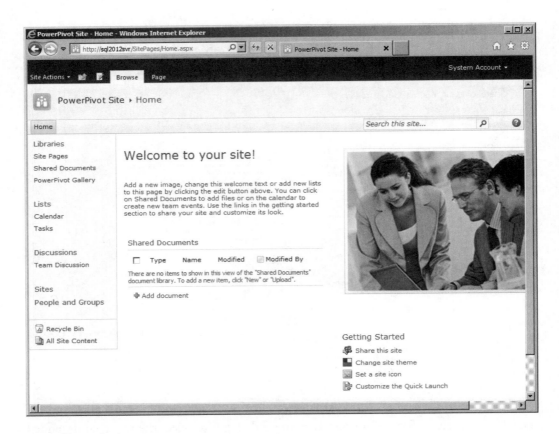

46.   Close the browser.

Step 5: Installing SQL Server 2012, Round 3

We are getting closer—over halfway done. Now that SharePoint is set up, we can go ahead and install the Reporting Services SharePoint Integration.

Learn By Doing: Installing SQL Server—Reporting Services SharePoint Integration

Video B-3

Creating a Virtual Learning Environment: Reporting Services, SharePoint Integration

1.   Click the Installation link on the left side of the SQL Server Installation Center page.
2.   Click the "New SQL Server stand-alone installation or add features to an existing installation" link.

3. On the Setup Support Rules page, click OK.

4. On the Product Updates page, click Next.

5. A second version of the Setup Support Rules page is displayed. Again review the information for any items that did not pass. It is not a problem to have a yellow triangle with an exclamation point next to the Computer domain controller and Windows Firewall items. After reviewing, click Next.

6. On the Installation Type page, select the option to Add features to an existing instance of SQL Server 2012.

7. Make sure MSSQLSERVER is selected in the drop-down list (this is the default instance), and click Next.

8. On the Feature Selection page, check the boxes for Reporting Services – SharePoint and Reporting Services Add-in for SharePoint Products.

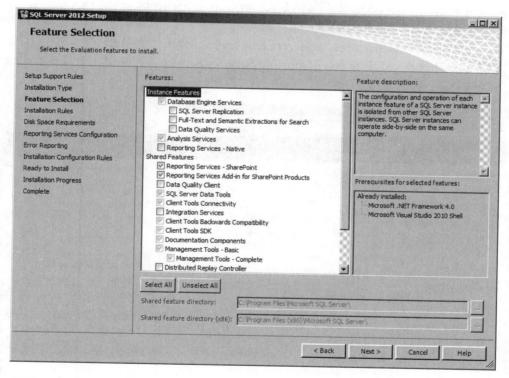

9. Click Next.

10. On the Disk Space Requirements page, click Next.

11. On the Reporting Services Configuration page, click Next.

12. On the Error Reporting page, click Next.

13. On the Installation Configuration Rules page, click Show details. Review the information for any items that did not pass. After reviewing, click Next.
14. On the Ready to Install page, click Install.
15. When the Complete page appears, click Close.
16. Close the SQL Server Installation Center page.

Step 6: Setting Up Reporting Services in SharePoint

The SQL Server installation is now complete. In this step, we go back into SharePoint and complete the setup of Reporting Services.

Learn By Doing: Installing the Reporting Services Application

1. Click Start | All Programs | Microsoft SharePoint 2010 Products | SharePoint 2010 Central Administration.
2. Click the Manage services on server link under System Settings.
3. Verify that the SQL Server Reporting Services Service is started. If it is not, click the Start link.

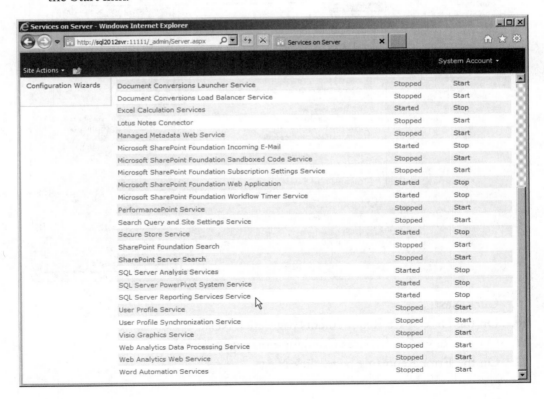

4. Click the Application Management link on the left side of the page
5. Click the Manage service applications link under Service Applications.
6. On the Service Applications tab in the SharePoint ribbon, click New to activate the drop-down menu.
7. From the drop-down menu, select SQL Server Reporting Services Service Application.

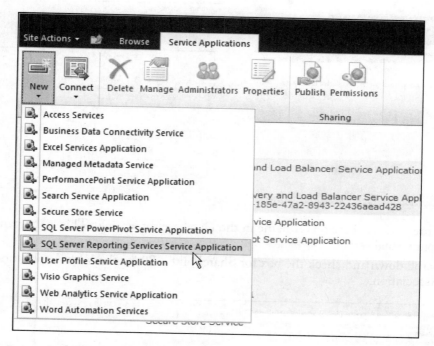

8. On the Create SQL Server Reporting Services Service Application page, enter **ReportingServicesApp** in the Name field.

9. With the Create new application pool radio button selected, enter **ReportingServicesAppPool** in the Application pool name field.

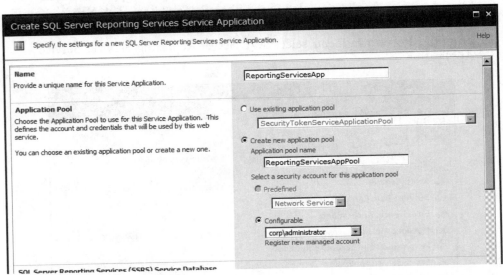

10. Enter the database server name in the Database server field. This is the name of your virtual server.

11. Scroll down and check the box for SharePoint – 80 for the Web Application Association.

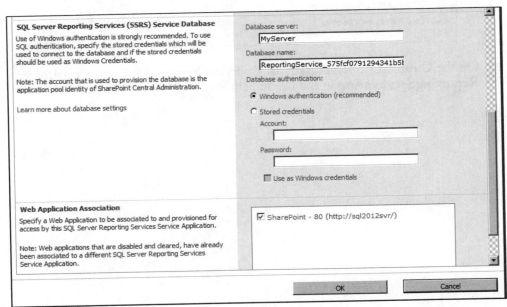

12. Click OK. After several minutes, you will receive confirmation that the SQL Server Reporting Services service application has been successfully created.

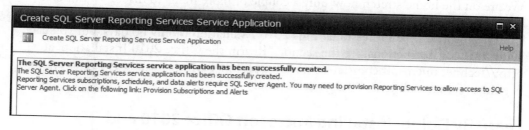

13. Click OK.

14. In your browser, navigate to the SharePoint Site Collection (use the Favorites link, if you created one earlier).

15. Click the Shared Documents link on the left side of the page.

16. Select the Library tab in the SharePoint ribbon, and then click the Library Settings button. (If you receive an Internet Explorer content blocked dialog, click Close.)

17. On the Document Library Settings page, click the Advanced settings link under General Settings.

18. On the Document Library Advanced Settings page, select Yes for the Allow management of content types option.

19. Scroll down and click OK.

20. Back on the Document Library Settings page, click the Add from existing site content types link under Content Types.

21. On the Add Content Types page, hold down CTRL and select the following in the Available Site Content Types list:

   ▶ BI Semantic Model Connection

   ▶ Report Builder Report

   ▶ Report Data Source

22. Click Add to move them to the Content types to add list on the right.

23. Click OK.

24. Back on the Document Library Settings page, click the Change new button order and default content type link under Content Types.

25. Uncheck the box for Document.

26. Click OK.

27. Close Internet Explorer.

This completes the setup of SharePoint and Reporting Services.

Step 7: Setting Up Microsoft Office 2010 and PowerPivot

We are on the home stretch now, only a couple of more items to install. In this step we set up Microsoft Office 2010 and then set up the PowerPivot for Excel add-in. The Microsoft Office Professional Plus 2010 Evaluation is only 60 days, but you can rearm this; for instructions, see the section "Rearm the Office 2010 Installation" at http://technet.microsoft.com/en-us/library/cc178964.aspx. This allows you to rearm five times for an additional 30 days each time.

Learn By Doing: Installing Microsoft Office 2010 and PowerPivot for Excel

Video B-4

Creating a Virtual Learning Environment: Office, PowerPivot Add-In, Silverlight

1. Open Windows Explorer and navigate to the PGHTSetup folder where you placed the installation software.
2. Double-click the Office 64-bit ProfessionalPlus executable.
3. Enter the Microsoft Office Professional Plus 2010 evaluation product key and click Continue. You should receive an Office evaluation product key as part of requesting and downloading the evaluation software.
4. Check the box to accept the software license terms, and click Continue.
5. Click Install Now.
6. When you are notified of successful installation, click Close. (You do not need to click the Continue Online button.)
7. Return to the PGHTSetup folder.
8. Double-click the vstor40_x64 executable to install the Visual Studio 2010 Tools for Office Runtime.
9. Click Next.
10. Check the box to accept the software license terms, and click Install.
11. After successful installation, click Finish.
12. Return to the PGHTSetup folder.
13. Double-click the PowerPivot_for_Excel_amd64.msi installation file to launch the setup program.
14. Click Next.
15. Check the box to accept the software license terms, and click Next.
16. Click Install.

NOTE

If you receive a message concerning the SQL Server Browser files being in use, use the Services application from the Administrative Tools to stop the SQL Server Browser service. After the installation is complete, restart the SQL Server Browser service.

17. After successful installation, click Finish.
18. Open Excel and verify the PowerPivot add-in loads on startup.
19. If the Microsoft Office Activation Wizard dialog box appears, click Cancel.
20. When the Welcome to Microsoft Office 2010 dialog box appears, select Use Recommended Settings and click OK.
21. Verify that the PowerPivot tab appears in the ribbon.

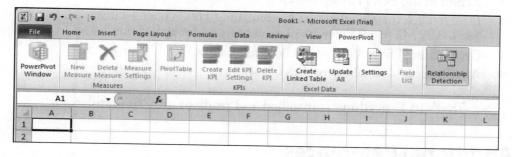

22. Close Excel.

Step 8: Setting Up Silverlight

This is it, the final step in the process. We just need to install Silverlight 5, which is a requirement for both Power View and some of the functionality in SharePoint.

Learn By Doing: Installing Silverlight 5 (32-bit and 64-bit)

1. In Windows Explorer, navigate to the PGHTSetup folder where you placed the installation software.
2. Double-click the Silverlight executable. (This is the 32-bit version that will be used by Internet Explorer.)
3. On the Install Silverlight page, shown in the next illustration, click Install Now.

4. After successful installation, click Close.
5. Return to the PGHTSetup folder.
6. Double-click the Silverlight_x64 executable. (This is the 64-bit version that will be used by Microsoft PowerPoint, which is a 64-bit application.)
7. On the Install Silverlight page, click Install Now.
8. After successful installation, click Close.

That's it! Everything is installed and ready to go. Congratulations!

Additional References

Table B-2 provides a few additional references you might find useful when going through this process.

Installing the Sample Data and Connections

Your learning environment is now equipped with all of the tools you need. The final step is to install the sample data necessary to complete the Learn By Doing exercises. Refer to Appendix A for the steps necessary to install the sample data.

Article Title	Link
How to Build a SQL Server 2012 Hyper-V Virtual Machine (KIWI build)	http://social.technet.microsoft.com/wiki/contents/articles/3402.how-to-build-a-sql-server-2012-hyper-v-virtual-machine-kiwi-build.aspx
Deployment Checklist: Reporting Services, Power View, and PowerPivot for SharePoint	http://msdn.microsoft.com/en-us/library/hh231687(v=SQL.110).aspx
Install PowerPivot for SharePoint on a Domain Controller (en-us)	http://social.technet.microsoft.com/wiki/contents/articles/1647.install-powerpivot-for-sharepoint-on-a-domain-controller-en-us.aspx
Install PowerPivot for SharePoint	http://msdn.microsoft.com/en-us/library/ee210708(v=sql.110).aspx

Table B-2   *Additional References*

Index

& (ampersand), 205
&& operator, 206
* operator, 203
+ operator, 203
/ operator, 203
< operator, 203
<> operator, 203
<= operator, 203
= operator, 203
> operator, 203
>= operator, 203
^ operator, 203
|| operator, 206
– operator, 203
100% stacked column charts, 71–72

A

ABS() function, 212
Add to Chart drop-down menu, 65
Add to Chart options, 63–65
ALL() function, 208
ampersand (&), 205
Analysis Services. *See* SQL Server Analysis Services
Analysis Services server, 11, 142, 144, 242
Analysis Services Tabular projects, 141–146
AND() function, 220
animating charts, 82–85
application design methodology, 4
arithmetic operators, 203–205
.asdatabase file, 254–256, 257
attributes, 177
AutoSum shortcut, 164
AVERAGE() function, 212

B

backup file, 256–257
backups, data, 143–144
bar charts, 72
BI projects, 4–5
BI Semantic Model (BISM)
    adding data to, 147–154
    adding data via queries, 152–154
    analyzing with Excel, 155–157
    cleaning up, 177–178
    connections. *See* connections
    creating from ground up, 131–146
    creating with PowerPivot, 131–145
    creating with SQL Server Data Tools, 141–145
    cubes, 6–7
    development environment, 117
    Diagram View, 168–174
    enhancing, 157–158
    getting started with, 111–127
    hierarchies, 179–183
    images stored in, 191–192
    importing data from new source, 147–150
    multidimensional. *See* Multidimensional BI Semantic Model
    overview, 6–8, 112–115
    perspectives, 185–187
    PowerPivot. *See* PowerPivot model
    refining, 174–190
    tabular. *See* Tabular BI Semantic Model
    testing, 155–157
    usefulness of, 154–166
    versions, 112–115
BISM. *See* BI Semantic Model

295

LICENSE AGREEMENT

THIS PRODUCT (THE "PRODUCT") CONTAINS PROPRIETARY SOFTWARE, DATA AND INFORMATION (INCLUDING DOCUMENTATION) OWNED BY THE McGRAW-HILL COMPANIES, INC. ("McGRAW-HILL") AND ITS LICENSORS. YOUR RIGHT TO USE THE PRODUCT IS GOVERNED BY THE TERMS AND CONDITIONS OF THIS AGREEMENT.

LICENSE: Throughout this License Agreement, "you" shall mean either the individual or the entity whose agent opens this package. You are granted a non-exclusive and non-transferable license to use the Product subject to the following terms:

(i) If you have licensed a single user version of the Product, the Product may only be used on a single computer (i.e., a single CPU). If you licensed and paid the fee applicable to a local area network or wide area network version of the Product, you are subject to the terms of the following subparagraph (ii).

(ii) If you have licensed a local area network version, you may use the Product on unlimited workstations located in one single building selected by you that is served by such local area network. If you have licensed a wide area network version, you may use the Product on unlimited workstations located in multiple buildings on the same site selected by you that is served by such wide area network; provided, however, that any building will not be considered located in the same site if it is more than five (5) miles away from any building included in such site. In addition, you may only use a local area or wide area network version of the Product on one single server. If you wish to use the Product on more than one server, you must obtain written authorization from McGraw-Hill and pay additional fees.

(iii) You may make one copy of the Product for back-up purposes only and you must maintain an accurate record as to the location of the back-up at all times.

COPYRIGHT; RESTRICTIONS ON USE AND TRANSFER: All rights (including copyright) in and to the Product are owned by McGraw-Hill and its licensors. You are the owner of the enclosed disc on which the Product is recorded. You may not use, copy, decompile, disassemble, reverse engineer, modify, reproduce, create derivative works, transmit, distribute, sublicense, store in a database or retrieval system of any kind, rent or transfer the Product, or any portion thereof, in any form or by any means (including electronically or otherwise) except as expressly provided for in this License Agreement. You must reproduce the copyright notices, trademark notices, legends and logos of McGraw-Hill and its licensors that appear on the Product on the back-up copy of the Product which you are permitted to make hereunder. All rights in the Product not expressly granted herein are reserved by McGraw-Hill and its licensors.

TERM: This License Agreement is effective until terminated. It will terminate if you fail to comply with any term or condition of this License Agreement. Upon termination, you are obligated to return to McGraw-Hill the Product together with all copies thereof and to purge all copies of the Product included in any and all servers and computer facilities.

DISCLAIMER OF WARRANTY: THE PRODUCT AND THE BACK-UP COPY ARE LICENSED "AS IS." McGRAW-HILL, ITS LICENSORS AND THE AUTHORS MAKE NO WARRANTIES, EXPRESS OR IMPLIED, AS TO THE RESULTS TO BE OBTAINED BY ANY PERSON OR ENTITY FROM USE OF THE PRODUCT, ANY INFORMATION OR DATA INCLUDED THEREIN AND/OR ANY TECHNICAL SUPPORT SERVICES PROVIDED HEREUNDER, IF ANY ("TECHNICAL SUPPORT SERVICES"). McGRAW-HILL, ITS LICENSORS AND THE AUTHORS MAKE NO EXPRESS OR IMPLIED WARRANTIES OF MERCHANTABILITY OR FITNESS FOR A PARTICULAR PURPOSE OR USE WITH RESPECT TO THE PRODUCT. McGRAW-HILL, ITS LICENSORS, AND THE AUTHORS MAKE NO GUARANTEE THAT YOU WILL PASS ANY CERTIFICATION EXAM WHATSOEVER BY USING THIS PRODUCT. NEITHER McGRAW-HILL, ANY OF ITS LICENSORS NOR THE AUTHORS WARRANT THAT THE FUNCTIONS CONTAINED IN THE PRODUCT WILL MEET YOUR REQUIREMENTS OR THAT THE OPERATION OF THE PRODUCT WILL BE UNINTERRUPTED OR ERROR FREE. YOU ASSUME THE ENTIRE RISK WITH RESPECT TO THE QUALITY AND PERFORMANCE OF THE PRODUCT.

LIMITED WARRANTY FOR DISC: To the original licensee only, McGraw-Hill warrants that the enclosed disc on which the Product is recorded is free from defects in materials and workmanship under normal use and service for a period of ninety (90) days from the date of purchase. In the event of a defect in the disc covered by the foregoing warranty, McGraw-Hill will replace the disc.

LIMITATION OF LIABILITY: NEITHER McGRAW-HILL, ITS LICENSORS NOR THE AUTHORS SHALL BE LIABLE FOR ANY INDIRECT, SPECIAL OR CONSEQUENTIAL DAMAGES, SUCH AS BUT NOT LIMITED TO, LOSS OF ANTICIPATED PROFITS OR BENEFITS, RESULTING FROM THE USE OR INABILITY TO USE THE PRODUCT EVEN IF ANY OF THEM HAS BEEN ADVISED OF THE POSSIBILITY OF SUCH DAMAGES. THIS LIMITATION OF LIABILITY SHALL APPLY TO ANY CLAIM OR CAUSE WHATSOEVER WHETHER SUCH CLAIM OR CAUSE ARISES IN CONTRACT, TORT, OR OTHERWISE. Some states do not allow the exclusion or limitation of indirect, special or consequential damages, so the above limitation may not apply to you.

U.S. GOVERNMENT RESTRICTED RIGHTS: Any software included in the Product is provided with restricted rights subject to subparagraphs (c), (1) and (2) of the Commercial Computer Software-Restricted Rights clause at 48 C.F.R. 52.227-19. The terms of this Agreement applicable to the use of the data in the Product are those under which the data are generally made available to the general public by McGraw-Hill. Except as provided herein, no reproduction, use, or disclosure rights are granted with respect to the data included in the Product and no right to modify or create derivative works from any such data is hereby granted.

GENERAL: This License Agreement constitutes the entire agreement between the parties relating to the Product. The terms of any Purchase Order shall have no effect on the terms of this License Agreement. Failure of McGraw-Hill to insist at any time on strict compliance with this License Agreement shall not constitute a waiver of any rights under this License Agreement. This License Agreement shall be construed and governed in accordance with the laws of the State of New York. If any provision of this License Agreement is held to be contrary to law, that provision will be enforced to the maximum extent permissible and the remaining provisions will remain in full force and effect.